WARNING!

ENTER AT YOUR OWN RISK!

THIS PIECE MAY BE THREATENING
TO YOUR EVERYDAY REALITY.

THIS PIECE MAY CAUSE QUESTIONING
OF THE COMMON MORALITY.

THESE SYMPTOMS MAY APPEAR DAYS
AFTER THE PIECE WITHOUT WARNING…
EVEN IF DURING THE PIECE, YOU MAY FEEL
AS IF NOTHING IS HAPPENING…
OR YOU MAY EVEN ENJOY IT.
BUT ABOVE SYMPTOMS MAY STILL APPEAR,
LEADING TO RESTLESSNESS,
AND EVEN TO RADICAL CHANGE.

ENTER

And within our cells
We have been digging
Throughout the ages
Underground passages
Linking passions together.
When we reach to touch one another,
The bars melt like butter.
We sing together
In words that the masters
Can't understand.
We create together,
Dream, imagine together.
We hope and make love
Together behind the dam
In evolution.

Frank Moore, from the poem,
"Locked In, Locked Out"

Frankly Speaking
A Collection of Essays, Writings and Rants
by Frank Moore
© Inter-Relations 2014

ISBN-13:978-1495443381
ISBN-10:1495443388

Cover photos
Top: Frank typing circa 1966. Photographer unknown.
Middle: U.C.B. Series, Berkeley, California, Winter 1984. Photo by Mary Sullivan.
Bottom: Frank at the computer 2013. Photo by Michael LaBash.
Book design by Michael LaBash.

Inter-Relations
PO Box 1931
Eagle, ID 83616

Printed by CreateSpace, An Amazon.com Company.

FRANKLY SPEAKING

A Collection of Essays, Writings and Rants

by **Frank Moore**

Preface

by Corey Nicholl

The "writings binder" is now a thick pink three-ring binder with color copies of Frank's digital paintings decorating the front and back covers, complete with index. Linda Mac, Frank's lover and partner in crime for 38 years, started putting it together years ago as a way to bring Frank's writings and poetry to his live performances, and to have available to read when they were talking to people. You never knew when Frank would call for a piece to be read, something that fit the moment and the person perfectly. The binder grew and grew slowly over the years as Frank kept writing and adding new and old pieces that he wanted to have available. Some years ago, it became too big and heavy to even lift! Linda and Erika (Shaver-Nelson), one of Frank's students, separated the one binder into two, one for Frank's poetry, and the other for his prose writings, and indexed both.

Frankly Speaking is really this binder of Frank's prose writings. It roughly covers the period from the late 1970s until Frank's death in 2013. It is not a complete collection of Frank's writings during that period, and it is not arranged chronologically; rather it contains the writings that Frank most wanted to have on hand. We are presenting it alphabetically, just as it was in the binder.

The scope of Frank's writing is truly amazing. As you open the pages of Frankly Speaking, you might first come upon Frank's "just makes sense" plan for the complete political and social transformation of American society (see *Platform for Frank's Presidential Candidacy 2008*)…then turn the page and Frank is passionately shaking up the "art world", urging fellow artists to truly live their calling and not accept censorship (see *Art is Not Toothpaste* or *The Combine Plot*)…and then another page, and Frank is drawing you deeply into the heart of magic, responsibility, shamanism, play and expanded sexuality (see *Dance of No Dancers* or *States of Tanpan*). Frank always had this way of joyfully and fearlessly digging into the meat of any issue to get to something deeper: intimacy, community, human liberation. These writings were often inspired by fellow artists and the work with his own students. Frank always focused on the small, personal, intimate level. But their wide-reaching effect is profound, and for many years, these pieces have influenced and inspired people around the world through their appearance in magazines, books, and online.

Sometimes during a performance, Frank would ask a person in the "audience" to read randomly from his writings binder. As they read Frank's words, the writing would become a "jam" with whatever else was happening. It always created new levels of depth, intimacy, meaning, what Frank was always going for!

"I used all my tricks and tools: slides, strobe lights, random readings of my writings, the gestures which I have made more explicit, etc. There were layers of different activities in the room. On one end of the room were Tomek, Shirt, Abigail, etc. playing music joyfully. On the other end were the dancers working through morality, individualism, freedom, going beyond the comfortable acceptable thing, or not! In the middle of the room readers were totally jamming, when they were not playing dress-up." (From Frank's write-up of "The Uncomfortable Zones Of Fun", Temescal Arts Center, Saturday, May 28, 2011)

On that note, in that spirit, enjoy!

TABLE OF CONTENTS

TABLE OF CONTENTS continued

Introduction

1994

This is not a logical, linear, or rational process towards some fixed set of goals. It is instead a mystical experience, a dream which will be created by various rituals...some silly, some intense. The dream experience will be different and unique for each person here. But the dream will include healing by ecstasy. It will be about performing passionately, and living fun. It is about creativity as channeling...creating as something which you open yourself up to, instead of something you do.

The rituals of this dream will probably seem to be unconnected fragments that I pull out of the air. These fragments will dance around, not making any sense at all. But slowly they will end up as a whole jigsaw puzzle. This may be a dramatic event or a small but important insight. This coming together of the fragments may occur days after we leave here.

We are leaving the world of time, of taboos, of reason. We will visit birth, childhood, playhouse, the dark side. It may be overwhelming in the normal reality. But this will be the magical state of all possibilities in which you can let yourself be carried away. In this realm, you can be that trusting...trusting yourself, trusting others, trusting the magic.

This is a gateway. This is a beginning. Once you have passed through this gateway, it is up to you where the path leads.

An update of the last 37 years of my life

March 2, 2006

Ok, here it goes...fast forward through the 35 years since Debbie and I left the community. A bus ride to D.C. to her family...the Jewish mother-in-law from hell [years later she sicced a hit man on me!]. I quickly called my friend Moe...whose head shop was in that book I was writing and which is lying unfinished in a trunk....but I did turn the material I was "channeling" into a book **the art of living**. [The metaphysical writing is in the same trunk.] Moe rescued us and put us on a plane to San Francisco. The first person we ran into as we stepped off the airport shuttle was another of my college friends who put us up for the night. The plan was for Debbie to go to the S.F. Art Institute [where I would go years later]... but she couldn't get in. After a week getting kicked out of rooms [crips weren't in fashion yet], we boarded a bus to Santa Fe before we ran out of money. Santa Fe is where I lived before I went to the community. We got into Santa Fe at 4am without any phone numbers of my friends. But a friend drove by and saw me...and woke my dear friend Louise up. She picked us up. We stayed with her for a while. But to get Vocational Rehab money, I had to get back into college. So we moved to Albuquerque, staying with my friend Steve in the mountains until we found a room in town. My channeling made a spiritual community interested in me...until my muckraking nature raked up muck! I got my B.A. much too soon in terms of our money. We met Jo, who we became intimate with. We three moved back to Santa Fe, where I got into an intensive film course. We met Ray. We four got married. After the film course, not having money to make films, I did nonfilm performances. I also started a drop-in workshop combining theater, ritual, intimacy, eroticism, etc. A community began to develop out of this. I began doing all-night audience-interactive ritual performances. We moved, with some of the workshop people, to N.Y.C. to continue the work in a loft off of 5th Ave. Both Debbie and Jo were pregnant. Louise flew out to deliver the boys at home after the hospital wouldn't let me even on the ward [again before crips were in fashion!]. The boys came three days apart. We raised them tribally...the sanest way! They are in their 30s now...one is becoming an acupuncturist; the other is a musician and an instrument maker. After they were born...and after

I did 2 nights of ritual performance in a ballroom...the tribal we moved to Berkeley...after a short attempt in San Bernardino. There I got a motor wheelchair. Imagine me mobile, driving myself all over the bay area, driving into all kinds of adventures. I even drove into a travel agency and met a sexy travel agent Linda who quickly quit to be my partner in crime for the last 35+ years!

A guy who saw a flyer for my workshop came to check me out. He didn't want to do the workshop. But he did want to come to me for weekly individual sessions where I kicked his ass about his relationships and his life...and he paid well! He turned out to be a psychic teacher. All of his students and clients wanted to see me! For a couple of years I worked 8 hours a day and had two weekly workshops going. Although I always charged just what the person could afford, money was good, especially when they started moving in with one another and came as households! I even got a masters degree just by documenting this work. But problem solving was boring. I wanted a community of deep intimacy. So I demanded more. A community of 30 in several households emerged. Sound familiar? Also quite a few successful businesses came out of this sexy coming together... not to mention a few millionaires [never me!]. We won a legal battle with the I.R.S. over getting church status. They were saying we didn't believe in a God. We had to go to D.C. with my channeled and metaphysical writings and the A.C.L.U.! But **Inter-Relations** was born, which has made doing the work much easier.

I started putting on events like free concerts and sexy parades, and directing plays at our storefront. I also started doing 48-hour improvised performances. Everything was small and underground. But then I directed what was supposed to be a one-night-only wacky tacky sexy take-off on beauty contests, **the outrageous beauty revue,** at the S.F. punk club **the Mabuhay.** The room held 500. It was packed. The first two rows were photographers and reporters [we were on the third page of the next day's S.F. paper]. Scary! The club's producer made me announce that it'll be a weekly show. So it became the ever-evolving early show every Saturday night [and often Thursday too] for three and a half years. So we opened for EVERY punk/hardcore/whatever band! And we got international coverage of all kinds...magazines, t.v., films, etc. I had to work hard to not let it get big or lose its edge...to keep it underground where you have the most effect and freedom...just popping up everywhere to interject bits of subversive alternatives. At the beginning, I was not in the show. But I started worming myself in. I added a live band, **the superheroes**...of course I was one of the lead singers! The band started getting gigs at other clubs. And we opened our own club, **the blind lemon,** in Berkeley. But by the second year of the show, the community began to decay. It took years for that painful process to play out.

In the meantime, I started making small films [after walking out of a "real" film deal!] and mainly put them in the closet...waiting for the internet and public access t.v. to give them outlets! The first film, **Fairytales Can Come True,** even was distributed. In the meantime I went to the S.F. Art Institute graduate program for "performance/video". I/the work freaked them out bad! But Linda and I stuck it out for two years... which landed me a cover story in the major performance art magazine... which made me the darling of *"THE ART WORLD"* for at the most two years, until they figured out I wasn't a nice safe thankful crip artist, but an artist who pushed limits. But during these two years, before the art world blacklisted me, Linda and I started touring the U.S. and Canada, doing both the long ritual performances and singing gigs. I also started being invited to lecture at colleges. I was one of the featured performance artists in the film **Mondo New York.** I also kept making videos [directing, acting, editing, even creating musical scores and Linda doing the camera work]. I began a performance series at the University of California. This series, which lasted for three years, gave me a lab where I could improvise/jam with other artists/musicians. When I got on the art world's blacklist, I moved into poetry readings and other underground worlds. But then Sen. Jesse Helms got me back into the art world's graces, kind of, by including me on his list of six targeted performance artists whom he considered obscene. That opened more possibilities for touring. I rode that pony for all that it was worth!

My writings, as well as articles about my work by other writers, began to be published in a wide range of magazines and books. In the early '90s, I began to offer shamanistic apprenticeships. My book, **Cherotic Magic,** came out of this. By this time, the community had shrunk to our household of five and the two boys. And even in our house, the original vision, principles, etc. had faded. Linda and I finally moved out...in with two of my apprentices, Mikee and Alexi. Debbie and the two others of the old household went into walking around town nude as **The X-plicit Players.**

I continued performing, directing, touring, etc. But we also started publishing an underground zine, **The Cherotic [r]Evolutionary**, which became very popular...which ain't saying it was a profit-making thing! The Work has always been a holy addiction that we pour money, etc. into to create community and to effect social change. We jumped into the web full force when it was born. **FreespeechTV.org** gave me free unlimited space to put up videos and audio content...that lasted for years! We put up the works of other artists as well as our own work. Our site, **eroplay.com**, expanded and expanded. Over 7 years ago I started doing a radio show **The Shaman's Den,** on a web station. But my muckraking their ambitions to make it big didn't sit well. They suggested not politely that I start my own web station. So we did within a week. **luver.com** started with a live music show web casting from Japan, followed by my 2-hour show on Sunday nights. But **LUVeR** quickly evolved into a radical 24/7 station with all kinds of music, news, whatever shows. It became a black hole for our time and money, forcing us to stop publishing our zine. In about a year **LUVeR** started webcasting video as well. My show started to be a video show of me either talking to a very interesting person or of bands from all over the world playing live at our house. Then I started doing shows on Berkeley's cable public access station. I use **the shaman's den** shows as the base of these cable shows, but throw in videos of my live performances, films, concerts, erotic explorings, poetry readings, whatever. For a year the City Council tried unsuccessfully to get me off the air. But now I'm on the channel every night of the week, up to 6 hours a night!

Now we have two houses on the same street. I live in the "Purple House" with Linda [we have been together for over 35 years!], Mikee [who has been with us for over 15 years], Erika [who has been working with me for 5 years and moved in over a year ago], and three cats. And in the "Blue House" Alexi lives with Corey and Cookie the Cat. The two houses are on the same block. We designed the Blue House, and Alexi and Corey basically built it. Alexi learned construction by working for a company that grew out of the community of 30. We have set him up with a successful handyman business. Corey works at the natural food store around the corner. Through it we have started an international food testing project for GMOs. Erika has become **the director of enrichment** at a large retirement community, injecting our sexy subversion in there. Linda, Mikee and I work at home keeping everything going. Mikee does the tech and graphic stuff [which, btw, he is available for hire cheap!]. Linda does all the practical stuff that makes everything possible. And me?...a cult leader always with big ideas! We are a good team, a tribal body.

Hey, I just found out that we are putting on a **LUVeR** benefit at the illegal infamous historical hardcore dive **burnt ramen** with my jamming erotic band **the cherotic all-stars** in May. Not bad for a crip turning 60 in June! True, we have pretty much stopped flying to places touring. But there is no sign of slowing down!

WHAT A LIFE!

Introduction to Cherotic Apprenticeship

1991

breaking taboos releases a magical freedom if done in certain contexts. this is true and important, but only in the first stages of magical training. taboo can be defined as social or moral forbiddens which maintain a dogmatic power structure by fear of what is outside that structure.

the things that are taboo, and hence are magically charged, in the normal social reality, are not taboo in the reality of the magician. there are no taboos or morals within the reality of the magician. for example, when i eroplay with someone, the eroplay itself is not taboo or transformative for me. the being with the other person in the eroplay is transformative, but not in the taboo dynamic. for me, eroplay, ritual reality, etc. is just everyday living. magicians will not do a lot of things, but this is never from a taboo/moral consideration, but from a practical ethical knowledge of how things work.

in what i do, breaking taboos is important in the first stages. in the public and private performances, as well as in my short-term work with people, breaking taboos plants seeds and time bombs, cracks the normal frame to let in a glimpse of an alternate reality.

but within the apprenticeship, there comes a time where, if the student relates to the magic life as breaking taboos, rather than as her everyday life, it becomes clear that she is taking a vacation from the normal social world, rather than truly living beyond taboos as her own personal reality.

the first ring of the chero apprenticeship, introduction to cherotic magic, lasts for 10 weeks. i meet with the student once a week for 2-4 hours. (for someone who lives outside the bay area, this ring can be done as a 10-day intensive.*) this ring focuses on the cherotic basics of the magical work. this is done one on one, focusing on how the student can use these basics in her life even if she does not go on to the advanced rings.

the break between each ring has proven to be vital. the minimum break period after the first ring is a month. there is no commitment to return from the break.

the second ring, practice and performance of cherotic magic, is 6 months. this is an intensely physical training, which includes both public and private ritual. this training will affect every aspect of the student's life profoundly.

the third ring, living magic, is 2 years and is focused on the student's devoting his life for the 2 years to the aiding of the shaman in the magic work. because of this, during the break between the second and third rings, after the student hears the calling for this devotion, he should arrange his personal life to make this devotion possible.

beyond these first three rings of magical training lie four deeper rings into the realm of the responsibility of the shaman. but it is important to stress that each ring is complete in itself, reaching a different level of shamanism.

* the out-of-towner may stay at the ashram/salon of all possibilities during this intensive. subject to availability.

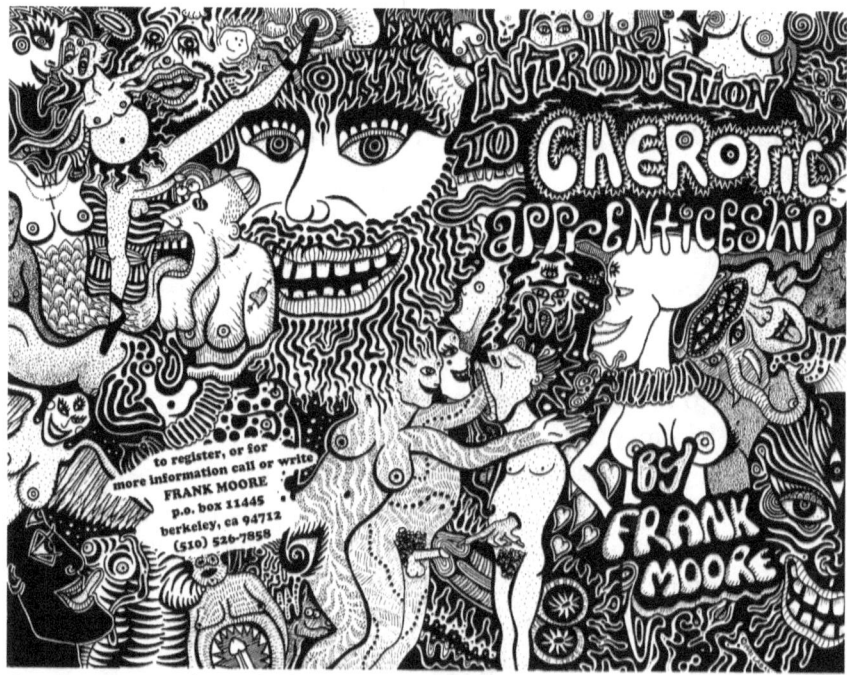

Brochure cover art by Michael LaBash.

Art is Not Toothpaste

Written in 1990. Published in *The Drama Review (TDR)* 1991.

This is in response to Catherine Schuler's "Spectator Response and Comprehension: The Problem of Karen Finley's Constant State of Desire" published in the Summer 1990 issue of *TDR*. My main aim in this is not to defend Finley's work. The content of the work should be the only defense needed. But art itself needs to be defended from being framed in as a commodity on the same level as toothpaste, politicians, and T.V. shows.

I was shocked and frightened at the kind of thinking which Schuler's writing represents. Schuler clearly does not like Finley's work. Schuler seems to pin her dislike on the symbols and words Finley uses, calling them "pornographic...angry, confrontational, and deliberately provocative...something vaguely obscene...she (Finley) uses language and images associated with the most repugnant forms of heterosexual sadomasochistic pornography."

Schuler does not say what the language and images are or why she thinks they are obscene and pornographic. The words "pornographic" and "obscene" are words which have high emotional content and very little, if any, content of definable meaning. They are words which the enemies of human freedom such as Senator Jesse Helms use as a smokescreen to justify suppression and repression. In these days of new McCarthyism, careless use of such words by people who consider themselves feminists and humanists can have most dangerous results.

Words and images in themselves are not either good or bad, healing or destructive. If Schuler feels that Finley in her work uses words and images to exploit or abuse people, then there would be legitimate grounds for critical discussion about Finley's art. To me it seems obvious that Finley has always used words and images in a subversive poetic way to battle such exploitation and abuse. There are legitimate questions about the angry intensity of the work jading people, and questions about does the work offer alternatives to what it is destroying...does it have to offer such alternatives?

Schuler does not focus upon the work itself and her personal reaction to the work. Instead, she focuses on the myth surrounding the work. This myth is created, not by the work nor by the artist, but by the press, by rumor, by word of mouth, by fragmentary bits of information escaping into the outer world. This myth is one of the materials that the artist has to work with. People may come to the work because of the myth, but what is important is what happens when people come in contact with the art itself. I learned a long time ago that the myth has very little to do with me as the artist. I can never live up to the myth. The art just takes some people who come to the art beyond the myth. This is what happens to me when I go to a Finley piece.

What is disturbing about Schuler's essay is her lack of understanding of what art does, how art works. Her basic point in the piece is the need that she sees for "more traditional, benign forms of feminist performance." But instead of exploring what these forms are or might be, she attacks Finley as a representative of the avant garde. We liberal/radical/ revolutionaries have always been prone to this kind of self-defeating cannibalization of our own kind.

What is scary about Schuler's article is she does not seem to think her own reaction to the art is enough to talk about. Instead, she invents a fictional character called "average spectator" or, better yet, "the average female spectator". If this fictional character responds "appreciatively" to the art, then the art works as "a vehicle for meaningful social and political analysis". But if the work leaves our average female spectator leaving the theater in confusion, frustration, anger, rejection, then the work has failed as a feminist piece because our average female spectator is, after all, a female. The logic is sexist. But it also creates a cardboard flat reality.

Schuler tries to breathe scientific life into this cardboard reality by conducting a pop exit poll after one of Finley's shows. Fifteen people are not a scientific sample even if art were something linear like a bar of soap, a politician, or a T.V. series. But this exit poll gives this fictional average female spectator an illusion of importance in some sociological anthropological unreality. What Schuler does not realize is the only important thing is what the art made her feel. Anything else is putting dangerous frames around the art.

During over 20 years of performing, I have learned that the apparent audience response during the performance or immediately after the performance is rarely the person's final response to the art. Some people who loved the performance experience as it was happening, go home and freak out. Other people who were bored, hostile, or even walked out, very often come up to me days, weeks, even years later to say the performance turned out to be an important event in their lives. This nonlinear dynamic is so common that I put a warning sign in the lobby outlining this dynamic. It may take years for someone to come to terms with a work of art. Because art uses so many channels of influence (many of these channels are subconscious and nonrational), good art plants seed and time bombs within the person. These seeds and time bombs may take years to bloom or to explode.

This is why it is so dangerous to link the art to the apparent "spectator response and comprehension". It would bring art to the level of a T.V. show whose worth is measured by the overnight ratings; down to the level of the politician who changes his image and views according to the polls; down to the level of the Hollywood movie that is recut after a negative test audience response.

Art is not just a "vehicle for meaningful social and political analysis". It is magic, working its change even in confusion, frustration, anger, and even rejection. There are many channels in art, some so occult that not even the artist understands all of the meanings. Trust the art, trust the magic, trust the ability of the people to ultimately absorb humanist art!

Art of Living

From Frank Moore's book, *The Art Of Living*, 1974.

You and your group take yourselves much too seriously and don't take your lives seriously enough.

You must do what most people want to do -- to do in their dreams, but they dare not bring down into reality. A few men have done what you are about to do, but they are exhibitionists and egoists, little men trying to project illusions to show their contempt for their fellow men. One of their motives is pride. But what is really driving them is fear -- fear that behind all of their illusions there is nothing. So while daring to stand out in an extreme way, they don't dare to drop their illusions and stand naked as themselves, in their selves. They live out of fear and doubt as much as the masses of which they are so contemptuous.

You must not live out of any kind of fear. If you do, you are not who you say you are and will not do what you said you would do. These people whom we have been talking about take their illusions very seriously, believing their illusions are their only selves. They have lost their real spirit, or life, in the reflections of reflections, the thought forms of their egos, their brains. Now you see what I mean by "don't take yourselves so seriously, but take your lives more seriously."

Now it is time for most of you to create an illusion to walk about in the world. It is the same process that you used in spirit after you chose the thought form of your present body. After all, your body is an illusion that you created yourself after you and the thought form were matched up. Now you are creating another illusion using thought forms. But your spirit must do the creating, and not your ego or brain. This is what is hard for most of you to grasp. You are told you are the only one who can create you, who knows what you require, and that you owe nothing to anyone else save love. You take this as a command to do what you want, what makes you "feel good". It does not mean this. Your wants can make illusions without, if you please, a "zipper". You get trapped in it, having to tear your way out finally, bruising yourself in the process. The illusion that you are creating must come out of you and not out of your wants or from what you think you should do.

What you have created may appear to be taking you into hardships. As soon as I say this, some of you think you have to have hardships and pain, and will start creating hardships and pain for yourselves. This is not what letting you create means; you are just creating another zipperless illusion out of which you will battle. You have to create an illusion that is like clothes that you can put on to deal with the world, and that you can take off to play naked with your friends. If you can't take the illusion off, you had better start ripping it off because you are trapped, no matter how fine the illusion may be. As the body is still there when it is clothed, you are still there under the illusions; it is impossible to create an illusion as beautiful as you. Know this because it will save you time.

*   *   *

Use your own judgment when you listen to what I say. Believe only what feels right to you.

*   *   *

Your group will be concerned with the creativeness which is in every human, every spirit. This creativeness is truly the God who is the reason for all life. This is so obvious. But Man has rarely understood the process of creating. He starts, let's say, a painting with a set idea of what he is going to paint. Sooner or later he makes a "mistake" -- a color or a line which doesn't fit in the original idea -- which "ruins" the painting. When this happens most people give up, thinking that they are not cut out to be artists, and withdraw back into the common existence. Others try to pretend that they didn't make the mistake, that the color or line isn't there on the canvas. They go on painting as before. When they are done, they have painted the shadow of what they wanted. Moreover, this shadow is covered with a haze. Others keep starting over whenever they make mistakes, not accepting any mistakes. They are rewarded for their endurance with the perfect copy of the thought form which they had held for all this time. They are rewarded by what they think they want to create. Their thought form has been brought down into the material plane. The creation is perfect. But it is not a masterpiece. It is perfect within the limitations placed around it by the rigidness of the artist. The work is perfect, but not free.

A masterpiece is perfect and free. The master artist paints an adventure in color, words, or notes. What others see as mistakes, he sees as challenges, boxes out of which he has worked as the basis on which he creates a totally new, fresh pattern. These challenges, boxes, keystones, keep appearing as he works, demanding the artist's flexibility. If the artist looks back, trying to hold on to what he thought the painting was or would be, he gets trapped in a box out of which he must battle or be turned into a rigid, bitter pillar of salt. The artist has to keep his whole attention on the swirling colors in front of him in order to be the creator.

To create a masterpiece, the artist has to use and risk every bit of himself. But he also has to create with God, for God is the one who creates what most people call mistakes, and that the master artist sees as his tools and materials. God does not create for the artist. God just provides the tools, the guiding bumps. It is up to the artist's free will whether he creates or gets dragged down by the weight of the tools. When the artist is creating, he feels no weight.

The most important masterpiece is a lifetime. This is a statement of hard fact. Creating a masterpiece in every day living is governed by the same rules as creating a masterpiece in paint, but much harder because the artist is also the canvas. In every period of time, in every land, there are a few masterpieces of art and writing. But a masterpiece lifetime is much rarer. Moreover, there has never been a time on your world where there has been a society where masterpiece lifetimes abound.

The Art Of Breaking Taboos

December 6, 1991. Published in *VOX Magazine* 1992.

Sensitive issues? Sensitive to whom? Sensitive within what historical time period? Raising these kinds of questions in an issue focused on "artists who deal with sensitive issues" is in itself raising and dealing with a sensitive issue. By seeing art in terms of "dealing with sensitive issues", it places art in the same shallow realm as journalism and fashion. What is a sensitive issue has to do more with the social context within which the art is done than with the art itself. So when the focus is on the social context rather than the art itself, the art gets limited by being tied to political correctness, to fashion, to the thinking by the galleries and other "art experts" that they have the right to dictate the form, style, content, and the subjects of the current art. It would be far better to let future historians analyze the art in terms of "sensitive issues", and let us artists get back to creating.

From what I have said so far, it might appear I am blasting this very magazine. I am not. What this issue of the magazine does is give me an opportunity to raise a major but hidden concern within my art...the liberation of art from the power structures of art. It is one thing for an artist to deal with, just for an example, AIDS because he personally, artistically is pulled into it by his emotions and his life...and quite a different thing when he does a piece on AIDS because galleries are booking "AIDS pieces" this year. When galleries and theaters impose the subject matter, form, and style of the art they present, it is the same as when they would not book any political art in the '40s and '50s.

A few years ago I was in a controversy with a gallery which tried to withdraw their booking of me. The reason that was given was that my art was old fashion because it used nudity, audience participation, rituals, and extended time lengths (5-48 hours)...all of which, according to them, went out of fashion with the '60s. Then they somehow heard I had within the piece a nude guy wearing a sign saying "I have AIDS." They said, "now that is interesting...we are booking that kind of art!" They did not ask why he was in the piece. He was a member of my cast who discovered he had AIDS. "The dying man" role was a part of an intense process of exploring death, for both Carlos and people in general, as a part of a lustful joyful life. Within the piece, Carlos talked to each person about dying in this context. Later in the piece, Carlos as a regular cast member erotically played with the audience. AIDS was just one aspect of the death process, which in turn was just one aspect of the alternative human experience which was the performance. Focusing on Carlos as an "AIDS victim" obscures him, cheapens him, objectifies him, fragments him away from humanity.

This is also true when we focus on a work of art or an artist in terms of objectifying labels such as gay, woman, black, disabled, etc. I have cerebral palsy, am in a wheelchair, move and sound uniquely. So that any art I do which uses my body just has to have an aspect of the disabled in it. But disability has never been the central theme of my work. However, disability has been a "sensitive issue" within the cultural frame to various degrees in the 20+ years that I have been performing.

When I was doing the tacky sexy gross cabaret show, *The Outrageous Beauty Revue*, in the late '70s, I just happened to have in the cast of 30 three disabled guys as well as myself. Some in the audience were upset because they thought we were "normal" actors making fun of crips. It did not help when they figured out that we were "real crips". They then assumed that somebody was exploiting us poor souls. When they discovered that we were the artists who had created the acts, they then accused us of self-exploitation. This is similar to when "feminists" tell women artists such as Annie Sprinkle and Karen Finley that they shouldn't use their own nude bodies in their own art. I ran into this again after I did a shamanistic erotic ritual in Philadelphia. At the end of the piece, a guy accused me of using a cheap tactic of shock by using my body. If this criticism was valid, it would deny me the use of my own body. Obviously the physical disability aspect of my reality, although it is on the fringe of my art focus, does give me a powerful tool to get to my true focus, that of human liberation.

When I started my performance journey in the early '70s, I was not interested in creating literary drama pictures, either fiction or based on real events. I wanted to create alternative realities which could be experienced and in which the normal rules and taboos do not apply. To create these awake dreams, I saw I had to break the traditional barriers between audience and performers, had to break the dramatic time structure (both the linear flow and the real time length) which has been held on to from the ancient Greeks down to modern movies and T.V. I was focused on creating within the interpersonal level both within performances and in working with groups of performers. I started doing street pieces, secret private pieces with one other person, public rituals which lasted from 5 to

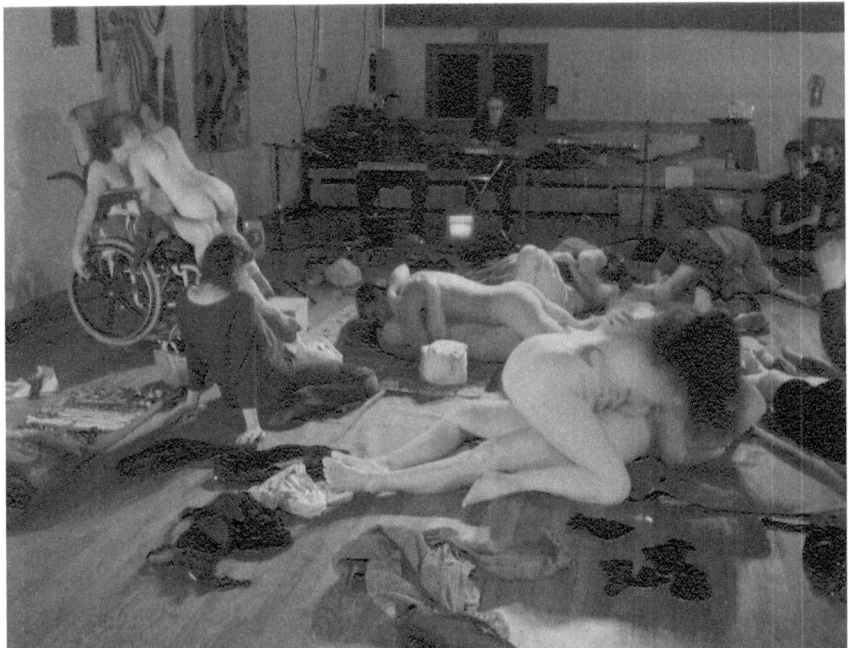

The Uncomfortable Zones of Fun, Temescal Art Center, Oakland, California, February 27, 2010. Photo by Michael LaBash.

48 hours. I also used low cost technologies and tactics which were in reach of everyone, but which were frowned upon by the art experts because of the lack of a "certain level of professional quality". The concern about "professional quality" has kept the creation of "real or fine art" in the hands of an art elite.

All of this breaks the taboos concerning form, time, and style. But the taboos concerning form, time, and style are in reality the main reason why I have had problems doing this art in "the art world" for most of my career. This was not as true when I started out. One reason for this was, instead of performing in galleries and theaters, I performed in rented dance halls, school gyms, rock clubs, and my own studios. But the main reason why I had an easier time doing my art was I was working within a different, more open, culture and artistic environment than the current one. My work was in the context of art done by Anna Halprin, The Living Theatre, the performance group of Richard Schechner, Grotowski, etc... and of course Artaud. I was working within an artistic context which was using the breaking of taboos within the traditional time/style format, breaking them to create a subversive alternative reality to the normal reality of fragmentation and isolation. Within this culture and artistic environment, what I did was less "sensitive"...and hence less subversive.

But what I did was made much more "sensitive" and subversive because of the artistic environment of performance in the late '70s shifting into personal monologues about the normal reality instead of creating an alternative experience of reality, shifting back onto the theatrical stage. Directors of galleries and theaters started telling me they were not booking me at their spaces because they are personally afraid of the audience participation, the extended time, and/or the trance experience. I always thought this is a valid honest reason for not booking me. These directors often voted for my work when they were on committees for venues other than their own.

But some galleries step over the line into looking at both the artist and the art as a packaged commodity by telling the artist what changes have to be made in the art in form, style, content, subject, time, to make the art suitable for the gallery. This assumes the artist has a choice or the power to mold the art.

This is a basic misunderstanding of the process of creating art. As a person, I have always needed to break out of personal and physical isolation. To do this, I need to bring other people into an altered reality to play in an expanded/extended "sexuality". All the forms and contents of the art flow uncontrolled from this depth of need. I am sure this is true of all good artists who are drawn into taboos areas. We do not see what we do as "dealing with sensitive issues", but as things we must do.

Intro for *Campus Quest*

An introduction written for Lee Gerstmann's book *Campus Quest*, February 24, 2001.

Here I am writing the introduction to this book...and maybe an introduction of you to Lee...and maybe of Lee to you...especially if you are a woman who lives outside of the NORMAL yourself...or at least are not fulfilled by THE NORMAL. Lee is shy.

I don't usually do this. The reason I am doing this is because Lee is one of my favorite poets. He writes, reads, exists in a "strange" state of purity, innocence, and an indirect directness which is fueled by a child-like passion. This state is not normal. It is very close to madness, to out-of-control homeless raging which threatens to destroy everything. But Lee's reality isn't madness. It is what a lot of artists and poets try to fake. Lee is real. I hope you bought this book from Lee after you heard him read/perform. Then you know what I mean. You probably also feel the warmth, the softness/gentleness, and the vulnerability that is the core of the planet Lee lives on. So get on stage and hold his hand...hold him like you would hold a scared puppy struggling to get away. This is why Lee writes poetry. This is the quest, hoping a woman out of uniform will hold him like this.

If you haven't been around Lee physically, if you just came across this book...well, before reading the rest of the book...take off all your clothes, lie down on your bathroom floor, kick your legs and flap your arms for five minutes at least...then read Lee's poems aloud, very loud, in the voice you would read Poe or Lovecraft with. Then you will have most...but not all...of Lee's intensity.

You don't need to do this to "get" these poems...especially if you are an outsider, a watcher looking in...not really wanting to be absorbed into THE REAL WORLD...just wishing to meet somebody to touch. I spent many years watching, on campus, on the sidewalk...unseen...desiring. If you have ever been an outsider, you are always an outsider, no matter what your outside "reality" presently is. Lee is the voice of us outsiders!

Censorship Address to the Berkeley City Council

Written September 8, 2002.

Hi. I am Frank Moore, the producer/host of the targeted UNLIMITED POSSIBILITIES and the sponsor of the targeted SUSAN BLOCK SHOW. It is interesting that this proposed ordinance is designed to target shows by an uppity crip and a smart sexy woman...or is it a smart sexy crip and an uppity woman? My show is politically, culturally, and artistically radical, offering in-depth conversations about issues that affect us all with a wide range of people, live music, and cutting-edge performances, films, and art. We throw everything in this stew for social change, explore everything, including eroticism, to find alternatives. This is what got me targeted by Sen. Jesse Helms in the early '90s. And this is why our shows are being targeted now. A few people, including some on the City Council, want to sweep these alternatives from public access because they are threatened by these alternatives.

Councilmember Betty Olds, who introduced this ordinance, has publicly proclaimed that if she had her way, she would ban these alternatives from our public access channel. She bemoaned the fact that it is illegal to censor or ban community shows on public access channels. This ordinance is an attempt to get around this legal fact. Olds actually has said she would take away B-TV, the channel of the community, if that was the only way she could force the removal of the shows that she doesn't approve of. So the real targets and victims of this ordinance are not our two shows, but the people of Berkeley, their freedom of expression on their channel.

This ordinance came about when both the staff of B-TV and the board of BCM refused to adopt a censoring scheduling policy, following their mission of promoting free speech and diversity. They knew getting some complaints is always a part of running a free speech channel. All of us producers were acting responsibly, requesting that our shows be aired after 10pm, the standard "safe harbor" for adult content. But the City Council, fueled by very few complaints, decided to ignore B-TV's staff and producers and the BCM board. It decided to issue rules controlling what could be shown on B-TV when. When politicians do this, it should always set off loud alarm bells.

This ordinance is a dangerous product of this misguided adventure. It purports to protect children from "indecent" programs. It doesn't do this. Again Olds has admitted that protecting children is just an excuse to get rid of shows that she and people like her find unsettling, etc.. This ordinance does not provide cheap hardware to concerned parents that allow them to block any program they deem unfit for their kids. Instead, it does away with the "safe harbor" of the 10pm-6am timeslot for adult programming. In its place there will be an "indecent" timeslot of midnight to 6am. Except for the shows which fall into a very narrow definition of what "indecent" is as defined in this ordinance, all other shows can be shown anytime! As Councilmembers Spring and Maio pointed out as they voted against the ordinance, the two targeted shows are not indecent. In fact, B-TV doesn't have any shows that are indecent as defined in this ordinance.

In reality, this ordinance is not about protecting children at all. It is about chilling free speech. It is about forcing people to do "acceptable" shows. Under this ordinance, a producer is expected to label her show as indecent or not. If she doesn't label it as indecent and somebody complains, there is a hearing. This hearing, its process, its rules, etc. are not remotely spelled out in the ordinance. If the show is found "indecent" in the hearing, the show is exiled to after midnight. But if the show is found not to be indecent...well, the complainer can do it again next week...until the producer is ground down into watering down her program. This is the real goal of this ordinance, not protecting kids!

Well, Suzy and I are not chillers. We do not chill. We boil. If this ordinance passes, we will fight lustfully! And we will win. We have to because, as Kriss Worthington keeps pointing out, this would give this and other city councils the power to control what we do and say on OUR public access channels...and freedom of speech dies!

By the way, are we going to let them limit our possibilities?

Chero

Chero is the physical life energy.
I created the word "Chero" by combining "Chi" and "Eros".
Magic is the science/art of nonlinear change.
In Cherotic Magic, it is the practical focus of the person
to reshape reality into more humane forms by using the
magical dynamics of relationships.

Cherotic Healing

Written March 28, 1998 for *P-Form* for their "Illness" issue. Published in *P-Form* #46, Fall 1998.

It is funny to be asked to write about art as healing. It is funny because when I went to grad art school, one of the main "criticisms" I got for the work I did was, because it "heals", it must be therapy, not art. That was news to me! I always thought one of the functions of art is healing.

For the purposes of this essay, my work consists of rituals. These rituals are in the contexts of public performances, of shamanistic training, and of private performances.

There is an attracting, pleasurable, excited, calming, healing energy that I call "chero". In these rituals of body play, one of the things that often occurs is a healing transformation. One of the channels of this trans-formation is aroused "chero".

In the western culture, chero is known as "sexual energy" or as the "sexual urge". This is because in this culture, adults usually call chero forth by means of sex and use chero mainly for sex. However, sex is just one way to use chero. Moreover, sex is just one of the ways to call forth chero.

Chero is the life force. It is what attracts. Chero is what attracts other people to you. It is what the shamans used to heal and melt other realities into the normal reality. It is what Tantric Buddhists used to reach the higher spiritual spheres. They use the sex act to arouse chero, which they then use in their spiritual quest. Sex is a cherotic act. But Chero is by no means simply a/the sexual energy. There are many ways of calling forth chero, and many ways of letting chero direct or guide you.

Within these rituals, chero is aroused by various physical/magical ("tanpanic") trances. One of these trances is eroplay.

Eroplay is not foreplay, even though foreplay is eroplay.

Kids play very physically both with their own bodies and others' bodies. They get turned on by this play, turned on both physically and mentally. This turn-on is not sexual in kids. Studies have shown that babies who are held, touched, and played with are more healthy and alert, weigh more, and have a lower rate of death than babies who are denied this eroplay. Studies also show that old people who live alone, who don't get physical and emotional contact, are less healthy and die sooner than people of the same age who live with others and get that physical contact.

When we grow up into adults, eroplay is linked to sex, maybe to assure procreation. But there may be different results when eroplay is not connected to the sexual orgasm.

Foreplay is eroplay, but eroplay is not foreplay. We need a certain amount of straight eroplay (not connected to or leading to sex) to be as healthy as possible.

Foreplay leads to orgasm...eroplay leads to being turned on in many different ways and in all parts of the body. It can be different every time.

Skin touching skin seems to be what releases the full impact of eroplay.

There are some physical health and lifestyle advantages of using eroplay to arouse chero in your body. These advantages are caused by the physical and psychic changes in the body started by aroused chero. Over the years of experimenting, we have often noticed that people's physical appearances change, sometimes radically, after they eroplay. Their physical features soften, the way they hold their bodies relaxes, their bodies have a glow very similar to the glow that many pregnant women have. All of these signs are visual, physical signals which attract open people to the chero-enriched person...and thus attract more opportunities to him. It is also important to point out that these changes are temporary, lasting from a few hours to a few weeks depending on the physical and emotional environment. Continued release of chero is needed to have these changes be longer and longer lasting.

There are other changes that occur during eroplay. By touching, rubbing, rocking, moving, the energy centers of the body are randomly activated, releasing a flood of blood with chemicals that produce the sense of well-being in all parts of the body. This is a warming well-being. This is deepened by the special breathing that is gentle laughing. This is why eroplay is playful and fun at its most healing level. Laughter has its own special healing quality.

Sometimes the release of chero is blocked by confusion and guilt when the person feels the pleasurable, turned-on feeling which he in the past associated with sex. But now he feels it in a nonsexual, nonromantic situation. If he can just let the pleasurable turn-on wash over him without thoughts, it carries him to a new realm of relaxed enjoyment.

Eroplay as a spiritual, healing technique balances chero through all the energy centers throughout the body. This is different than other techniques such as Kundalini Yoga in which the energy which I am calling chero is raised through a very dangerous process from the base of the spine to out the top of the skull. In eroplay, chero is called forth in all parts of the body, creating an energy center out of the whole body.

There is a widely held misconception that the physical and the spiritual planes are in opposition to each other, that to reach the spiritual, you have to avoid the physical. This is overlooking a great number of disciplines that use the physical in various aspects to reach spiritual treasures. The physical is one aspect of the spiritual, the aspect most accessible to us.

As we eroplay, many changes take place. The changes are both physical and psychic. We have already talked about some of the physical changes. One of the physical signs that can occur is the male erection when certain energy centers (and not necessarily the cock) are aroused in certain ways. This male erection has become the most sexual symbol in our culture and perhaps the most taboo. The female erection is not outwardly visible, and hence is usually ignored. But in reality, the "sexual" organs are no more or no less sexual than any of the other energy centers in the body. In eroplay, erection should not be thought of as sexual or a turn toward sex. This region of the body is just one of the main centers of energy.

The other physical changes caused by the arousal of chero through eroplay are a slight enlarging of the pupils, a slight change in scent from the sweat glands and nipples, the chero blush, and a difference in body tone. All of these are so slight that they usually are only picked up on the subliminal level. The changes in one body can be transferred to the bodies of others through these subliminal sensory signals. This is one reason why physical nudity is important in this work. It gives these signals a more direct channel to affect others.

But to understand better what is happening when chero is aroused by eroplay, it should be remembered that the physical is only one aspect of what we are. Around our physical body there is a force field made up of thoughts, emotions, and other psychic material. This field is usually a fraction of an inch out from the body, but we have the ability to broadcast this psychic force outward.

When we release chero through eroplay, we focus this force and with the willingness to be unlimited, we radiate this force outward, creating a rapport into which others can be drawn. This rapport has physical, mental, and psychic qualities.

In my performances, this rapport, in the form of an altered reality or a spell, is created by arousing chero between two people by rubbing bodies, by rocking together, moving together, making noises. These two generating people are sometimes isolated in a tent or a box. But the rapport generated physically and psychically by these two leaks out of the enclosed space, putting those on the outside into an altered state. The deeper the chero rapport is between the two, the more complete the outer reality will be.

At first, the generating chero rapport may feel uncomfortable, forced, and/or strange. This is because we are using things that in the western culture are usually contained only in sexual and/or romantic contexts. One should not be thrown by this forced, uncomfortable feeling. It is the breaking of old patterns. It is one of the first stages of this work. Each energy center "breathes" several kinds of energies in and out, very much like the lungs-nose breathe air in and out. Each center both takes energy in and projects energy out. Some energy centers are commonly thought of as one-way channels. The eyes obviously let in visually the outer world to our brain, our mind, our inner reality. But the eyes also visually let out what is happening inside us, who we are, and our personal power into the world. All of the centers work on this breathing principle.

Chero healing as eroplay is a two-way channel whether in play, art, magic, or everyday living. It must be this way to be effective. To create this deep two-way chero breathing you must be willing to both deeply project and deeply take in chero with anyone who is willing to do the same.

In eroplay, the centers of the body are randomly opened up so that this chero breath can be free and deep. Eroplay creates a complete cycle of chero. This cycle is created when you touch your own body. But it becomes more dynamic when this chero cycle is between two people. This interplay opens and relaxes the centers of both people, letting them both cherotically breathe deeper and easier. This deep, easy breathing is what is healing. (We will get into the difference between healing and curing later.) Both people get healed in this interplay and the energy released through the interplay helps to heal the outer world. This is important to understand because many people think healing is a one-way helping/giving channel. Because of this, they are careful "not to give too much". "I must protect myself and my personal power; maintain my own space, my control over the situation." This attitude is thought to be individualism.

We are now turning to how to use cherotic rituals in healing. The principles are the same whether we apply them to apprenticeship, performances, or bodyplay as a healing method.

Healing is not necessarily the same thing as curing. Modern western medicine is focused on curing illness, solving health problems, restoring normalcy. It is a very logical, goal-oriented process.

When we talk about healing, we mean becoming better able to cope with and adapt to the life situations we find ourselves in. This may or may not mean curing. When we are healed, we are in the position of actively accepting the situation. This puts us into the realm of all possibilities in which we are more open to cures, if the accepting itself has not become the "cure", or we find happiness within the situation.

We will get technical in this. But we should always remember that at the root, the student comes to the teacher, the audience comes to the performance, the person comes to the bodyplay to be deeply and intimately with a flesh-and-blood person or a group of flesh-and-blood people in a way that is usually denied to her in normal polite social life. She comes for touching, holding, rocking, playing, having fun, and healing. This has been usually forgotten under rigid serious rituals, techniques and theories. Again, western medicine is a prime example of this forgetting. But even spiritual methods of healing in our culture have put the rituals and techniques over the playing and fun.

This is why, before we get into the techniques of chero bodyplay, we have to be clear about what we are doing. By doing the apprenticeship, by doing performances, by doing bodyplay, we are calling forth the liminal state of controlled folly. Controlled folly is liminal because it is a combination of the awake reality and dream reality. Rituals make this combination possible.

In the state of controlled folly, the activities of playing and creating fun are intensified and expanded, because rituals take the place of the normal rules, taboos, fears, and inhibitions. This makes it possible to go into the unknown where anything is possible. Ritual is what makes this magical playing safe by giving the playing a living, breathing structure. Playing is only possible within a structure. But when ritual becomes important in itself, rigid and serious, it starts limiting and killing the play and fun. So it is important to remember that the ritual is just the channel of the play and fun.

Playing is a primal state in which things are drained temporarily of their normal meanings. Life goals for a time fade in importance in this state. Tensions and stresses of normal life are safely transmuted into creativity. In play, newness appears. This newness is translated into inspiration, into new ideas, new ways of doing things. The young, both in the higher animals and humans, learn the most through the state of play. Both man and the higher animals use play to transform violent energy into safe acting out. The human mind and civilization were evolved by playing.

In bodyplay, chero is aroused by playing with the body. Fun is created and released by this play into the world directly. Fun is energy focused upon itself, rather than upon some goal. The fun we are talking about in this work is a deep, intense fun that corrects imbalances and induces newness. This kind of fun comes from risk-taking and work. This deep fun feels very different from the surface, light, fast fun of the world of politeness, glamour, romance, and social rules. This difference confuses people.

In bodyplay, this deep fun, which is focused chero, brings about a balance where there was an imbalance; it slowly moves things into balance. People usually think the healer heals the sick, the teacher teaches the student, the performer entertains the audience. This mistaken concept has the chero that heals flowing from a source (the healer) to a passive container (the sick) for the benefit of the receiving party. The truth is the two, by touching and playing, create a complete chero circuit, allowing the chero to flow freely finding the needed balance in both. When this balance is reached in the two people, the special fun of controlled folly is released into the world, inching the outer world into balance. This world balance is the ultimate purpose of these healing rituals of magical play. This ultimate purpose is usually hidden from awareness by focusing on healing the person.

To understand the nature of balancing, we must understand the true qualities of Yin and Yang. The popular notion about Yin and Yang is they are feminine and masculine with tints of negative and positive. Yin and Yang really are parts of a continuum, called the Tao. Everything has a Tao. When we were talking about the chero breath, inhaling is Yin and the exhaling is Yang. Contractions are Yin; expansions, Yang. The backbrain is Yin with its deep, intuitive, long-range vision; the frontbrain is Yang with its practical knowledge of how to live day by day. Within each person there is the Tao of Yin and Yang. There is a certain point in each personal Tao where there is a balance between Yin and Yang. This point is different in each person. It is rarely at the middle of the Tao. When a person can find and maintain this balance, he has erour, the vulnerable strength. The vulnerability in erour is Yin; the strength is Yang. As a rule of thumb, in our modern western culture, imbalance is usually caused by too much Yang.

This means "health" is not a fixed point of perfection or normalcy that you reach and maintain. Health is the ever-changing dance of balance among the dynamic taos of the body. This dance of balance is the state the body tends to be. Healing is putting the body back into this dance. Within this picture, "illness" is often one of the paths back to health. Also death may be the natural outcome of health. This flies against the western misconception that holds that health is a static state, something you get to, maintain, or lose...that health is being unsick, untired, balanced, grounded, normal, undying. But the truth is health is a dynamic state of interaction of the seven centers, each operating as close within its Tao as possible. Sickness, contractions, mistakes, death are as equally parts of the state of health as wellness, expansions, doing the right things, and life are. There will be no state of perfection, only the process of living, the art of living.

Through bodyplay, erour is slowly reached by calling forth chero in all parts of the body by eroplaying. This is true not only in the "receiver", but also in the "healer". Moreover, through the energy released through these magical sessions, a collective social erour is gradually created for the general world. This is the ultimate reason for this work. The chero released as focused fun "writes" upon the place in which this magical play is performed. It transforms the place into a magical site. The more play is done in a place, the more chero is stored in the physical site. The more chero that is contained in a physical site, the easier it is to perform more intense play.

Each touch and gesture and movement in bodyplay has its own Tao of Yin and Yang...its own qualities of calming and arousal. Each touch has both calming and arousal within it. One of the secrets of bodyplay is finely using these two qualities in the right balance within each firm touch of playing.

The hands are transmitters of chero. This is because your hands are the only parts of your body that can touch almost all of your body. They are healing wands of chero. Laying on of hands is powerful magic. But rubbing body centers together is much more powerful, therefore more taboo. This magic requires two or more people being physically intimate together.

Cherotic bodyplay releases, frees, creates new possibilities. This is true for the people who are actually directly playing together. But this is also true for the society, the people, the world, the outer reality surrounding the eroplaying people. This makes bodyplay not just an individual problem-solving therapy. Instead, it is a playful but powerful ritual that has effects on many different levels. There is a danger in focusing too much on what it will do for the individual, how it will affect his life, what it means in terms of his life, how it will help him.

You who are reading this are aware to some degree that you create at least your own reality. But you look around at the reality that you find yourself in, and it does not match your ideal of how things should be. This has given rise to bad logical thinking which has sealed many people (especially in the growth movement of the '70s) back into being victims. According to this bad logic, since a person creates his own reality, he must somehow want the reality he finds himself in. If the reality does not match what he thinks should be, then he must not really want what he thinks should be, what he wishes should be. So he does not really want what he thinks he should want, what he wishes he wants. Just writing down this bad logic is confusing!

This way of thinking is a padded cell. It comes from the premise that there should not be any "shoulds". This premise originally applied to false "shoulds" coming from outside of the person. But over time, it bled into the personal inner shoulds, what is right inwardly. This leaves no base upon which the person can create. He is left with guilt for creating a reality that should not be...or worse, he proudly takes "responsibility" for doing what he knows he should not do...takes responsibility for continuing to do it until sometime in the future when he magically can start doing his ideal. This is absolutely false "taking responsibility", the worst kind of double-think.

It takes one magical fact, the fact that you can create your own reality, and uses this fact as the foundation for a prison of victimization. It simplifies freedom, power, and real responsibility out of life again. If you really do not want what you yourself think you should want, what you wish you want, your only option is to give up on yourself, to see yourself as inferior to your ideas, to settle for less, to be less, to wallow in self-indulgence within guilt and fear and doubt. So you project guilt, fear, and doubt out into the dynamic interplay of ultimate reality. So you are personally responsible for guilt, doubt, and fear in all reality.

What this bad logic does not take into account is the influences of the dynamic interplay on the person. If a person gets cancer, it does not mean that he secretly wanted to get sick or that he did anything wrong to cause the illness, or that this sickness is a lesson that he has refused to learn in any other way. If he thinks these things, if he thinks in this cause-effect linear logic, he takes on the illness as himself. This makes healing much harder to take place because there is no place within which to do battle. It is him...it is the cause of his doing, his fault, or God's wrath.

In reality, there are many, many factors that create such a situation. Many of these factors are "invisible", impersonal. For an example, in our cultural frame, there is an expectation that has the title of "statistical probability" that a certain number of people within a certain time frame will have cancer and die. Reality tends to fulfill strongly held expectations, so that number of people will die within that time frame. This is just one of the factors. The person does not need to understand these factors.

We have said a major secret in healing is acceptance. What the person with cancer first (as any healer) needs to do is to accept the situation (but not the surrounding expectations) he finds himself in, accept the cancer, accept death, but more importantly, accept living. This acceptance creates a level battleground. Next, he should find out what he envisions should happen (but not just should happen for him, but what should happen)...how should he live, how should he die, what should the cancer do, what should life be like, what should dying and death be like, what should things be like. Then he has to act and live in passion and in faith as if things are as they should be. There is always a risk of failure, of losing the battle. But by doing this healing battle, even if the person "loses", he is still within power.

I explore these ideas more fully in my book *Cherotic Magic*. And I'd love to hear from you.

Frank Moore

The Combine Plot

Originally written in 1990, The Combine Plot was widely published in such publications as *P-Form Magazine* and *Short Fuse*.

For months I have been thinking about writing a piece about what I call the plot of fragmentation. It would be about the aspect of the plot that focuses on making us think that to do anything meaningful, to be an effective force for change, you have to reach a large number of people, commonly known as THE MASSES or THE MASS MARKET. I was going to talk about how this aspect of the plot has limited art by making artists and galleries think that to reach this market, or at least a fraction of it, artists have to reach levels of educational, technical, and marketing skills which are set by, and acceptable to, the real world of mass communications.

Moreover, the subject matter was set to certain "in fashion" areas such as AIDS, feminism, the homeless, the environment, etc...what are "in fashion" subjects keep changing every six months or a year (obviously, the homeless people did not get homes nor did people stop dying of AIDS...rather, the glamour attention-span wears off and the focus quickly switches before things crack through the surface into the uncomfortable depth of universals where issues explode, leaving us trying to live together).

This aspect of the plot leads artists on a chase of college degrees, of skills to operate high-tech art-making machines, of money or positions that will give them the opportunity to do art, even when the style, the subject matter, and maybe the content of the art is dictated by this chase, by the combine plot.

This was what I was planning to write about. I was going to call it THE PLOT OF BIGNESS. But the plot has overtaken me during my thinking about the article. I see in the press that Sen. Jesse Helms and Rep. Dana Rohrabacher have nominated me, along with Annie Sprinkle, Karen Finley, Johanna Went, Cheri Gaulke, as well as other unnamed artists, to be the next target in their war on art. By doing so, Dana and Jesse have given us artists a platform from which to fight the plot. Because doing battle with the combine plot is one of the main functions of an artist, I am flattered to be nominated as one of the top ten on the new McCarthy hit list. I was feeling left out. All my heroes in the past were banned, jailed, harassed for their work. Artists such as Finley who I respect have been fighting the censors for years. My ego was crushed when I saw Rohrabacher on CNN label Annie Sprinkle a threat to the established moral order. After all, my work is as threatening as hers. But days later, someone sent me the *NEW YORK CITY TRIBUNE* (Feb. 5) special report that named names, and my name was there. What a relief! I only wish Dana and Jesse had invited me to testify. Jesse, I am available.

I know the last paragraph sounds like light humor...not taking the war seriously. It is a serious war with the high stakes of freedom and liberty for everyone. But you must understand the nature of the combine plot. It does not understand humor or the personal level. It can crush you if you operate by the mass rules and try to fight it on its terms. But once you drop out of the mass headset, the plot becomes very fragile, very threatened. This is why the plot's Helms is after me and you. Because of this, my article is forced to take on a larger scope and a certain nonlinear quality. Please bear with it.

To understand what is really going on under this "sex" witch-hunt, it is important to understand the nature of the general plot of fragmentation, the combine plot. I took the word "combine" from the novel One Flew Over the Cuckoo's Nest by Ken Kesey. In the book, the combine is a fear machine network which secretly installed pacemakers of fear, doubt, and mistrust in almost everyone in childhood. This made people much easier to control. It isolates people into cells padded with fear and doubt, making the people part of the combine. There are some misfits whom the combine missed with its fear pacemakers. In others, the fear pacemakers blow their fuses. These people without the fear pacemakers are very dangerous to the combine because if they are not checked, destroyed, discredited, isolated, or enfolded into the combine, they can show others how to blow out their own fear pacemakers, can show others how to be free humans linked to other free humans. The combine rarely has to directly destroy the misfits itself. Just direct eliminations would reveal the existence of the combine. So such direct eliminations are kept to the minimum. The real tool of the combine is a vague sense of uncomfortableness, of inferiority, and of mistrust within the victims of the combine. The setting of the novel is a mental ward in which most of the patients are self-committed. They believe themselves weak, unable to cope with the outside world. They believe the fear comes from themselves, not from the pacemakers. They just have to start believing in themselves, and they could pull out the pacemakers and walk out of the hospital. But every time they reach this threshold of freedom, the combine, by clever remote manipulation, turns up the vague uncomfortableness and mistrust. The victims themselves do the destroying of the misfit either in themselves or that con man pied piper who laughs at their fears and limits, who shows them the way to freedom. It is the victims who do most of the censoring.

One of the main functions of art is to be that misfit who reveals and fights against the combine, to show the way back to freedom and self-trust. This misfit function of art is the real target of this attack of the combine in the form of Jesse and Dana.

The sexual layer of the attack is a misleading ploy. As Lisa Duggan says in her excellent article in the October 1989 *ARTFORUM* on the history of this attack of art, "sex panics, witchhunts, and Red scares are staples of American History....they have been enthusiastically taken up by powerful groups in an effort to impose a rigid orthodoxy on the majority." Understand, each of the layers of the attack are important and must be met directly and with full-force. The use of sex censorship to disguise political censorship is recent in our history, starting in the 19th century. It is based on our puritan national background. It depends on the belief that sex is somehow innately bad, or at least suspect. So if you want to shut someone up, it is easier if you can paint the issue in sexual terms...better yet, in terms of sexual deviance. Then the people who should stand up and full force beat back this threat, are strangely silent, strangely half-hearted. My liberal Senator Alan Cranston replied to my letter about the Mapplethorpe/N.E.A. issue by saying he (Cranston) is totally against Helms' attempts at censorship, but that the N.E.A. did make mistakes which needed to be looked into, making sure it does not happen again. With friends like this, who needs Helms!

THE VILLAGE VOICE defended my work from Helms just on the grounds that I am physically disabled. I have not figured out the logic of that even now. Duggan says, if you are banned as sexually deviant, "No one will defend your action, only your right to due process and a good lawyer."

There is a martial arts principle that when you are attacked, that is the point that you have most force potential. This is because you can combine the opposing force with your own, and reshape this new, more powerful force into your advantage. Helms has given us an opening to create a greater freedom. I refuse to defend my work from charges of obscenity.

There is no such thing as sexual obscenity. It is an undefinable concept invented to limit freedom and to promote the established moral order. If I protest that my work is not obscene, I would be admitting the valid existence of sexual obscenity. There is nothing wrong with using sex, nudity, and all the bodily functions as art. It is time to do away with the legal concept of sexual obscenity once and for all...and for good. Dana and Jesse are just giving us artists an opening to accomplish this.

But sex is just the top layer of this attack. Sex is what Communism was in the McCarthy Era. In the '50s, people thought those who were blacklisted for being Communists or fellow travelers somehow deserved to be blacklisted, were asking to be blacklisted by going too far. People thought it was O.K. to sign the loyalty oath, O.K. to not hire the blacklisted, O.K. to play along with the corrupt system...O.K. because they were not and never had been Reds.

But what they did not understand was that the real focus was not Communism, but controlling power. The same is true today. Let us peel away the layers.

I have not heard anyone talk about the visual beauty of "Piss Christ"...only about Serrano's right to do "obscene" and "blasphemous" art. In our society in which the church and state are supposed to be separate, any attempt by the governmental agency to label images and subjects as "blasphemous" and "sacrilegious"...or, for that matter, "sacred" and "holy"...and act upon these labels, is intolerable. Religious material has been traditionally a rich vein of artistic inspiration, whether the art itself is religious, anti-religious, or using symbols from religion in a non-religious context. This is a basic artistic and religious freedom which must not be taken away.

Why Serrano is on the hit list is because his images are seen by some to be anti-Christ or anti-Christian. I think this religious layer of the attack on artistic freedom is as deep, if not deeper, than the sexual layer. In the "Name Names" special report on "Funds Descending into Cesspool of 'Art' Filth", the right wing N.Y.C TRIBUNE listed five objectionable performance artists (Annie Sprinkle, Karen Finley, Johanna Went, Cheri Gaulke and myself). An interesting pattern appeared. All five use trance process in our art; all five can be considered to be shamanistic. By reading this article, it became clear that this layer is not a coincidence. There are many artists who use sex and nudity in their art. What set these five apart is their use of trance, of ritual, of the body, of taboo to create a magical social change. This is also true for the "Modern Primitives" exhibition. What this reveals is that "sexual obscenity" is just a cover for the religious, artistic, and political battles. We are on the list not because we are sexually obscene...but because our intention is not to just sexually arouse. And that is what is threatening to the combine.

Under this religious layer, there is the political layer. As V. Vale and Andrea Juno, whose RE/SEARCH PUBLICATIONS is under the Jesse/Dana investigation, said in their open letter in the S.F. CHRONICLE (March 23, 1990): "Art is not always comfortable to society. One of the major powers of art is to stimulate dialogue on psychological and other issues society neglects...is it just a coincidence that the victims on Helms' 'investigation' are all members of oppressed communities? Mapplethorpe was gay, Annie Sprinkle, Karen Finley (Cheri Gaulke), and Johanna Went are women dealing frankly with sexuality. With such groups now finding their voices in society, it must strike fear in the hearts of Helms and his ilk." It is important to see the attack as a tactic in the movement to "Repress anything controversial: to get rid of the 'fringes' and purge the country of eccentricity, cultural diversity and minority identity," to again use the words of Vale and Juno.

Truth is the N.E.A. controversy is just a move in a game for political power. It is not really about defunding the N.E.A. Even though the N.E.A. does a lot of good, it is one of the best ways that the combine powers have to control the arts. The issue of defunding the N.E.A. is a ploy to direct the attention of both artists and the general public away from what is really going on. Dana and Jesse, and the forces behind them, have no intention of cutting or killing the N.E.A. It would make no political sense. It would be like a drug pusher threatening to cut off the junkie's supply. The pusher will not permanently cut off drugs to the junkie... unless it is as a warning to other junkies. The drugs are the pusher's control over the junkie. The N.E.A. money is the medium of the combine's control over artists and their art.

The threat of killing the N.E.A., the cutting funds, creates a manageable flap to focus people's attention upon, to drain artists' protesting energy into, and to set up a dummy issue. Then when the peak of outrageousness in this media event has passed, a "compromise" is offered. The N.E.A. will not be done away with. There will be money for the arts. Artists will be painted as winners. Of course, there is a price for this "victory". The "compromise" will be new rules, both spelled out and hidden, willingly accepted by artists. These rules, these fears, these limits will make artists agents for the established order. This is the real goal of the combine.

This real goal and the basic dishonesty of the plot that Jesse and Dana represent becomes increasingly clearer the closer we look under the surface. In the CNN piece on his attack on Annie Sprinkle, Dana said he does not want to censor this "obscene" art...he just wants artists to do this kind of art on their time and money, not on the government's. This would be outrageous in itself. But it is a lie. The real goal of this attack is to make all art, not just N.E.A. funded art, the agent for established order, to deball all art, to tame down all art.

Annie, Vale and Juno, and some other artists on the hit list have not received a penny from N.E.A. money. The Kitchen, which does get N.E.A. funding, did not use any of that money for the Sprinkle show. Dana's logic for wanting to cut the Kitchen's government funding is: since the N.E.A. sponsors some of the Kitchen's programs, it enables the Kitchen to produce on its own other shows, some of which may be objectionable to the N.E.A./Combine. Since the N.E.A. indirectly supports these independent productions, it can express its displeasure of these independent productions by cutting the funds to the offending gallery or artist.

We have seen this line of mislogic before. What comes to mind is the forbidding of federally funded family planning centers from talking with their clients about the abortion option. After all, historically in America, abortion and birth-control have been tied with obscenity.

The message is clear: eliminate controversial, experimental, and avant-garde art. This purely artistic level of the attack by those who do not care about art is revealed in the TRIBUNE article. The elimination of the politically and artistically controversial work is to make the N.E.A. into a vague system of rewards and punishments based on "correctness" ... be it political, religious, artistic, or sexual/moral. The example of this reward/punishment system is the threat by the N.E.A. to withdraw a $10,000 grant to ARTISTS' SPACE for a show about AIDS because of an essay in the catalog criticizing Jesse and other public officials. The N.E.A. chair John Frohnmeyer tried to justify this by saying, "Political discourse ought to be in the political arena and not in a show sponsored by the endowment." This outrageous attempt to limit the scope of art makes it clear that John is no friend of art. It is also clear that obscenity and N.E.A. defunding are smoke screens.

Let me put it bluntly. What we have here is another McCarthy era.

Jesse is losing his favorite enemy, the Communists, which he has used as an excuse for trying to limit personal freedoms. Dana needs an issue to make his reputation on. And John just wants to keep his job. When the outside enemy began to crumble with the Berlin Wall, they looked inside for new enemies to sink their teeth into. First, they focused on the war on drugs. Although that was a good start for invasion of privacy with drug testing and "Just say no" ..after all, drug pushers make great bad guys...it was too limited. Same was true with abortion. But suppression of expression under the guise of a war against obscenity opens a wide range of possibilities.

Understand, I am using Helms, Rohrabacher, and Frohnmayer as symbols; as they are using me and the other artists on the hit list as symbols. And frankly they are easy targets. They are dishonest men who do not really care about art or morality. They are not the real culprits. The real culprits are us artists, us liberals. It was us who opened the door to the Helms attack by surrendering the artist's control of art over to what is called "politically correct". When feminists tried to ban artists such as Karen Finley from art shows because of using objectionable words and images, when blacks, gays, and the disabled tried to change the stereotypes by trying to censor them out of existence, it gave Helms the opening he needed. The only real way to get rid of evil, bad, stupid stereotypes and ideas is to give them freedom of expression in an open marketplace of ideas where all ideas have equal access to people. This requires the trust and the faith that the truth will be ultimately chosen.

I am a slow typist. As I write this, events have overtaken me. The combine has struck again with its remote control of fear and with its drugs of bigness and money. The Cleveland Public Theater Performance Art Festival had invited me to do my "Journey to Lila" ritualistic piece with audience participation. Two weekends before I was to perform, the city's vice squad sat in on the festival's show of Annie Sprinkle and made it clear that if she did certain things which are regular parts of her art, she and the director of the festival would be arrested. For personal, practical reasons, Annie decided to change her act.

We should be outraged that the vice squad came. We should be outraged against the government undercover spying on art and theater, against the use of a bad law in a manner it was not intended, against what makes it impossible for us to see truly free art and theater in this festival. There was a lot of pressure on me from the festival director to not be unreasonable, to give up control of the art over to some political game.

(I need to make a distinction between the festival and the Cleveland Public Theatre. The festival is an event that takes place at the theatre for two months, once a year. The festival director, Tom Mulready, is not a regular member of the theatre organization's staff. Any references here to the festival and/or its director refer only to the festival and its director and do not reflect in any way on the Cleveland Public Theatre or its director and staff. I found the Cleveland Public Theatre Director and staff to be a great example of what a group of people can do when they are committed to art.)

The law was used in a very strange way. The law says performers and their audience cannot touch one another on certain so-called erogenous zones. In ritualistic audience participatory performances in general and in my work in particular, this prohibition destroys any hope of doing the work. As I write this, I do not have copies of all of Cleveland's laws that are wrongly being applied to works of art. I do not know if there are laws in Cleveland against nudity in performance. But it is clear it is not possible for me to do the art without getting arrested or seriously compromising the integrity of the art. I am not willing to do this. I am willing to be arrested for the art.

I would understand if the director did not want to get arrested along with my company. After all, the curator in Cincinnati is facing a possible five-year sentence for having the Mapplethorpe exhibition. Most people do not have that kind of courage. If that was the fear, I would have created with the festival an artistic protest against the law that would have neither broken the law nor compromised.

But it was not fear of arrest, but the fear of losing funding, fear of how the festival would look, fear of inconvenience. The focus was how to protect the festival, its size, its importance, its financial health. What was right for the art was forgotten. In fact, both the art and the artist became nuisances to be dealt with, to be sacrificed. The headset is it is the duty for artists and for every citizen to obey the law, even admittedly unjust laws. After all, it was stated by the director that he, Mulready, is not Martin Luther King. King, Jefferson, Gandhi, and all of the artists and just plain folk who broke unjust laws in order to evolve things to a better place are turning over in their graves. This is one of the main functions of art. It was stated by Mulready that it is impossible to present in Cleveland what is presented in big cities such as New York, Los Angeles, San Francisco...but we have also done the same performances in small cities such as Denver, Buffalo, and Rochester.

He said it as if this situation is acceptable, if regrettable, in the Midwest. This attitude places the festival in the role of being the agent of the established order, rather than on the side of change. I was told by Mulready that this kind of art would be shown privately in Cleveland. But the festival could not be remotely linked to it unless the art is mutilated to fit the status quo. I kept being told to think of what the festival gives me and the other artists in terms of money and exposure. I should not blow it. What is forgotten in all of this is if the art is not intact, if the content of art is not firmly in the hands of the artists, then artists, art festivals, art galleries and theaters, and even art itself will become just window-dressing for the established order. I am thinking of the artists. If I gave up control of the art directly or indirectly either to the vice squad or this festival, I would be putting a frame of untruth around the artists and the audiences of the Festival. I will not do that.

After two days of pressuring me to change my performance, Mulready suddenly reversed his position. He did not do it from a flash of integrity, but because he was getting pressure from both inside the Cleveland Public Theatre and the national art community. I did the performance as it was originally created without incident.

The combine plot has Mulready hooked on the drug of bigness, on the funding habit. In our talks on the crisis over my performance, things were talked about in terms of how big the festival was, how the funding could not be risked now that the Festival has reached this level of size and importance. Hidden within this is the pacemaker of fear that the combine can use by remote control. This drug of bigness is why, to get N.E.A. money, artists are signing what amounts to a loyalty oath to the established order, agreeing to not do patently offensive work. The combine can only pull off this slow giving up of the artists' control by using the drug of bigness and the pacemaker of fear.

It is easy to get hooked on the drug of bigness, as I found out when I received an N.E.A. fellowship for $5,000 in the early '80s. I had been doing art, performance and theater for about ten years with little or no money. So the N.E.A. money was just extra money. I soon noticed the work shifted from human-intensive to a more money-intensive focus. This shift was slight because I work on a small grassroots scale. But the scale began to expand. In a way, this expanding scale was fun, exciting, glamorous. But the change did not organically come from the art. Moreover, as my N.E.A. year drew to a close, I became more and more anxious about where I would get more money, thinking about applying for more grants, worrying about what I could not do if I did not get more grants. All of this took away from the art. It made me much more vulnerable to compromise, much more likely to become a part of the combine. The old richness of possibilities and alternatives began to dry up, being funneled into a possibility of grants. One day I began to wonder how I could have done art for all those years, and now I was full of fear. I decided to not play the grant game.

If this addiction can happen to an artist like me, who operates on the small scale, I can only imagine what a temptation of addiction someone like the festival director, Mulready, has to cope with. But when the drug of bigness and fear of losing funds compromise art, it is time to protest ... it is time to bring it all back down to the basic core of the artistic experience which is the art coming directly through the artist to the society without any censoring influences, so that art can cause evolution in the society. It is extremely dangerous when artists sign loyalty oaths to the established order to become paid agents, when art festivals and galleries find it acceptable for vice squads to spy on art and theater, to use blue laws to forbid art.

To fight back this full-scale attack on creative expression, the attack that may surpass that of the McCarthy era, we artists must be willing to make sacrifices to become independent of the combine. Many galleries and performance companies have died when their grants were cut. This is because bigness and money-intensive art which grants promote drain possibilities from us, blind us to the possibilities that are outside the combine. It has become increasingly important for us artists to start devolving art back to the human personal scale and away from high-tech mass bigness. This devolution will create alternatives that our society needs, and which is the function of art.

I usually perform at grassroots spaces which have created independent alternatives to the combine. For example, Karen Briede ran a multi-level visual and performance gallery in Denver. She brought in nationally known but controversial artists by using the money she made in her hair salon. She was always selling art to her hair clients. She now is having nationally important exhibitions in her apartment in Chicago. In Seattle, A.F.L.M. (A FLIMSY LACE NIGHTIE) is doing the same thing by being a coffee house during the day and a gallery by night.

In these and other similar small places, cutting-edge art finds homes because people like Karen personally take risks for the art. But as Martha Wilson of FRANKLIN FURNACE has shown, it is possible for established galleries to show controversial art. It is extremely important that both artists and art administrators be willing to lose everything, including funding, in order to save freedom. This is the only way we will win back our full freedom from the combine, take back our full range of possibilities.

I want to close this by quoting from a letter from Kyle Griffith, an author. The Combine "is counting on the majority of creative people to stay on the sidelines until the anti-art movement gains real support among the general public, saying 'Well, my work isn't that controversial, so why should I take the trouble to support a bunch of really hard-core people who are deliberately asking for trouble from the blue noses, anyway?'" The combine plot "encourages consumer art while discouraging all art forms that turn the consumers of art into artists themselves. What people like you are REALLY being attacked for is drawing the audience, the art consumer, into the creative process."

The Combine Plot Thickens

An email conversation published in *P-FORM* Number 42.

Thu, 30 May 1996
From: Frank Moore <fmoore@lanminds.com>
To: fmoore@lanminds.com

Well, gang....I'm blown out, am cracking up...I have heard every-thing now. I recycle my writings...cut them up to use the ideas. Remem-ber that I sent out THE COMBINE PLOT 96 a few months ago as a response to the telecom bill? It was really a part of a larger piece. I cut out the last half of the old piece...in that half I talked about how a certain ass-hole director of a performance festival was trying to force me to mutilate/censor my performance...yeah, right! I finally did the performance there uncensored...and THE COMBINE PLOT was published in a lot of art magazines. That was '90.

Guess who called today. The asshole! Guess why he was calling. He is creating a website for the festival...and he wants to put THE COMBINE PLOT, along with "other scholarly papers", on the site!

Here's the second half. Can you tell me why he wants to put this on his site?

I am a slow typist. As I write this, events have overtaken me. The combine has struck again with its remote control of fear and with its drugs of bigness and money. The Cleveland Public Theater Performance Art Festival had invited me to do my Journey to Lila ritualistic piece with audience participation. Two weekends before I was to perform, the city's vice squad sat in on the festival's show of Annie Sprinkle and made it clear that if she did certain things which are regular parts of her art, she and the director of the festival would be arrested. For personal, practical reasons, Annie decided to change her act.

We should be outraged that the vice squad came. We should be outraged against the government undercover spying on art and theater, against the use of a bad law in a manner it was not intended, against what makes it impossible for us to see truly free art and theater in this festival. There was a lot of pressure on me from the festival director to not be unreasonable, to give up control of the art over to some political game.

(I need to make a distinction between the festival and the Cleveland

Public Theatre. The festival is an event that takes place at the theatre for two months, once a year. The festival director, Tom Mulready is not a regular member of the theatre organization's staff. Any references here to the festival and/or its director refer only to the festival and its director and do not reflect in any way on the Cleveland Public Theatre or its director and staff. I found the Cleveland Public Theatre Director and staff to be a great example of what a group of people can do when they are committed to art.)

The law was used in a very strange way. The law says performers and their audience cannot touch one another on certain so-called erogenous zones. In ritualistic audience participatory performances in general and in my work in particular, this prohibition destroys any hope of doing the work. As I write this, I do not have copies of all of Cleveland's laws that are wrongly being applied to works of art. I do not know if there are laws in Cleveland against nudity in performance. But it is clear it is not possible for me to do the art without getting arrested or seriously compromising the integrity of the art. I am not willing to do this. I am willing to be arrested for the art.

I would understand if the director did not want to get arrested along with my company. After all, the curator in Cincinnati is facing a possible five-year sentence for having the Mapplethorpe exhibition. Most people do not have that kind of courage. If that was the fear, I would have created with the festival an artistic protest against the law that would have neither broken the law nor compromised.

But it was not fear of arrest, but the fear of losing funding, fear of how the festival would look, fear of inconvenience. The focus was how to protect the festival, its size, its importance, its financial health. What was right for the art was forgotten. In fact, both the art and the artist became nuisances to be dealt with, to be sacrificed. After all, it was stated by the director that he, Mulready is not Martin Luther King. King, Jefferson, Gandhi, and all of the artists and just plain folk who broke unjust laws in order to evolve things to a better place are turning over in their graves. This is one of the main functions of art. It was stated by Mulready that it is impossible to present in Cleveland what is presented in big cities such as New York, Los Angeles, San Francisco...but we have also done the same performances in small cities such as Denver, Buffalo, and Rochester.

He said it as if this situation is acceptable, if regrettable, in the Mid-west. This attitude places the festival in the role of being the agent of the established order, rather than on the side of change. I was told by Mulready that this kind of art would be shown privately in Cleveland. But the festival could not be remotely linked to it unless the art is mutilated to fit the status quo. I kept being told to think of what the festival gives me and the other artists in terms of money and exposure. I should not blow it. What is forgotten in all of this is if the art is not intact, if the content of art is not firmly in the hands of the artists, then artists, art festivals, art galleries and theaters, and even art itself will become just window-dressing for the established order. I am thinking of the artists. If I gave up control of the art directly or indirectly either to the vice squad or this festival, I would be putting a frame of untruth around the artists and the audiences of the Festival. I will not do that.

After two days of pressuring me to change my performance, Mulready suddenly reversed his position. He did not do it from a flash of integrity, but because he was getting pressure from both inside the Cleveland Public Theatre and the national art community. I did the performance as it was originally created without incident.

The combine plot has Mulready hooked on the drug of bigness, on the funding habit. In our talks on the crisis over my performance, things were talked about in terms of how big the festival was, how the funding could not be risked now that the Festival has reached this level of size and importance. Hidden within this is the pacemaker of fear that the combine can use by remote control. This drug of bigness is why, to get N.E.A. money, artists are signing what amounts to a loyalty oath to the established order, agreeing to not do patently offensive work.

It is easy to get hooked on the drug of bigness, as I found out when I received an N.E.A. fellowship for $5,000 in the early '80s. I had been doing art, performance and theater for about ten years with little or no money. So the N.E.A. money was just extra money. I soon noticed the work shifted from human-intensive to a more money-intensive focus. This shift was slight because I work on a small grassroots scale. But the scale began to expand. In a way, this expanding scale was fun, exciting, glamorous. But the change did not organically come from the art. Moreover, as my N.E.A. year drew to a close, I became more and more anxious about where I would get more money, thinking about applying for more grants, worrying about what I could not do if I did not get more grants. All of this took away from the art. It made me much more vulnerable to compromise, much more likely to become a part of the combine. The old richness of possibilities and alternatives began to dry up, being funneled into a possibility of grants. One day I began to wonder how I could have done art for all those years, and now I was full of fear. I decided to not play the grant game.

If this addiction can happen to an artist like me, who operates on the small scale, I can only imagine what a temptation of addiction someone like the festival director, Mulready, has to cope with. But when the drug of bigness and fear of losing funds compromise art, it is time to protest ... it is time to bring it all back down to the basic core of the artistic experience which is the art coming directly through the artist to the society without any censoring influences, so that art can cause evolution in the society. It is extremely dangerous when artists sign loyalty oaths to the established order to become paid agents, when art festivals and galleries find it acceptable for vice squads to spy on art and theater, to use blue laws to forbid art.

To fight back this full-scale attack on creative expression, the attack that may surpass that of the McCarthy era, we artists must be willing to make sacrifices to become independent of the combine. Many galleries and performance companies have died when their grants were cut. This is because bigness and money-intensive art which grants promote drain possibilities from us, blind us to the possibilities that are outside the combine. It has become increasingly important for us artists to start devolving art back to the human personal scale and away from high-tech mass bigness. This devolution will create alternatives that our society needs, and which is the function of art.

I usually perform at grassroots spaces which have created independent alternatives to the combine. For example, Karen Briede ran a multi-level visual and performance gallery in Denver. She brought in nationally known but controversial artists by using the money she made in her hair salon. She was always selling art to her hair clients. She now is having nationally important exhibitions in her apartment in Chicago. In Seattle, A.F.L.N. (A FLIMSY LACE NIGHTIE) is doing the same thing by being a coffee house during the day and a gallery by night.

In these and other similar small places, cutting-edge art finds homes because people like Karen personally take risks for the art. But as Martha Wilson of FRANKLIN FURNACE has shown, it is possible for established galleries to show controversial art. It is extremely important that both artists and art administrators be willing to lose everything, including funding, in order to save freedom. This is the only way we will win back our full freedom from the combine, take back our full range of possibilities.

I want to close this by quoting from a letter from Kyle Griffith, an author. The Combine "is counting on the majority of creative people to stay on the sidelines until the anti-art movement gains real support among the general public, saying 'Well, my work isn't that controversial, so why should I take the trouble to support a bunch of really hardcore people who are deliberately asking for trouble from the blue noses, anyway?'" The combine plot "encourages consumer art while discouraging all art forms that turn the consumers of art into artists themselves. What people like you are REALLY being attacked for is drawing the audience, the art consumer, into the creative process."

Date: Fri, 31 May 1996
From: Barbara Golden <barb@c2.org>
To: Frank Moore <fmoore@lanminds.com>
cc: fmoore@lanminds.com

go frankie.

WIGband found out years ago, that there was no use applying to play in major art venues, and have to defend our work, it was much easier to rent a space and have total freedom, then we got asked a bunch of times to do openings and so forth, but the act of having to write a proposal to do our performances was anathema to us.

Date: Tue, 4 Jun 1996
From: keith848@sirius.com (Keith Hennessy)
To: Frank Moore <fmoore@lanminds.com>

Frank
I've been enjoying your e writings and have been sending them along to other freedom spirited artists and activists. I'm disappointed that you're calling Thomas Mulready an asshole. He is no big art dealer. He's produced all of the controversial artists he can afford including many of our visionary kinky taboo breaking friends. Including me and you. He is making different choices than you or I about how to survive during this anti-art wartime. And he may play some games that you think are more

destructive than healthy. In my opinion he's more ally than asshole. Not just an ally of mine but of performance artists in general and controversial sexual liberationists most of all. When I was in Cleveland, most of the African-American theater's staff (Karamu house) wanted to close me down before we opened because in my show about racism and homophobia I pulled a text — inside a condom — from a naked man's butt. A white queer writer from the alternative press called me a racist colonialist because I was going to collaborate with a black gay man from Cleveland. I felt severely unwelcome. Thomas backed me all the way. I changed my piece because I went to Cleveland to be in a conversation with a community of people. I ignored the petty attack by the writer and focused on meeting with the mostly Christian black staff at Karamu. Several of them came to my show because I took out the nudity. I am a community-based artist who makes site specific work. In Cleveland the site included the community I was performing in. I adapted my work to the environment. I told the audience during the show about the changes I made and why I made them. I challenged the edges and my work changed people. It was a major personal success for me. Thomas sat with me in intense meetings. He never asked me to back down. He tried to protect his ass and he respected every move I made.

That is my experience and I respect Thomas for all that. And I just wanted you to add this story to your accumulated information about him. Thanks for reading.

Keith Hennessy

Date: Tue, 04 Jun 1996
From: Frank Moore <fmoore@lanminds.com>
To: Keith Hennessy <keith848@sirius.com>
cc: fmoore@lanminds.com

i just call 'em as I see 'em.

Date: Fri, 07 Jun 1996
From: Frank Moore <fmoore@lanminds.com>
To: Keith Hennessy <keith848@sirius.com>

Keith, more thoughts:
Maybe the bottom line reason why I don't let outside forces/pres-

sures dictate the form or the content of the art is because I do not see myself as the creator of the art, but the servant to the art. One of my functions as a servant is being the bodyguard to the art. I am just following the evolution of the art. I don't really know what an element, image, aspect magically does. I trust that each is there for a host of reasons. So I sit back and watch the interplay and the organic change in the art. I don't feel it is my place to tamper with the art out of reasons of convenience or politics. This is just my personal philosophy of art.

But on the practical level:

It is one thing to create a performance especially for a certain site, event, or audience; or change the performance within [and based on] the dance of you, the art, the audience, the space, and whatever else.

It is a totally different thing to change a piece because of pressure from a censor, an offended person, or a timid producer. The changing of a piece under pressure sets up all kinds of bad and very dangerous precedents, and sends all kinds of bad, dangerous, misleading messages. It says a piece of art is not a united whole, but just a collection of bits of business not really important; so there is no big deal in taking some of the bits out. This is like saying a poem is a collection of words so you can take out the certain offending words and read the poem. It is no longer the poem [probably not even a poem]. People, the community, have been denied the real poem, the real experience. And they are being denied the knowledge of poetry/art.

Moreover, if we change art because of outside pressure, we are saying people have the right to not be offended, to not be made uncomfortable; that it's bad and harmful when art and life offends them. This so-called reasonableness and being careful and staying within the lines becomes the standard order: "be reasonable, change the art!" And then we wonder why someone like Jesse Helms gets started! It seems to me that one of our functions as artists is to make it clear that people can live without censoring limits.

Finally, I have never found that the offended people and censors represent the community. They really look down on the community. In Cleveland, after I spent a week in an intense fight to get the actual performance to the community, the community was hungry for it! It was my largest audience for that kind of long ritual performance: over a hundred people who very actively participated, causing the performance to last over six hours. The censors always sell the people short, looking down on the people. I think artists should keep the control over the content and the form of the art within the art; not surrender the control over to the government, the galleries, the backers, or any pressure group. We as artists owe that to the art, to the people, and to other artists.

Date: Sat, 8 Jun 1996
From: keith848@sirius.com (Keith Hennessy)
To: Frank Moore <fmoore@lanminds.com>

Frank

Thanks for excellent articulation.

I am inspired by your commitment to the art, the image, the magic. I too see myself as servant to the image and to the audiences/communities/peoples.

Censors and producers and leaders in general are more conservative and afraid than the people they (claim to) speak for. Nonetheless there are many people who identify with the censors. I think that artists can make choices about who they are including within the sphere of influence of a given work. Collaborating with the fears and projections of a community is like a risky dance on shaky ruins. The potential for beauty is everywhere and inviting.

Like most body-based artists I work the edges, not the centers. I seek the "resilient edge of resistance"* the place where stretching or reshaping the boundary is possible. This is, of course, located differently for different folks.

All power to the sensualist neo-shaman anti-fascist magicians all power to you and me and performance artists everywhere.

Keith

* a quote from Chester Mainard

Conditions

First written for *FAERIES*, a performance with/for Linda Burnham, 1982.

We will use words, people, ideas, erotic excitement, images, messy fun play to fight the plot that has been brewing ever since the Roman days. For women, the plot has gone on longer except for whores and sex priestesses...ever since the cave days when she lost her equality. The plot of...of what...of romance, of thinking you can't do something because you have no talent or no money...the plot of not trusting, not trusting yourself and not trusting others. The media, politicians, churches have been pushing it. You are not good enough. He is not good enough for you. Buy Topol toothpaste because smoking is a sexy front to hide your unworthiness, but yellow teeth and bad breath give it away. This is about trust. It will get pretty gross, fun, intense, boring, sexy, turned on, everyday... do you trust yourself? Do you trust me? I am a dirty old man who wants to get your clothes off, roll around with you naked...and other disgusting but fun things like making the whole universe disappear by playing cards. But trust is where the magic comes from...so will you revolt by trusting?

I am the director, I like to direct, I like women, I like to be turned on, I like to scream and be a spoiled bastard...I hope I have not forgotten any bad things...all the rumors about me are true. If all of these things are ok, stay. If not, go. If they become not ok during the piece, leave. But don't interrupt or interfere with the piece. I may be lying. I am saying these things to save time. Time is a vital element of this magic. The longer the time that we are in the piece, the greater the magic. Don't tell anyone about anything that went on in this piece, except if you add that you may be lying.

I will use bits and pieces which I will channel, not knowing why, not knowing how an individual bit fits into the whole. So I can not explain them. In some of these bits I will use some of you, using who you are, sometimes sending you to places outside of the cave of this room. Some bits only you and I can do alone. Nobody will see all of the parts. But in the end, there will be a whole. I will not use violence to create this magic. You will not be hurt.

We are putting an arrow in the dragon; we are tripping up the plot that has been trapping us for so long. One obvious way is the piece will change we who are involved, changing our lives and relationships...and that change, no matter how small, will cause a chain reaction in the outside world.

But there is another way that what we will do here will effect and affect the outside world. Science has come up with a theory which explains why one group of a species in another part of the world, with no physical or material contact with another group, picks up change that occurs in the first group. In the past, it would have been called magical. But what some scientists are now saying is that in DNA there is what amounts to a broadcasting unit which both sends out and receives data to and from every member of that certain life form...and perhaps to other life forms and maybe even to non-living material as well. It also has been long known that the observer effects what he observes.

The core of this piece is you and I will set a power erotic wave with each other that will be transmitted on the DNA network. It does not matter if you believe this. But the bits...or rather one of the bits...which I will have people other than you and I do, will create an open channel for our broadcast. So what the other people do in the piece is very important. Now I am talking to everyone else except you. If you feel threatened and want to leave, do so. Don't argue, or judge. Don't try to protect other people in the piece. If you do leave, I am counting on you to honor your commitment to not tell anyone anything about this piece without stating that you may be lying.

Back to the plot which we are fighting against today. If we had freedom to touch each other erotically without limits, without romance, they could not control us, they could not have power over us. They know this. If we know we can do anything we want...that we don't have to wait for enough money before doing what we want...that it ain't true that we have to have talent to do things that we want to do...then their power over us would vanish. That is why they make commercials promoting ideals and images that you cannot fit unless you use their product. "It's so easy to get their attention...it's so easy to lose it...use Head and Shoulders." That is why they keep changing fashions. That is why they say wait for Mr. Right. That is why they say art takes talent and skill...which most people don't have, and say those who are blessed with it must refine it before using it...why they say films must have a certain technical quality before people will see them...why they say don't touch your cock in public, don't stare, don't ask, don't need, don't rub. The people who are on the top and the people who have accepted that they cannot do what they want, have ganged up to preserve this plot of snobs, experts, and morality. It is easy to see why those who are in power want to keep the plot going. But why the schmucks who spend their whole lives not doing what they want, thinking they aren't good enough...why do they want the plot to keep going? Imagine someone like this seeing someone who...like me...is not as smart, skilled, good-looking as they are...so dumb that he doesn't know that the plot says everything is hard. He bumbles through life doing what he wants, making movies and art...playing with sexy girls...all easy. They want to kill him because he, as a symbol, says they could have done what they wanted all along.

Premises:

Pleasure, arousement, excitement are good in themselves.

Curiosity is good.

Religious-political-business-establishment is keeping its power over us by promoting romance through the mass media.

There is no Mr. or Miss or Mrs. Right.

We can fight the plot through magic.

Creating A Masterpiece

January 19, 2000. Published in *Lummox Journal*, March 2000.

An artist starts, let's say, a painting with a set idea of what he is going to paint. Sooner or later he makes a "mistake" -- a color or a line which doesn't fit in the original idea -- which "ruins" the painting. When this happens most people give up, thinking that they are not cut out to be artists, and withdraw back into the common existence. Others try to pretend that they didn't make the mistake, that the color or line isn't there on the canvas. They go on painting as before. When they are done, they have painted the shadow of what they wanted. Moreover, this shadow is covered with a haze. Others keep starting over whenever they make mistakes, not accepting any mistakes. They are rewarded for their endurance with the perfect copy of the thought form which they had held for all this time. They are rewarded by what they think they want to create. Their thought form has been brought down into the material plane. The creation is perfect. But it is not a masterpiece. It is perfect within the limitations placed around it by the rigidness of the artist. The work is perfect, but not free.

A masterpiece is perfect and free. The master artist paints an adventure in color, words, or notes. What others see as mistakes, he sees as challenges, boxes out of which he has worked as the basis on which he creates a totally new, fresh pattern. These challenges, boxes, keystones, keep appearing as he works, demanding the artist's flexibility. If the artist looks back, trying to hold on to what he thought the painting was or would be, he gets trapped in a box out of which he must battle or be turned into a rigid, bitter pillar of salt. The artist has to keep his whole attention on the swirling colors in front of him in order to be the creator.

To create a masterpiece, the artist has to use and risk every bit of himself. But he also has to create with God, for God is the one who creates what most people call mistakes, and that the master artist sees as his tools and materials. God does not create for the artist. God just provides the tools, the guiding bumps. It is up to the artist's free will whether he creates or gets dragged down by the weight of the tools. When the artist is creating, he feels no weight.

The most important masterpiece is a lifetime. This is a statement of hard fact. Creating a masterpiece in every day living is governed by the same rules as creating a masterpiece in paint, but much harder because the artist is also the canvas. In every period of time, in every land, there are a few masterpieces of art and writing. But a masterpiece lifetime is much rarer.

Credit Card Morality

Excerpted from *Cherotic Magic* by Frank Moore, July 1998.

Do to others as you would want to be done to you. Treat people as yourself. Love your neighbor, your enemy, others as yourself. You will reap what you sow. The law of karma. These are all nice abstractions with the loopholes of individualistic choice and time built into them. That is, they secretly imply that there is a choice about seeing the other as separate from yourself, from your personal body...imply that there is a karmic credit card on which you can in effect charge "wrong" action to be paid, with a certain rate of interest, in either good works or suffering at a later date. This creates a judging, an evaluating, a choosing, a questioning whether a "wrong" action is worth the charge on the credit card, how it affects your credit rating. Worst yet, it, like the bank's Mastercard, tends to hide the real costs of the "wrong" actions, hiding it within the easy payment plan, hiding the wide-ranging resulting effects of the "wrong" actions.

"Wrong" actions are different both from mistakes and from "bad" action in a morality system. Mistakes are learning tools within life's evolution. Mistakes are vital, unavoidable, and vulnerable because true mistakes are the result of creative risk-taking. A "mistake" that is repeated over and over is not a mistake at all, but a "wrong" action. A wrong action is an action which harms, does not promote life-affirmations...it is in fact a life-denial, broadcasting life-denials. Morality is an itemized list from the moral visa card...a list of all the possible sins and the form of payment required for each sin. But nowhere on this list is there any mention of the real results, both personal and dynamic, of the so-called sin.

This moral/karmic easy payment plan is one of the main means by which the life-denying power-combine abstracts us out of the direct involving experience of life. It puts the results outside of the personal present into an impersonal future. It puts the "payment" result of a sin outside of the personal present into both an impersonal past and impersonal future...that is, in a moral system of payment. You are paying for past sins in the future. This is fragmenting the reality of experience. A credit card makes it much harder to experience the reality of buying something because it fragments the exchange, the relationship, between two people. There is no exchange of what/who you are in the present. So it is very much harder to feel, experience, the real worth or result of the buying experience. It is much harder to feel, experience who you really are. So you spend more than you would if it had been a physical exchange, a physical relationship, between you and another person. Moreover, the medium of the exchange, money, has been abstracted into unreality, put outside the personal reality. This makes spending casually a matter of course. Creating this casualness is a main reason for credit cards, poker chips, and sins.

But the abstraction does not end at the purchase experience. Without the context of the relationship of exchange, the actual experience of the result of the exchange...for example, the concert which the ticket is for...takes on an unreality to it. Moreover, when it comes time to pay, the experience of the concert has long ago happened, faded into the past. The payment is no longer a personal physical involvement in the actual experience of the concert. The payment is now an involvement with the abstraction, the power system, of the credit card. This involvement with the abstraction is the concept of duty, "should" duty. Because the experience of the concert has been long ago made over into an abstraction before payment time, it is difficult to feel the real effect of the concert. So you dutifully, casually pay the credit card bill.

This basic credit card dynamic is at the root of all moral systems. All moral systems are systems of power, of abstraction, of fragmentation. A moral system contains a framework of shoulds, should nots, taboos. This moral framework is substituted for the direct experience of life. The reasons for the shoulds, should nots, and taboos are not revealed or explained. Love thy neighbor. Thou shall not kill. But there is not a real sense of why. This is true of the modern anti-moral systems of "going with the flow" and "do your own thing"...these anti-moral systems are just moral systems dressed up in mirrors. The should/taboo framework is a con for power.

A saint takes on a moral system so completely that he becomes the social system. Living within a moral framework as a saint does limits the personal ability to shape reality, hence transferring this ability in the form of power to the abstract social structure.

But a life of a saint is not the real goal of any moral system. If everybody lived as saints, the power that was thus generated would not be anywhere near enough to keep an abstract structure in existence. This is why real saints are always in a very tiny minority or a false myth. Saints are decoy models projected in front of people by the abstract power structure.

The real goal of any moral system is personal failure. This type of failure is different from the failure within evolution or creativity. It is the failure of a victim or a loser. A moral system is set up to be almost impossible, if not in fact impossible, for humans to live within. At the heart of the con of morality is to convince the people that they should do what they are not empowered to do. Convince them by creating a system of rewards and punishments which is based on the fragmentation of time into past and future. Once a person is plugged into this reward/punishment system, he stops shaping his actions by the concrete experience of the results, both linear and nonlinear, of his actions. Instead, he starts focusing on the rewards and punishments within the moral system...starts focusing on the past and/or future...starts doing/not doing based on the promised reward/punishment. This abstracts the person out of the direct present experience of his life action and its resulting effects. This abstraction is the root cause of personal casualness. Once he is thus abstracted out of the direct experience, he can be sold whatever prepackaged pictures of reality that the abstract power structures issue, will pay whatever price for forgiveness, protection, for a piece of power (no matter how small). In this way, the person is convinced by the power structure that he needs it, needs to belong to it, to conform to its prepackaged deck of pictures of reality.

Our modern social world is made up of the combine of moral systems. Each power system...be it political, religious, social, economical, or sexual...issues its own deck of reality pictures and moral credit cards. This moral combine includes power systems that we do not usually think of as moral systems. What I am thinking of are the systems of romance, glamour, and education. A moral system is a system that abstracts reality into mental pictures into the past/future.

Love others as yourself. Why? If you do, you will be rewarded sometime in the future. If you do, you will be paying back for something bad you did sometime in the past...or, for that matter, for something bad you will do in the future. This is the logic of morals. It is individualistic ego-centered. It abstracts your dynamic relationship with the other out of reality.

Deep love can be defined as: treat the other as yourself, love the other as yourself, because the other is in fact yourself, is part of your body. So what you do to/with/for the other, you are doing to yourself within the point of action of now. Deep love goes back to the pre-shamanistic personal awareness of the land, the plants and animals, the others in the tribe, and in fact the whole physical existence as parts of the personal body, and hence within personal responsibility.

Cultural Subversion

1991. Published in *New Observations* Issue #1, May/June 1994 and many other publications.

This will be personal. But the personal level is the key to understanding the cultural, artistic, and political movement which is taking back technology into the personal control of anyone who has something to say, something to create. It is personal technology, anarchistic technology. It is not like cable T.V. which we were told ten years ago would liberate the person by giving him intimate and direct information and communication channels...but which today is simply more channels for the money types who have always controlled the communication flowing through mass media...just more monopolized channels for passive entertainment, selling, and manipulation of information and of reality. The only exception to this is the local access channels which are kept in the closet and are always in danger of being axed by the cable company. These access channels are a part of the personal technology.

Personal technology is basically a slip up of what I have called elsewhere "the combine plot". I took the term "combine" from the Ken Kesey novel One Flew Over the Cuckoo's Nest. The combine plot is a hidden dynamic system of power, control, and interest that keeps the tools of creation and of effective change out of the hands of the common people. This keeps the people powerless, keeping the power within an elite. The tools of effective change have been kept out of the hands of the common people by false rituals of education, money, and bulky expensive equipment which took a cult knowledge to operate. Added to this maze of creative blocks were the false myths about talent and the acceptable quality levels needed to reach people, acceptable quality levels below which people are trained to not watch or listen.

All of this is too abstract and philosophical. In this article, I will try to pull these issues down into the real world by using my own artistic experiences as a context. But it is important to realize at the beginning that personal technology, anarchistic technology is still technology. All technology has hidden, built-in links to the established order of isolation and fragmentation. These links can frustrate attempts to use technology to subvert the established reality. Only by being always aware of these links to isolation and fragmentation inherent in all technology, can technology be safely used as a tool of cultural subversion. This fact again banged me over the head when I was talking to a successful musician who didn't understand why all performers do not stop touring, considering the pollution caused by traveling...and do what he does, which is do everything through telecommunications. I just said you can not touch through phones, computers, videos...and even through writing. To restore humanity to our culture by using technology, we must know and admit the limitations of that technology.

All technology is a double-edged sword. This includes the very first communication technology...writing/reading. We usually think of the invention of writing as extremely liberating. And in so many ways it was. But in so many other ways it confined humanity. For one thing, it placed a fixed linear frame of thinking within the human brain much more than spoken language had done. Moreover, writing/reading created a very exclusive elite for most of the known human history. Before writing, everyone knew the tribal language...everyone knew how to paint, sing, dance. Information flowed both between people and within time to the future through this tribal accessible language both of spoken word and of art. If information did not flow through this tribal channel, that information was lost. All of this changed when writing was invented. Now there was a channel that was not accessible to everyone, a channel that did not easily lose information. Those who could access this channel had power. Because of this, for most of recorded history, the skill of reading/writing was monopolized by the ruling elite to maintain its power. This was true even after a larger minority gained limited access to the flowing channel of writing. One of the ways the elite maintained its control was by withdrawing the important ideas...dangerous ideas...both sacred and profane, away from the common people, withdrawing the dangerous ideas into a dead language such as Latin or Greek. Only the members of the elite who went through the rituals of education of the established order (be it religious, political, and/or class) could read or speak this dead language of power. There was another channel of flowing information which was folk art, folk music, and folk words, be it written or spoken. This folk channel was accessible to everyone. It was a dynamic, interactive channel of communication. But the full force of this folk channel was always kept in check by the elite channel with the myth that anything which comes through the folk channel was not worthy or important because it did not come from the hidden knowledge.

This control by the elite did not start to break down until the printing press became cost-accessible to the members of the common people.

This opened to the common people a communication channel which was not rooted in physical time...that is, you write something and someone within another time, another place reads exactly what you thought. This is the real force which was unlocked by the printing press, and not the ability to reach mass amounts of people. Without the printing press being to a large degree accessible to the forces of change, the American and French Revolutions may not have happened.

But the elite quickly developed strategies to limit access for the common people to this printing channel. The elite spread the myth that to be really effective, a writer had to go through the rituals of the educational system, and then be blessed by being recognized by the publishing factory, which became increasingly massive and impersonal. Self-publishing was labeled "vanity press". The presses that offered this service were seen as cons, as scams. Writers who used this service were thought of as untalented fools who got conned. The individual who believed in this myth of the power of the corporate media system to bestow access to communications, and to bestow validity through acceptance, was frozen out of any real position for subversive change.

All of this is an historical background on which I can talk about the issues of personal technology, anarchistic technology in the context of cultural subversion.

I started out in the late '60s writing for underground papers as a political columnist...sneaking into the mimeograph room at school to run off a hundred copies under the protection of a friendly teacher. Of course, the teacher always, as well as us, got into hot water...and the access to the mimeograph machine was closed. No access, no underground paper. There was not any question about our buying our own mimeograph machine...no money.

But it took only a year or so for the underground press to move from the mimeograph stage into being run off at offset print shops. The underground press had its roots going back through the radical press of the '20s and '30s and in the poetry press. The kind of person who put out these papers poured all their personal money into it, then hoped by selling ads, selling papers, by magic, the paper would stay afloat. There was rarely any question of making money on it. But when your nest egg, your dead aunt's money, ads, sales, or whatever was supporting your rag ran out, that paper of visions died. But there was always a new paper being born to fill the empty space.

There was a rejection of the old standards of quality of both form and content which had kept the common people from creating. As a result of this rejection, a new way of looking at art, politics, and life was thus created. The underground press became so effective that by the early '70s there were over 700 of these papers and an underground press network. It became so effective that the F.B.I. targeted the underground press for destruction by a covert war. By using the fact that the underground papers rarely had direct access to a printing press, and by using the organization which developed around the underground press, the F.B.I. and the rest of the combine could bring the underground press into control, into the fold.

Around this time, I rejected politics as a means for effective subversive change, and began looking towards art and magic for an effective channel. I took a film-making course, learning the technical rituals of 16mm. 16mm was then the home movie technology. But when I did the technological rituals of lighting, shooting, splicing, etc., they took me away from the actual magic of doing. Hidden within these technological rituals are deadening roadblocks to direct personal creative communications. Roadblocks can be gotten around. But why bother when there are direct alternative routes?

After the film course, I still had no money to make films. One road would have been to put my time and energy into getting money or a position to make films. But I always have mistrusted the myth of changing the system from within. It never works. Once you compromised, modified, changed, distorted both yourself and your message to get the media channel, why bother sending the message? The system myth is a major vacuum that sucks creative power away from people by putting vast amounts of time between the person and the act of creation. Whether the myth is of waiting to get enough money, education, or power before you create, the effect is the same...waiting for Godot.

For these reasons, I created a no/low tech form of live performance which did not need money, theater space, sets, stage lighting, approval, or a particular audience size. This no/low tech form is vital to work which is culturally subversive by expanding the concept of sexuality and reality beyond the frame of taboos.

For me as a no/low tech artist, the personal technology, anarchistic technology is a very important dimension. I first realized this when I was trying to get established in N.Y.C. in the early '70s. I could not find out about art events until after the fact when I read about them in THE VIL-LAGE VOICE. So I couldn't go to them. So I couldn't meet people with whom I could have gotten something going. One reason for this was there was very little flyering. In N.Y.C., organized crime has a monopoly on putting up posters. I did not realize how much no flyering isolated people until I moved to Berkeley where on every telephone pole, there were 10, 20, 30 flyers. Anyone who has an event, a group, a cause, something to say, can go to a xerox place, run off hundreds, or even thousands of flyers and staple them up all over town. This direct two-way form of the press plugged me immediately into the community where I could do my work.

We have to start seeing flyering, be it on telephone poles or on computer bulletin boards, as a form of personal press, and as such is protected under the freedom of press. Big Brother comes in many forms from the mafia to government (down to the anti-flyer laws as part of a city's "beautification" campaign) to corporations such as A.T.&T. and Blockbuster Videos.

Just recently I saw the power of this direct personal press. For years I have not been able to be booked in the "alternative" performance galleries in the Bay Area for various reasons...so I put 500 "too controversial for the Bay Area" flyers up asking for leads to spaces in which to perform. From the very first flyer we put up came three good leads into the true alternative art scene. Moreover, the flyer directly exposed the true condition of the established "alternative" art world.

This direct exposing is one of the strengths of the personal technology, anarchistic technology in the context of cultural subversion. Be it a camcorder capturing police brutality or a xerox zine publishing radical heretofore unpublishable material, the effect is to decentralize power, putting it into the personal level. I noticed this again last year when Senator Jesse Helms targeted me for investigation for my art. With only one exception, no one from the regular press contacted me to get my reaction or story. Some of the art magazines printed my open letter to Helms and my article on censorship. But I reached a wide national audience when THE SPIRITUAL REVOLUTIONARY (TSR), a newsletter zine by S/R PRESS, printed both. While TSR has a small readership, other zines reprinted my two pieces from TSR, without my permission but without editing. Then still other zines reprinted the material from those zines. The effect of this anarchistic grapevine of xerox zines is I had exposure to a wide national audience which was made up of small subcultures.

The combine recognizes the uncontrollable force represented by the direct personal communications through the anarchistic technology. The combine is trying to put this genie back in the bottle. The easiest, and the most obvious way to do this is to censor the physical channels...be it phone lines, the mail, or T.V./radio waves.

But there are hidden means by which the combine can thwart the direct personal use of technology. One of these is making equipment such as computers, obsolete every six months, not for any real functional improvement, but for progress. The effect of habitual upgrading is not only that we keep having to buy new soft/hardware, but it also creates a false mystery around the computer very much like the dead language of Latin did in the Dark Ages.

But the best way for the combine to curb the use of personal technology is by the standards of "professional quality".

When I xerox-published by first two books, I did not run into this wall of "professional quality". This is because I sold them directly, personally at my performances, as well as by the mail through a review in BOX OF WATER.

But when S/R PRESS xerox-published by book, CHEROTIC MAGIC, we took it, along with my zine THE CHEROTIC rEVOLUTIONARY, around to bookstores. The reason why a lot of the bookstores gave for not carrying the book was not the written or the visual contents of the book, but that it had a spiral binding, rather than a regular binding. Having a regular binding would boost the cost out of the realm of personal level and into the traditional publishing with its concerns of mass sales. Kyle Griffith is fond of saying that if the book's format is too revolutionary for a bookstore, then the content is also...so it would serve no purpose for us to try to package it differently. I must quickly add that there are quite a few bookstores that are not locked into buying solely from a distributor, that will carry personal xerox-published books and zines. Moreover, there are bookstores devoted to personal xerox publications...for example, METROPOPHOBOBIA in, of all places, Phoenix! These outlets for personal publications will multiply in the coming years.

I have dealt with the barriers of format and technology to personal direct human involvement in every medium I have tried. A lot of people have assumed this was because I was poor, did not know how to get grants, did not know how to use technology, or did not know how to use the system. In reality, even if I had tons of money, I would still use the same no/

low tech, because that is the best way to take back the creative force from the combine...back into the hands of anyone with a creative urge...or, for that matter, a destructive urge.

Since we are communicating on the personal level, you can send feedback, inquiries, or whatever to me at:

Frank Moore
P.O. Box 11445
Berkeley, CA 94712
e-mail: fmoore@eroplay.com

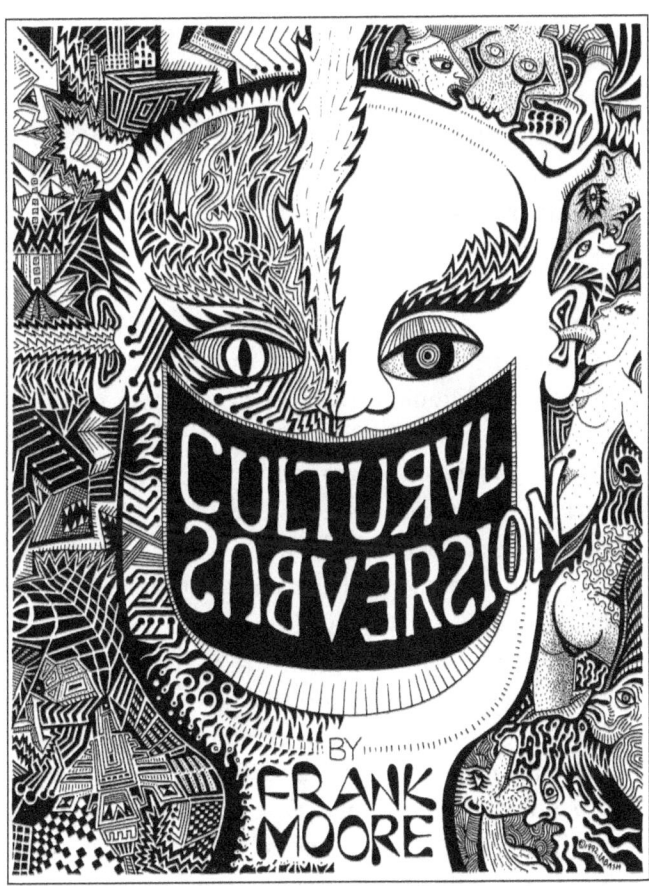

Cover for photocopied handout by Michael LaBash.

Dance Of No Dancers

From *Cherotic Magic Revised* by Frank Moore, 1993.

Matter is symbol, is metaphor containing possibilities. Chero is the physical life energy in the form of packets of possibilities. These packets shape matter. These packets, in turn, are reshaped by each body or object they pass through. This is why we are affected by the stars, for example, (and the stars are affected by us)...and why we affect the Tarot cards or the I-Ching coins we cast...why the physicists affect the subatomic particles they observe. This is the alchemical secret: by reshaping these inner packets, the material reality is reshaped.

These inner rivers of possibilities are two-way on the linear level. This means the magical effects are always two-way. The light of the sun warms us; but we affect the sun through the same channel. Again, we have entered the level of the dynamic web of relationships in which the individual does not exist. In place of the individual, there appear points of personal responsibility in a dance. It is not the sun that warms, nor is it us who are warmed. It is the dance of no dancers, the dance of relationships that warms, and that is warmed. Individualism hides this fundamental truth from most people.

These rivers of inner possibilities do not run only in a two-way linear manner. They also travel nonlinearly. This creates a deep ocean under time-space. In this ocean, there are nonlinear waves of possibility which pass through the points of personal responsibility which most people mistakenly see as individuality. When a wave passes through this, it is possible to personally amplify, mute, or change the wave. This makes the point of personal responsibility the moment of the universal creation. To accept this responsibility of the universal creation, we cannot step back from the ocean to claim the responsibility or judge.

We are then just water drops...individual water drops, not the ocean. To be in the moment of universal creation, in being the point of personal responsibility, we need to melt into being the ocean for all time, letting the dance happen through us, not thinking we are the dancers. In this point of personal responsibility, everything we do, think, and say is universally important, and not in the individually important sense.

Each center of the body is connected to many of the rivers of possibility. The nonlinear flow of the packets of possibilities within these rivers is chero. By transforming, transmuting, the packets of possibilities, it is actually possible to change matter, to change the material world. This alchemical fact is just the opening for the more important fact that reality is created, recreated every second by and within us.

We have said reality creation is a dance and that we are the dancers. But in truth, it is a dance without dancers. If we really take on personal responsibility for the dance, we surrender to the dance, give up individual "control", give up individual linking with the results. By taking on the personal responsibility for the dance, we are the dance. We melt with the dance. We are only the dance. We admit these facts. It is not a question of becoming, but of remembering and admitting. It is a question of being, living, dancing lustfully, without controls or limits in responsibility. This quality is called "extensic". The extensic life dance is beyond morals or limits. It joyfully digs into the dance to the juicy black core.

There is the magical principle of inter-penetration, the spiritual fact that the universal existence is enclosed in everyone and in everything. To start to grasp this, we have to remember that the cherotic rivers flowing within matter run in a great many directions, both linearly and nonlinearly, both inward and outward. This is the web dance. The cherotic packets of possibilities, effectively changed within the person, are taken by these rivers throughout the entire web, affecting the entire web.

So you are never hopeless or without effect. You can always shift reality away from doubts, fears, and other mistaken creations. You can always transform, transmute yourself, situations and the universal currents into joyful dancing by extensic melting, which is the heart secret of using erour, the vulnerable strength.

Kinds of transmuting and transforming of situations and of self is the real purpose of alchemical art. You are not the source of effect, the dance of the web is. You melt forever with the dance within personal responsibility. The effect is caused by the everlasting interplay, inner dance, of the whole web of all possibilities with one another, creating seven dimension waves. You must enjoy the dance for its own sake, not some goal as an end. There is no end to the dance. Since the dance is everlasting, the holding-on to any guilt, any doubt, any fear is just creating these things in the whole web, for which you are personally responsible. If you let go of these limited frames, your personal responsibility for them will vanish; moreover, their reality force will fade to a certain degree in the web.

When you admit you are melted into the dance, that you are the dance, and that every act and nonact, no matter how "small", is profound, then reality shifts. The focus shifts from what you do, what you appear to be like, what effect you are having...shifts to enjoying extensically life, claiming any and all responsible act or thought as your own no matter who does it.

A Dance Ritual

January 26, 2003

Lower the lights.

Squat in the center of the room, holding yourself very tightly, rocking, fully dressed, maintaining boundaries, making whatever sounds, all tight, all "self-contained".

When you are ready…it doesn't matter how long this takes…let yourself expand into the room, while still squatting and rocking. Relax.

Let yourself expand into me when you are ready…it doesn't matter how long this takes…and take me into you when you are ready…it doesn't matter how long this takes…all the while squatting and rocking.

When you are ready, move around the room, making deep sounds within a relaxed freedom. Slowly remove your clothes… when you are ready…it doesn't matter how long this takes. Let yourself expand outside of the studio, taking everything into you.

When you are ready…it doesn't matter how long this takes…dance with me, drawing everything in the room into the rapture state of our combined being, making deep sounds within a relaxed freedom.

When you are ready…it doesn't matter how long this takes…sit on me and rock/rub our combined being into a rapture state, making deep sounds within a relaxed freedom. Remain in this state.

Deep Love

Deep love can be defined as:

Treat the other as yourself, love the other as yourself, because the other is in fact yourself, is part of your body. So what you do to/with/for the other, you are doing to yourself within the point of action of now. Deep love goes back to the pre-shamanistic personal awareness of the land, the plants and animals, the others in the tribe, and in fact the whole physical existence as parts of the personal body, and hence within personal responsibility.

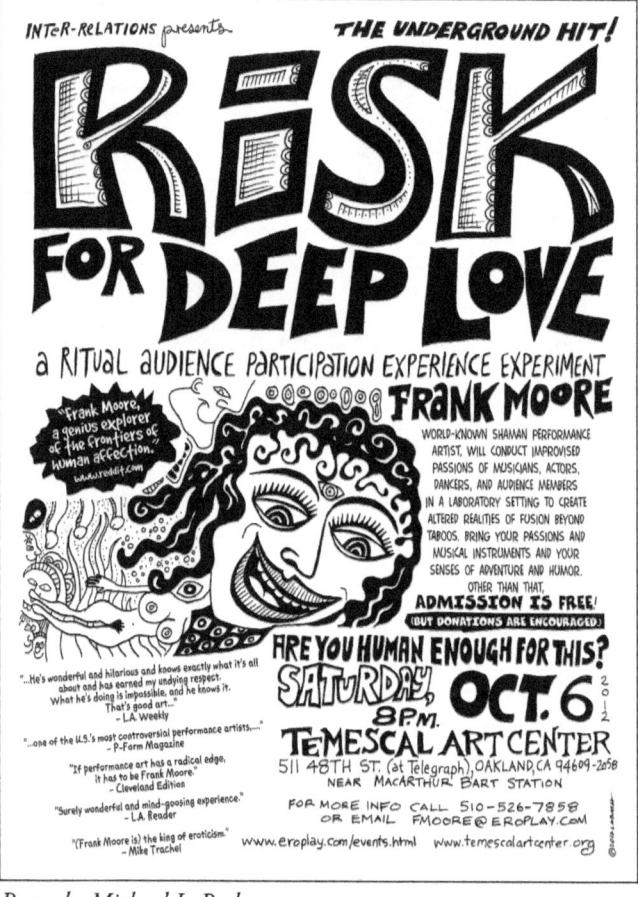

Poster by Michael LaBash

Eroart, Not Porn

December 11, 1996. Published in *Open Forum* #13, Greece, in 1997, and in *Lummox Journal* in February 1997.

In June 1988, Annie Sprinkle put out a call and some of the leading artists who use sex in their work came together in Veronica Vera's N.Y.C. apartment to sign a manifesto which talked about an art movement which "celebrates sex as the nourishing, life-giving force" which these artists use, in the self-empowering "attitude of sex-positivism" to "communicate our ideas and emotions...to have fun, heal the world and endure." This was a declaration of war against the censoring forces of anti-art, anti-human, anti-sex, anti-fun, anti-love, and truly anti-life...forces of darkness in power in the world today. We called ourselves Post Porn Modernists. This was very limiting because it linked us not only to dying deadening porn, but to the glum post modern art movement, setting ourselves up to be just a reaction, just the limb of a dead tree. We needed a name like Living Pleasure Artists...or Eroartists! By using the word "porn", it wrongly suggested that eroart somehow came out of what is very sloppily called "porn". Historically, there has always been eroart...and if truth be told, most artists have done at least some eroart. Eroart celebrates sex, love, the body, and the human passions. But porn was born in the Victorian Era with its repressive anti-sexual/anti-pleasure morality. What we eroartists were trying to do was to get back to the healing liberation of eroart.

What we are interested in is art that creates in people the desire to go out and play with other people, and to enjoy life. This is eroart. Historically, one of the tools of this art has been the sex act. But sex has only been a tool, not the goal. And it is just one of many tools.

Isadora Duncan is a person whom I would call an artist in the eroart tradition. She used nudity (especially at private parties where she could dance without feeling moral judgments) and movement to turn people on physically to their own bodies and to passion for life. This is the true goal of eroart. Most books on eroart have missed the true purpose of such art. There has always been sexual erotic art. This kind of art is universal and can be traced back to the caves and beyond.

We artists who signed the manifesto wanted to offer alternatives. We wanted to do art that would satisfy people's natural desire to see other people nude getting turned-on...to satisfy their child-like curiosity to see other people's bodies, to see what they are really like under those clothes. These are healthy human desires.

The time was, and is, right for an art form that addresses these healthy desires. The women's movement has changed people's standards with regard to sex and the quality of relationships. This is true of both men and women. They have scrapped, or are scrapping, the old sexist ways and attitudes. People want to see new ways of relating between humans both in and out of bed. Eroart in all media can show this way of relating.

Unfortunately, in recent years many eroartists have embraced the label of PORN...which is like embracing the label BAD COMMERCIAL ART. It is unfortunate because labels affect both the art and the artists. I don't know about you, but when I hear the word "porn", my mental pictures are...big-dicked jerks and big-titted bimbos fucking bored, unreal, dumb...tubes going in and out of holes...as many tubes going in and out of holes as possible...as close-up as possible...without any real human passion. This picture sets up undermining blocks for eroart. Eroart aims to liberate people. This picture makes the artist forget the idealism and importance of the eroart..."oh it's just porn."

This effect of the label of PORN can be seen on many of the female sex artists who have come on the scene since we signed the manifesto. The sex world has become in-grown. There is even a level of not liking/enjoying sex in this circle. Sex has become again the means to power, fame, money...and the means to avoid relationships, intimacy, needing other people. At a recent party of famous sex artists, one woman actually said, "I don't like sex, I like faking it!" Most of the people just nodded their agreement. Just shows the gender of the pornographer doesn't affect the porn!

We need to get back to the idealism of eroart...get back to changing/liberating society through eroart. Breaking taboos has always been a part of art, at least the area of art that seeks to change consciousness, change morality, change reality. This is one of the functions of art.

EROPLAY

As published in *The Drama Review* (TDR), Spring 1989. During this period, before accessibility software was available to him, Frank typed in all caps. TDR also published the piece in all caps.

MY FIRST STROKE OF GOOD LUCK WAS I WAS BORN SPASTIC, UNABLE TO WALK OR TALK. ADD TO THIS GOOD FORTUNE THE FACT THAT MY FORMATIVE YEARS WERE IN THE '60S—MY FATE WAS ASSURED!

YES, I ALWAYS HAVE BEEN LUCKY. I HAVE A BODY THAT IS IDEAL FOR A PERFORMANCE ARTIST. AND I HAVE ALWAYS WANTED TO BE A PERFORMER. WHEN I WAS A KID, MY YOUNGER BROTHER USED TO GET MAD WHEN PEOPLE LOOKED AT ME WHEN HE PUSHED ME TO THE MOVIES OR TO THE TEEN CLUB. HE CRIED. BUT I LIKED PEOPLE LOOKING AT ME. THAT IS WHAT I MEAN BY "I AM LUCKY." I AM LUCKY I AM AN EXHIBITIONIST IN THIS BODY. ONE TIME, I WAS WORKING OUT ON THE JUNGLE GYM OUTSIDE OF OUR HOUSE—A KID CAME BY AND ASKED IF I WAS A MONSTER. I JUST ROARED LIKE A MONSTER. IT WAS FUN.

I WAS LUCKY. I WAS NEVER UNDER PRESSURE TO BE GOOD AT ANYTHING, TO MAKE MONEY, TO MAKE IT IN "THE REAL WORLD", TO BE POLISHED—OR THE OTHER DISTRACTIONS THAT OTHER MODERN ARTISTS HAVE TO, OR THINK THEY HAVE TO DEAL WITH. SO I COULD FOCUS ON HAVING FUN, ON GOING INTO TABOO AREAS WHERE MAGICAL CHANGE CAN BE EVOKED. IN FACT, A MAJOR REASON WHY I AM WRITING THIS IS TO ENCOURAGE ARTISTS WHO HAVE NOT BEEN SO BLESSED WITH BODIES THAT MARK THEM AS MISFITS, TO ASPIRE TO BE MISFITS ANYWAY, TO DO MISFIT ART ANYWAY—EVEN IF YOU ARE HANDICAPPED BY YOUR NORMAL BODY. YOUR ROAD IS DEFINITELY HARDER THAN MY ROAD. BUT THAT'S LIFE.

MY ART IS ROOTED IN BREAKING OUT OF ISOLATION. UNTIL I WAS 17, I DID NOT HAVE ANY WAY TO COMMUNI-

CATE EXCEPT THROUGH MY FAMILY MEMBERS. FOR A COU-
PLE OF MY TEENAGE YEARS, I WAS VERY HARD OF HEARING.
MY HEARING CLEARED UP. I INVENTED MY HEADPOINT-
ER WHEN I WAS 17. MY COMMUNICATION ISOLATION WAS
THEN DISPELLED. BUT IT TOOK ME ANOTHER 10 YEARS
TO SHAKE OFF THE ISOLATION CAUSED BY MY ATTITUDES
AND SELF-IMAGE. THIS EARLY ISOLATION ALLOWED ME
TO OBSERVE LIFE AND PEOPLE AS AN OUTSIDER. I ALWAYS
WANTED TO BREAK PHYSICAL, EMOTIONAL, AND SPIRITU-
AL ISOLATION—FIRST FOR MYSELF, BUT THEN FOR OTHER
PEOPLE.

THERE ARE OTHER ADVANTAGES TO MY BODY. PEO-
PLE PROJECT ONTO ME CERTAIN MYSTICAL POWERS—LIKE
SEEING THROUGH THEIR FRONTS TO THEIR REAL SELVES
—SEEING THE PAST AND THE FUTURE—AND WHAT THEY
SHOULD DO. THEY ARE REACTING TO SOME SYMBOL OF
THE DEFORMED MEDICINE MAN. THEY USE ME AS A MEDI-
UM FOR GETTING THROUGH TO OTHER DIMENSIONS.
BECAUSE OF THE SLOWNESS OF MY COMMUNICATION
BOARD, THEY ARE FORCED TO SLOW DOWN. THEY CAN
PROJECT WHATEVER THEY WANT, MISREAD ME WHEN IT
FITS THEM. I AM A SYMBOL. AND BECAUSE THEY GIVE ME
POWER AS A SYMBOL, THEY ARE AFRAID OF ME. IT WAS JUST
MY LUCK TO BE BORN INTO THE LONG TRADITION OF THE
DEFORMED SHAMAN, THE WOUNDED HEALER, THE BLIND
PROPHET, THE CLUB-FOOTED "IDIOT" COURT JESTER.

THERE ARE ALL KINDS OF ART. THERE IS ART THAT
CALMS, ART THAT PACIFIES, ART THAT SELLS, ART THAT
DECORATES, ART THAT ENTERTAINS. BUT WHAT I AM COM-
MITTED TO IS ART AS A BATTLE, AN UNDERGROUND WAR
AGAINST FRAGMENTATION. THE BATTLE IS ON ALL REAL-
ITIES. THE CONTROLLERS HAVE ALWAYS TRIED TO FRAG-
MENT US FROM EACH OTHER. IMPRISON US IN ISLANDS
OF SEX, COLOR, RELIGION, POLITICS, CLASS, LABELS, ETC.,
ETC., ETC., ETC., ETC.—THEY FRAGMENT OUR INNER
WORLDS, THEY BLOW OUR INDIVIDUAL REALITIES APART

AND PLAY THE PIECES AGAINST ONE ANOTHER. THEY ARE US, OR A PART OF US. THEY ARE THE CONTROLLERS, THE POLITICIANS, THE SEXISTS, THE WOMEN'S LIBBERS, THE PORNOGRAPHERS, THE CENSORS, THE MORALISTS, THE CHURCH, THE MEDIA, THE BUSINESSMEN, EDUCATORS, THE VICTIMS, AND THE POWERFUL.

THEY ARE US.

I THINK PERFORMANCE IS BEING RUINED BY TRYING TO PACKAGE IT AS ENTERTAINMENT, AS OFF-BEAT CABARET. WHEN SOMEONE GOES TO A CABARET, HE KNOWS THERE ARE CERTAIN LIMITS INVOLVED SUCH AS THAT EACH ACT MUST END BEFORE ANOTHER BEGINS; BUT IN PERFORMANCE, ANYTHING IS POSSIBLE. A PERFORMANCE CAN LAST FOR A MINUTE OR IT CAN LAST FOR DAYS. PERFORMANCE CAN START IN ONE SPACE BUT THEN MOVE TO ANOTHER. PERFORMANCE CAN BE STORYTELLING, IT CAN BE A GUY THREATENING YOU WITH A BASEBALL BAT, IT CAN BE A GUY HANGING BY HIS SKIN, OR THROWING FOOD, OR ANYTHING. IN PERFORMANCE ALL THINGS ARE POSSIBLE. AND THAT IS WHAT GIVES YOU AN EXTRA EDGE TO CREATE DREAMS.

PERFORMANCE, LIKE ANY AVANT-GARDE ART, IS THE WAY SOCIETY DREAMS; IT IS THE WAY SOCIETY EXPANDS ITS FREEDOM, EXPLORES THE FORBIDDEN.

THIS WAS WHAT SEALED ME INTO A PERFORMANCE LIFE.

IN 1972 I HAD JUST FINISHED TAKING A VERY INTENSIVE FILM COURSE IN SANTA FE. I HAD NO MONEY TO MAKE REAL FILMS. SO I STARTED LOOKING FOR A WAY TO WORK WITH PEOPLE. I WANTED TO SEE PEOPLE NUDE, AND TOUCH THEM, AND CREATE AN INTENSITY BETWEEN US. PAINTING WAS THE FIRST ATTEMPT. I USED TO SELL PAPERS ON A CORNER TO FIND PEOPLE TO PAINT. BUT ONCE THE PERSON WAS POSED THE SITUATION WAS STILL, NOT MOV-

ING. SO I DID WHAT I CALLED NONFILMS—FOR WHICH I
ASKED PEOPLE I MET WHEN I WAS SELLING NEWSPAPERS TO
ACT OUT INTENSIVE EROTIC SCENES WITH ME. ALTHOUGH
I HAD PLAYED WITH MY FRIENDS BEFORE IN NONSEXU-
AL EROTICISM, THIS WAS THE FIRST TIME I TRIED TO USE
"SEXUAL" ACTS IN A NONSEXUAL ART FORM. I WAS SUR-
PRISED WITH THE POWER THAT THIS RELEASED. BECAUSE
OF THESE SCENES, THE PEOPLE STARTED TALKING ABOUT
THEIR LIVES DURING THE SESSIONS AND SAID IT HELPED
THEIR OTHER RELATIONSHIPS. NOT ONE PERSON MINDED
THAT THERE WAS NO FILM. THESE NONFILMS WERE THE
BASE FOR MY CAREER IN RELATIONSHIP COUNSELING IN
THE LATE '70S.

BUT I WAS NOT SATISFIED WITH THESE NONFILMS
BECAUSE THEY WERE BRIEF RELATIONSHIPS THAT DID NOT
GO ANYWHERE. SO I STARTED LOOKING FOR SOME OTHER
WAY TO WORK WITH PEOPLE. I TRIED TO CAST A PLAY, BUT
I COULDN'T FIND ENOUGH PEOPLE. I STARTED THINKING
OF AN INTIMATE THEATRE WHERE THE LINE BETWEEN
AUDIENCE AND ACTORS WOULD BE ERASED. I STARTED
THINKING ABOUT HOW IF THAT LINE WERE ERASED, IT
WOULD PLACE MUCH MORE RESPONSIBILITY ON THE
ACTORS. THEY WOULD HAVE TO DARE TO TRICK THE AUDI-
ENCE INTO THE INTENSE MAGICAL STATE.

I DIVIDED MY WORK—THE WORD "WORK" IS WEIRD—
IT IS LIKE PLAYING—INTO TWO PARTS. THE FIRST PART IS
PLAYED IN "REAL LIFE"—FOR INSTANCE, I GO UP TO A PER-
SON ON A STREET AND ASK HIM TO BE IN SOME PROJECT
WHICH MAY CONTAIN SOME NUDITY AND PHYSICAL PLAY.
THE NUDITY AND PHYSICAL PLAY AS AN IDEA IN THIS CON-
TEXT IS A GREAT TOOL TO GET UNDER THE POLITE CHAT-
TER SURFACE TO THE MORE MEANINGFUL THINGS, AND
OFTEN MORE INTIMATE, MORE PERSONAL STUFF—WHICH
IS, AFTER ALL, THE AIM OF THE PIECE. I CAN SEE THIS KIND
OF PIECE LASTING ANYWHERE FROM A FEW SECONDS TO
SEVERAL HOURS.

THE SECOND PART IS A PIECE IN A CONTROLLED SPACE, SUCH AS MY STUDIO, IN WHICH THERE IS A FORM GOING ON, GIVING THE PERSON A REASON TO BE THERE WITH ME.

THIS KIND OF PERFORMANCE IS DIFFERENT THAN NORMAL THEATRE. IN THIS KIND, THERE IS NO REAL SCRIPT. EVEN IF YOU HAVE A SCRIPT, IT REALLY IS A PROP. THE REAL COURSE OF ACTION IS SHAPED BY THE PERFORMER SO THE FLOW OF THE PIECE WILL GO FORWARD AND DEEPER.

WHAT IS IMPORTANT IS WHAT HAPPENS BETWEEN ME AS THE ARTIST AND MY AUDIENCE, HOW I CHANGE THEM AND HOW THEY CHANGE ME, THAT MAGICAL STATE IN WHICH WE INTERACT WITH EACH OTHER. I, AS THE PERFORMER, MUST CREATE AROUND THE PEOPLE, BY PLAYING FOR AND TO THEM, BY LETTING THE PERFORMANCE TAKE ME OVER AND GUIDE ME—EVEN WHEN IT LOOKS LIKE THE OTHER PEOPLE ARE DOING ALL OF THE ACTION. THE ULTIMATE GOAL IN MY PERFORMANCE IS TO CREATE A REALITY, NOT AN ILLUSION, WHICH THE AUDIENCE AND I ARE IN— EVEN IF I HAVE TO USE ILLUSIONS TO GET TO THIS REALITY.

THIS RAISES THE QUESTION OF MANIPULATION. ALMOST ANY TIME YOU PERFORM TO AN AUDIENCE, YOU MANIPULATE THE AUDIENCE. LET'S GET BEYOND THE NEGATIVE CONNOTATION OF THE WORD "MANIPULATE". PEOPLE GO TO THE THEATRE, MOVIES, CONCERTS, DANCE COMPANIES, ETC., TO HAVE THEIR EMOTIONS MANIPULATED. THEY COME INTO THE PERFORMANCE AREA WITH A WILLINGNESS TO BE MANIPULATED BY THE ARTISTS WITHIN CERTAIN LIMITS. BUT IN MY PERFORMANCES, THE ONES WHICH ARE NOT DIVIDED FROM THE REST OF LIFE BY A THEATRE OR A STAGE, THERE IS NO WAY TO TELL THE PERSON SHE IS ENTERING A PERFORMANCE. WHEN I HAVE A FORMAL STRUCTURE, A THEATRE SPACE, AND A SET TIME ENDING—WHAT IS REALLY GOING ON IS NOT WHAT IS SAID TO BE HAPPENING. ALSO IT IS A REALITY THAT IS HOPEFULLY BEING CREATED—PEOPLE WILL BE AFFECTED, INFECTED, AND EFFECTED BY THIS REALITY.

PERFORMANCE OBVIOUSLY GOES MUCH FARTHER BACK THAN 1909 WHEN IT BECAME A FORMAL ART FORM. I THINK PERFORMANCE CAME INTO EXISTENCE TO FILL A VOID IN WESTERN LIFE. THE VOID WAS THE LACK OF MAGIC AND INSPIRATION. THE TWO AREAS OF CREATIVITY, THEATRE AND RELIGION, THAT TRADITIONALLY WERE THE SOURCE OF THIS MAGICAL INSPIRATION HAD LONG AGO MOVED FROM MAGIC TO ENTERTAINMENT AND POLITICS. THIS VOID ALSO GAVE BIRTH TO PSYCHOLOGY DURING THE SAME TIME PERIOD. I OFTEN GET THE CRITICISM THAT MY WORK IS REALLY PSYCHOLOGY AND THERAPY, AND NOT ART. WHEN IT IS REALIZED THAT PSYCHOLOGY AS A FORMAL SCIENCE AND PERFORMANCE AS A FORMAL ART WERE BORN AT THE SAME TIME, THIS CRITICISM CAN BE ANSWERED. PERFORMANCE AND PSYCHOLOGY ARE BOTH INVOLVED IN SPIRITUAL HEALING.

I SEE PERFORMANCE AS EXPERIMENTS IN HUMAN POSSIBILITIES. TO DO THESE EXPERIMENTS, I FORMED IN SANTA FE IN 1972 A WEEKLY DROP-IN WORKSHOP TO DO RITUALS LASTING MANY HOURS. A YEAR LATER, PEOPLE FROM THAT DROP-IN GROUP MOVED WITH ME TO N.Y.C. TO BE THE CORE OF A COMMITTED GROUP. BUT IT WAS IN BERKELEY THAT WE FOUND A PERMANENT HOME IN 1974. THERE, THE WORKSHOP SLOWLY DEVELOPED INTO A GROUP OF 30 PEOPLE.

IN THE LATE '70S WE STARTED OUR PUBLIC PERFORMANCES BY DOING LONG RITUALISTIC PLAYS. OVER THE YEARS, THE GROUP BRANCHED OUT TO DO MANY DIFFERENT KINDS OF LIVE AND VIDEO PIECES, INCLUDING *the outrageous beauty revue* [1978].

THE *o.b.r.* WAS A CABARET SHOW THAT TRIED TO SHORT-CIRCUIT THE CABARET LIMITS OF TIME AND STAGE. IT DID THIS BY BEING A SHOW OF PEOPLE WHO WERE HAVING FUN AND WHO WERE LIVING THEIR FANTASIES—A SHOW THAT INCLUDED THE AUDIENCE DIRECTLY IN THE ACTION—AN UNPOLISHED SHOW THAT FLAUNTED NUDI-

TY, EROTICISM, AND GORE IN A SILLY, CHILDLIKE PLAY-
FULNESS—AN EVER-CHANGING SHOW WITH PREGNANT
SEX SYMBOLS, NUDE GIRLS, CRIPPLED ROCK STARS, MEN
AS WOMEN AND WOMEN AS MEN WITHOUT ANY SEXUAL
MEANING. THE *o.b.r.* RAN FOR THREE YEARS AND WAS BY
FAR MY MOST POPULAR WORK IN TERMS OF HOW MANY
PEOPLE SAW IT. BUT THE SUCCESS OF A PIECE SHOULD NOT
BE JUDGED BY HOW MANY PEOPLE SEE IT, BUT BY HOW FAR
IT WENT BEYOND THE TABOOS, BY ITS MAGIC POWER FOR
CHANGE. BY THIS STANDARD, MY BEST WORK WITH THE
GROUP WAS OUR 48-HOUR DREAM PERFORMANCES IN THE
LATE '70S.

SINCE 1983, I HAVE BEEN DOING A PERFORMANCE
SERIES AT U.C. BERKELEY WHICH HAS GIVEN ME A LAB
WHERE I CAN DEVELOP PIECES BY DOING THEM OVER
AND OVER WITHOUT THE PRESSURES OF MAKING MONEY
OR ENTERTAINING. THESE PIECES ARE WHAT GOT ME THE
N.E.A. FELLOWSHIP, AND THEY ARE THE ONES I DO ON MY
TOURS.

IN MY WORK, I ALWAYS HAVE USED NUDITY AND PHYS-
ICAL ACTS WHICH MOST PEOPLE WOULD CALL SEXUAL. IT
IS JUST ONE OF MY WAYS OF BREAKING NORMAL REALITY
INTO NEW WAYS OF COMMUNICATING AND RELATING. I
COMBINE THIS WITH BREAKING TIME/SPACE TABOOS, MY
UNIQUE BODY, AND OTHER TOOLS. BUT THE "SEXUAL"
CONTENT OF MY WORK GRABS MOST OF THE ATTENTION.

THERE IS A COMMON MISCONCEPTION ABOUT THE
DEFORMED SHAMAN TRADITION—THAT IT GETS ITS POW-
ER FROM THE MENTAL AND THE SPIRITUAL PLANE, SINCE
THE PHYSICAL AND SENSUAL ARE ALMOST NONEXISTENT.
IN TRUTH, THE WOUNDED HEALER USES HIS PHYSICALITY
AS A CHANNEL TO UNITE THE SPIRITUAL WITH THE PHYS-
ICAL.

I HAVE ALWAYS BEEN A VERY PHYSICAL AND SEXUAL
PERSON. THIS WAS HEIGHTENED BY MY EARLY PHYSICAL

ISOLATION. IN THE EARLY '70S WHEN I WAS NOT YET OUT OF MY SEXUAL ISOLATION, I OBSERVED AS AN INTERESTED OUTSIDER THAT FREE SEX (CONFUSED WITH FREE LOVE) WAS NOT WORKING. IT WASN'T MAKING MY HIPPIE FRIENDS HAPPY. THIS OBSERVATION WAS AGAINST MY PHILOSOPHY OF FREEDOM. BUT I COULD NOT DENY THE FACTS. I STARTED LOOKING FOR NEW WAYS OF RELATING AND TOUCHING. I WAS LOOKING FOR A NEW FREE LOVE. MY PERFORMANCES, BOTH THE PUBLIC EVENTS AND THE PRIVATE NONFILMS, WERE MY RESEARCH, MY EXPERIMENTS.

I EXPERIMENTED IN USING THE EXCITED, AROUSED, PLEASURABLE ENERGY IN THE CONTEXT OF ART, OF PLAYING, RELATIONSHIP-BUILDING—NOT THE CONTEXT OF SEX. THIS RESEARCH REACHED A CLIMAX IN MY BERKELEY WORKSHOP DURING THE YEARS OF the outrageous beauty revue.

IT WAS FAIRLY CLEAR TO 30 OF US THAT THERE WAS A DIFFERENCE BETWEEN PLAYING AND SEX. WE SAW IT HAD SOMETHING TO DO WITH SEX AND "MARRIAGE" (THE WORD marriage IS ANOTHER WORD THAT HAS NEGATIVE CONNOTATIONS HIDDEN WITHIN IT). SO WE DECIDED TO COMMIT OURSELVES TO HAVING SEX ONLY WITH THOSE TO WHOM WE WERE MARRIED. BUT WE EROTICALLY PLAYED (FOR LACK OF A BETTER TERM FOR IT) WITH ALL OF THE PEOPLE IN THE GROUP.

THE EROTIC PLAY GOT WACKIER, MORE PHYSICAL. IT GAVE US A GREATER FREEDOM NOT ONLY WITHIN OUR GROUP, BUT IN SOCIETY IN GENERAL AS WELL. EROTIC PLAYING INTENSELY BUT PLAYFULLY RELEASED CREATIVITY WHICH WE USED IN MANY WAYS. SUCCESSFUL BUSINESSES WERE ESTABLISHED. WE DID SEVERAL PUBLIC PERFORMANCES, AND A WEALTH OF PRIVATE PERFORMANCES. THERE WAS NO JEALOUSY OR POSSESSIVENESS BECAUSE IT WAS CLEAR THAT SEX WOULD NOT BE INVOLVED. THIS WENT ON FOR THREE YEARS.

AT A CERTAIN POINT, WE STARTED QUESTIONING THE CONCEPT OF MARRIAGE. WE DID NOT SEE ANY DIFFERENCE BETWEEN WHAT WE 30 HAD TOGETHER AND BEING MARRIED. NOT SEEING ANY DIFFERENCE BETWEEN MARRIAGE AND WHAT WE HAD AS A GROUP, THE NEXT LOGICAL QUESTION WAS, "WHY NOT HAVE SEX?" SO WE STARTED TO HAVE SEX OUTSIDE MARRIAGE, WITHIN THE GROUP. ALMOST IMMEDIATELY CHANGES APPEARED IN THE GROUP. JEALOUSY AND POSSESSIVENESS APPEARED. THE GROUP QUICKLY BEGAN TO FALL APART.

AFTER THIS BREAKUP, I FOCUSED MY WORK ON DEFINING THE UNIQUE PHYSICAL-SPIRITUAL ENERGY WE HAD USED, FORMALIZED IT IN MY ART TO TAP AGAIN INTO THE INTENSE, PURE PLAY WITH PEOPLE, USING THE RESULTING CREATIVENESS IN ART WITHOUT BEING DERAILED BY SEX.

I REALIZED THAT ONE OF THE THINGS THAT WAS UNDERMINING MY WORK WAS THE ENGLISH LANGUAGE. THERE WAS NO WORD, NO NAME, FOR THE FORCE I WAS DEALING WITH. MY FIRST TASK WAS TO CREATE A NEW WORD: eroplay.

OUR MIND NEEDS LABELS. THERE IS SUCH A FORCE OR ENERGY, WHICH I HAVE LABELED EROPLAY. BUT THERE HAS NOT BEEN A WORD FOR IT. THE WORD sex HAS BEEN THE DUMP FOR EVERYTHING SENSUAL, ROMANTIC, PHYSICAL, OR FOR SHOWING MORE SKIN THAN USUAL. CARS ARE CALLED SEXY. POSES THAT DO NOT SHOW THE SEX ACT ARE CALLED SEXUAL. WEARING CERTAIN THINGS, MOVING CERTAIN WAYS ARE ALL CALLED SEXUAL, EVEN WHEN IT IS NOT LEADING TO THE SEXUAL ACT—EVEN WHEN THERE IS NO INTENT TO HAVE SEX.

EROPLAY IS INTENSE PHYSICAL PLAYING AND TOUCHING OF ONESELF AND OTHERS. EROPLAY IS THE FORCE OR ENERGY RELEASED BY SUCH PLAY. IT IS ALSO THE HAPPY, PLAYFUL ATTITUDE TOWARDS LIFE THAT COMES FROM

SUCH PLAY. EROPLAY IS NOT FOREPLAY, EVEN THOUGH FOREPLAY IS EROPLAY.

FOREPLAY LEADS TO ORGASM—EROPLAY LEADS TO BEING TURNED-ON IN MANY DIFFERENT WAYS AND IN ALL PARTS OF THE BODY—INCLUDING, BUT NOT LIMITED TO, PHYSICAL AROUSAL. IT CAN BE DIFFERENT EVERY TIME. SKIN TOUCHING SKIN SEEMS TO BE WHAT RELEASES THE FULL IMPACT OF EROPLAY. EROPLAY CAN BE INTENSE. IT IS LIKE WHEN YOU RUB A PUPPY ON ITS BELLY AND THE PUPPY GOES INTO A STATE OF RAPTURE, BOTH TOTALLY TURNED-ON AND RELAXED. EROPLAY IS THE BLISSED-OUT, WARM, RELAXED, TURNED-ON, TOTALLY SATISFYING FEELING OF A GOOD HEAD RUB.

EROPLAY IS FUN!

EROPLAY IS INNOCENT AND CHILDLIKE.

EROPLAY'S FOCUS IS ON PHYSICAL ENJOYMENT.

EROPLAY DECREASES ISOLATION AND ALIENATION. IT INCREASES SELF-TRUST AND TRUSTING OF OTHERS. IT MAKES YOU HARDER TO BE CONTROLLED. EROPLAY LEADS TO A LIFE-STYLE WITH ALL THESE CHARACTERISTICS. THE LIFESTYLE LOOKS STRANGELY LIKE THE LOVE GENERATION, BUT WITHOUT DRUGS OR FREE SEX.

IN RECENT YEARS, OUTSIDE FORCES HAVE AFFECTED MY WORK. EDWIN MEESE'S POLITICAL WAR OF SEXUAL SUPPRESSION AND THE BLANDNESS OF YUPPIES HAVE GIVEN MY ART SOCIAL ISSUES AGAINST WHICH I CAN DO BATTLE.

BUT IT IS AIDS THAT HAS STARTED PEOPLE SEARCHING FOR NONSEXUAL WAYS TO FIND, TO SHOW, AND TO GIVE PHYSICAL INTIMACY. EROPLAY IS A SAFE, FUN, LUSTY CHANNEL FOR FREE PHYSICAL TOUCHING. IT IS SAFE BECAUSE THERE IS NO PHYSICAL INTERCOURSE. IT IS NOT AN AVOIDANCE, AS CELIBACY IS. IT IS NOT SOMETHING SECOND RATE. EROPLAY IS SATISFYING IN ITSELF.

I HAVE DEBATED WITH MYSELF ABOUT NO LONGER RESISTING THE LABEL sexual. BY INSISTING WHAT I AM DOING IS NOT SEXUAL, I AM OPENING MYSELF TO PEOPLE QUESTIONING MY HONESTY AND INTEGRITY. IF I ACCEPT THE SEXUAL LABEL, PEOPLE WOULD JUST HAVE TO DECIDE WHETHER OR NOT THEY LIKE SEX IN ART— DECIDE WHETHER IT IS ART OR NOT. THAT WOULD BE THE DEPTH OF THE QUESTIONING. THEY MAY FEEL UNCOMFORTABLE SEEING SEX AS ART—BUT THAT UNCOMFORTABLENESS WOULD BE JUST FROM BREAKING THE TABOO OF SEX— WHAT'S THE BIG DEAL? WHAT I AM DOING IS TAKING NUDITY AND ACTS THAT ARE USUALLY CONSIDERED SEXUAL AND GIVING THEM A NEW, NONSEXUAL CONTEXT. THAT CREATES A TENSION, A CONFLICT, AN EXAMINING, A LEAP INTO SOMETHING NEW. THAT IS WHAT I AM AFTER. THIS LEAP INTO NEWNESS IS WHY PEOPLE WHO ARE NORMALLY COMFORTABLE WITH CASUAL NUDITY AND CASUAL SEX SOMETIMES GET VERY UNCOMFORTABLE WITH THE NUDITY AND EROPLAY IN MY WORK. BY TAKING "SEXUAL" ACTS AND SINCERELY PUTTING THEM INTO A DIFFERENT CONTEXT, I CREATE ANOTHER REALITY, ANOTHER WAY OF RELATING. I ALSO CREATE CONFLICT WITH THE NORMAL REALITY—AND THAT CONFLICT MAY CHANGE, IN AN UNDERGROUND SORT OF A WAY, THE NORMAL REALITY. I THINK ART—OR AT LEAST THIS KIND OF ART—SHOULD CREATE CONFLICT AND CHANGE. AND I LIKE RELATING WITH PEOPLE IN THIS "UNNORMAL" WAY. THIS IS WHY I DO PERFORMANCE.

Eroplay in Life and Art

As published in *Shades of Grey* (1985) & *Smut* (1991).

Eroplay is a made-up word for intense physical playing and touching of oneself and others. Chero is the force of energy which is released as the result of eroplay.

Usually the word sex has been the catchword for people to dump on almost everything sensual, romantic, physical, or showing more skin than usual. Cars are called sexy. Poses that do not show the sex act are called sexual. Moving in certain ways is called sexual even when it is not leading or intending to engage in the sexual act...

In magic, words create. If you use sexual words for non-sexual playing, they will create a false sexual confusion.

Eroplay is not foreplay, though foreplay is eroplay.

Kids play very physically both with their own bodies and others' bodies. They get turned-on by this play, both physically and mentally. This turn-on is not sexual in kids. Studies have shown that babies who are held, touched, and played with are more healthy and alert, weigh more, and have a lower rate of death than babies who are denied this eroplay. Studies also show that old people who live alone, who don't get physical and emotional contact, are less healthy and die sooner than people of the same age who live with others and get that physical contact. We may need a certain amount of straight eroplay (not connected to or leading to sex) to be as healthy as possible.

Eroplay can be intense. It is like rubbing a puppy on its belly: the puppy goes into a state of rapture, both totally turned-on and relaxed. To use something that is not normally confused with sex, eroplay is the blissed-out, warm, totally satisfying feeling of a good head rub.

Sex seems to be connected to mating; whereas the combination of both physical and psychic forces released during and after eroplay seems to be connected more to communication and attracting people to you.

Eroplay is satisfying in itself, in relaxing intensity. There is no build-up of pent-up energy in one climactic act. In sex, however, there is a point where foreplay (eroplay) ceases to satisfy and energy gets pent up and built up to be released in the sex act. This build-up is a clear and broad dividing line between the turn-on of eroplay and sex.

Eroplay starts when the possibility of the physical eroplay arises, the possibility of breaking normal rules, social conventions, and morality. But the turn-on of the possibility of breaking the taboos, rules, and the common morality is not a natural part of eroplay. It has been added on to eroplay by social repression. Anytime you break a taboo, there is a release of energy almost like a high. But sooner or later you have to go back into the system where that taboo still exists. Then, more often than not, you will get a backlash from breaking it. It may come from inside you or from others. If you can ride out this backlash -- if you have it at all -- you will be a stronger person, and you can modify the moral system to fit how you want to live.

Breaking taboos has always been a part of art...at least the area of art that changes consciousness and reality. The breaking of taboos ideally should not be a part of everyday eroplay, but it is. One of its functions is to take eroplay out of the taboo area. Eroplay's focus is on physical pleasure for its own sake. This is why it is taboo: religion teaches that physical pleasure for itself is bad. Eroplay connects you more with your own body and with other people. It decreases isolation and alienation. It increases self-trust and trusting of others. It makes you harder to be controlled. This is another reason why eroplay is taboo.

Most of the so-called sex problems in sexual relationships have to do with trying to do with sex what eroplay can do, trying to fill needs with sex that sex can't fulfill. This leads to the downward spiral of frustration, self-doubt, trying too hard, and blame.

Since eroplay may release certain chemicals in the body, to get familiar with what eroplay itself does, not adding other chemicals will help. Since eroplay is not mate oriented, it is possible to have a relationship with a friend in which eroplay is an important part, but in which the possibility of sex and romance is very clearly excluded. This kind of relationship will have good effects on your other relationships. In the '70s, I had a group of about thirty people. It was fairly clear to us that there was a difference between playing and sex. By eroplaying intensely, but playfully, it released a certain creativity which we used in many ways. But at a certain point, we started questioning the concept of marriage: what was the difference between what we thirty had together and being married?

We did not see any difference. I now see that we should have used the word "mating", which does not refer to child-bearing, but to bonding. So we started to have sex. Almost immediately changes appeared. The playful creativity which came from eroplay dried up. Playing and the physical freedom between the people quickly ceased to be. The group quickly began to fall apart.

Thanks to the repressive, anti-sexual, anti-pleasure morality, romanticism, and pornography, the traditional area of eroart -- art that uses physicality, and/or sex to turn people on to life -- has been ripped off by pornography. The true goal of eroart is to turn people on physically to their own bodies and to passion for life.

It is fashionable to be against porn. But it is not fashionable to offer an alternative to porn. To make videos that satisfy that child-like need of seeing nude bodies and seeing people playing, making out, and having fun is not as profitable as either what Hollywood does or what the porn makers do. This child-like need is the healthy human desire that is perverted in porn.

The time is right for an art form that addresses this healthy desire. The women's movement has changed people's standards with regard to sex and the quality of relationships. This is true of both men and of women. They have scrapped, or are scrapping, the old sexist ways and attitudes, and now they find the old style porn is not meeting their needs and desires. They want to see nudity and be turned on without stupidity; they want to see new ways of relating between humans both in and out of bed. Eroart in all media can show this way of relating...can show both purely nonsexual eroplay and eroplay as foreplay in sex.

The desire to see nudity and intimacy and to be turned-on is not being satisfied. Hollywood is caught between being ruled by taboos and being in the business of teasing. Hollywood has been doing a 40 year striptease, showing a little more each year to get people to come back.

But breaking taboos has always been a part of art, at least the area of art that seeks to change consciousness, change morality, change reality.

This kind of art creates a kind of bubble in which the forbidden can be done with immunity, releasing energy of the broken taboo...energy which then affects society as a whole.

The best way to undermine sexism and porn is to take back nudity, pleasure, sex and eroticism...but only if it comes from some warm, playful place can it be good eroart. Unless we put ourselves, our creativity, our minds, and yes, our bodies into eroart, the pornographer, the sexist, and the moralist will win by default.

Evolution Ritual

1993. This is one of the many ritual "modules" that Frank created for his performances.

We are going on a journey to Lila. Lila is an inner island. On Lila there is no isolation or competition or fear. But to get to Lila, we have to let go of our personalities and fears and inhibitions. We have to pass through the transition that is death, through rebirth, through losing our old personalities in the form of our clothes, then going playfully through all the stages of evolution until we are reborn on the island of Lila in the bodies of babies who will grow up slowly into teenage Lilans, and then will do rituals of play. Death is not something to fear. It does not hurt. It is not an end.

But this journey is only for heroes...only because heroes are the only people crazy enough to make this journey. Heroes think that only by risking, they will find the hidden treasures and the hidden meanings of Life. Heroes actually think taking risks and going beyond limits is fun! Sane people do not think like this.

We will now divide the ritual community into those of you who think of yourselves as heroes and those of you who think you are sane. The heroes should sit in the middle of the ritual space, and those of you who are sane should sit against the walls. The heroes will actively take this journey both for themselves and for the sane people. As heroes, you will go on an adventure of risk and vulnerability. As heroes, you will be stripped of your old personality and approach death in nudity and vulnerability. You will have personal guides who will move you into death in a soft and gentle way, into the floating reality of between lives. You will then experience the evolution of life.

Those of you who are too sane to be heroes, please sit against the walls. You are now the watchers...which may be much more risky. As the watchers, you should just watch. Please do not talk.

Now, you heroes, lie down on the mat and close your eyes. Lila is an inner island, warm and green. The people are playful. They know no isolation, no fear, no violence. Lila is cut off from our world by death...so, to reach Lila we have to die. Death in itself is not painful, it is not an end. It is a transition. Soon the guide of death will come to help you through the transition.

Now those who are along the walls make soft sounds, gentle noises to help the death process. The guides should gently lift the heroes/spirits into a sitting position. The guides should hold the heroes/spirits and rock them. Melt into one another as you rock. When the heroes/spirits are melted, both the heroes/spirits and the guides should stand up. Because we are now beyond time, there is no reason to rush. To prepare the hero for death, the guide will take the old personality in the form of clothes from the hero, slowly undressing the hero and then will lie him back down.

Now Death is approaching...quietly, gently. It is like a soft, warm blanket. It will slowly cover you. It will start at your toes and travel up your body like caresses. When it reaches the top of your head you will be in an in-between state where you will not have either your old body or old personality. Enjoy floating. Some of you are floating in a cozy dimension. Explore that bodiless state. Do not try to get up because there is no up. The floating is the womb of life, all life, all matter. You are all life, all matter.

Now, keeping your eyes closed, roll in slow motion towards the center of the room, stopping only when you are surrounded by a web of warm soft skin.

You are now parts of a huge rock. Act, sound, move, and relate as parts of the huge rock. Most people think the inorganic is not aware. We now know different.

Time freezes.
Time flows by.

You are now parts of a single-cell organism. Act, sound, move, and relate as parts of a single-cell organism.

Time freezes.

Time flows by.

The single-cell is now dividing. You are now cells in a multi-cell organism. Act, sound, move, and relate as cells in a multi-cell organism.

Time freezes.
Time flows by.

You are sea weed. Act, sound, move, and relate as sea weed.
Open your eyes.

Time freezes.
Time flows by.

You are snails. Act, sound, move, and relate as snails.

Time freezes.
Time flows by.

You are a school of fish. Act, sound, move, and relate as a school of fish.

Time freezes.
Time flows by.

You are dolphins. Act, sound, move, and relate as dolphins.

Time freezes.
Time flows by.

You are jellyfish. Act, sound, move, and relate as jellyfish.

Time freezes.
Time flows by.

You are frogs. Act, sound, move, and relate as frogs.

Time freezes.

Time flows by.

You are snakes. Act, sound, move, and relate as snakes.

Time freezes.
Time flows by.

You are ants. Be, act, sound, move, and relate as ants.

Time freezes.
Time flows by.

You are mice. Be, act, sound, move, and relate as mice.

Time freezes.
Time flows by.

You are birds. Be, act, sound, move, and relate as birds.

Time freezes.
Time flows by.

You are vegetarian dinosaurs. Be, act, sound, move, and relate as vegetarian dinosaurs.

Time freezes.
Time flows by.

You are kittens. Be, act, sound, move, and relate as kittens.

Time freezes.
Time flows by.

You are chimps. Be, act, sound, move, and relate as chimps.

Time freezes.
Time flows by.

Close your eyes.

You are newborns on Lila.

On Lila, there is only one family. All are brothers and sisters, mothers and fathers. You are in a playpen. Act and sound and be newborns.

Time freezes.
Time flows by.

You are now six months old.

But even at six months old, you will notice the difference from the old life. There is no violence or competition on Lila. Act and sound and be six months old. Open your eyes. What cute babies!

Time freezes.
Time flows by.

You are now one year olds and the differences are more obvious. Be and sound and act and relate as one year olds on Lila. But stay in the playpen of the mat.

Time freezes.
Time flows by.

You are now two year olds. Not the terrible twos you vaguely remember but the fun, playful twos of Lila. Be and act and sound and relate as two year olds.

Time freezes.
Time flows by.

You are now five year olds. Act and be and relate as five year olds.

Time freezes.
Time flows by.

You are now sixteen years old and it is time for the ritual of eroplay and becoming a full member of the Lilan community. You will always be sixteen years old on Lila even after this dream has faded. Now for the ritual. We will now do the eroplay ritual of Gestures.

Experiments in Magical Change

Written for and published in *The Act* in 1989.

I always have a problem when someone who has not experienced one of our performances asks, "Well, what was your performance about?" Within this question, there are a number of concepts about performance which are undermining limitations.

I became sucked into performance not to tell stories, not to paint pictures for others to look at, not even to reveal something about myself or about the state of things, and certainly not for fame or fortune. It was simply the best way that I saw to create the intimate community which I as a person needed and that I thought society needed as an alternative to the personal isolation....

O.k. Let's cut the b.s. The above is true, but boring. In a lot of my performances, I spend the first hour boring people, usually by asking what each person does, how did he hear about the performance, etc. I drive in my wheelchair up to each person and tap out these questions slowly on my letterboard. Talking to this strange person in this strange way may be interesting as a confrontation. But listening to trivial chatter between this disabled man and each person in this "painfully slow" way can become an active boredom in a room which looks as if nothing else will ever happen. This active boredom is a slow increasing shock that makes people who want quick-paced, high-energy entertainment suddenly bolt out of the door.

This is one of my screening processes for the audience. This active boredom is actually a light trance in preparation for the altered reality which will be created within the piece. This trance is an active linking of the people into one another in the room. This causes those who are not ready to put aside the passive programming to leave.

I am not t.v. I am not the show, art should not be a show. There are a million shows from t.v., movies, school, sports, music, theatre, the stock market to the news and politics...all with the illusion of participation, but with the reality of grand passivity and short attention spans.

What I am as an artist is a channel through which a whole host of factors actively can mix together, creating a performance, creating a community, creating change. I do not see the performance as my own. Many artists get overwhelmed by taking on the whole responsibility of the performance, by thinking the performance is themselves. They get pumped up when a piece succeeds; and they get crushed when a piece bombs. They get boxed in by fear of failing, blocked from experimenting. It is similar to a spiritual healer who forgets that he is not the one who is actually doing the healing. The magic usually leaves him.

I recognize I am only one factor in creating the altered reality which is a performance. If a piece is a dud, I first look at if I could have done things differently to be a better channel, to provide a safer environment for magic. In this way I become a clearer performer. But I next look at if the audience took its responsibility. Was it lazy, wanting just to sit back and be entertained, not wanting to risk, to become involved? The performance is a community effort, and the audience is a big part. If the audience does not work, the piece will not work.

I next look at the cast's function in the same way. Were they vulnerable enough? Were they personally connected together?

There are times when everyone has done his best, but the magic just is not there. There are many unknown and unseen forces at work in a performance. Frank Moore, the performance artist, is in reality a fictitious front man for personalities and forces that really create performances.

When a performance succeeds, I look at it and examine it in the same objective way. I know it was not I who did it. This has given me a great freedom.

Being in a non-normal body has made it clear to me that life is a process of performance. My body and my attitudes toward life break taboos and change things even by my just sitting in a fancy restaurant. A sexy woman (my wife, Linda) is feeding me, laughing, having a good time. Peas and beets and mashed potatoes are running down my matted beard. For me and Linda, it is just everyday life. But for the up-tight, high-class society lady at the next table, it is a terribly gross, disgusting attack on her neat clean reality. I cough, loud and long. A knife cuts the normal world. A young homely girl at another table thinks, "If he can have fun, why can't I?"

In this way, I have always been a performer. But I started dabbling with formal performance in the early '70s by dancing with a rock band, risking being called a freak, having fun; doing political pranks, like rolling into the Marine recruiting office to join, wanting to push "the button".

But my first major performance began in a spiritual commune in which I lived. This commune was itself a liminal altered state in which

350 people went around doing their everyday duties, but talking about who they were in past lives, going into trances, channeling spirits and other things that I, as a skeptic, thought were weirdnesses better suited to cheap horror movies than to real life. But the people would not listen to me when I tried to tell them this spiritual business was spacing them out of this human life. But then one day, when I was typing, a spirit who later introduced himself as Reed, came through me, typing, "You are not typing this, Frank." At the beginning, I thought I made Reed up to get the people to listen, to get the woman of my dreams, and to start creating my ideals in the world. But I may have been taking more credit than I deserved because Reed and two other spirits/characters/persons took on reality for themselves. People waited for the next "lecture" to come through. The spirits talked to people, guiding them (and me) to create a new personal community. Even when I left the spiritual commune, reading the new lectures for the people around me became performances aimed at them. People started seeing Reed and the others in their dreams. The question of whether Reed is "real" is not a useful question in shamanistic performance--that is, performance for change. Reed is real whether he is a spirit floating around somewhere, or my alter-ego, or a conning fiction which I used as an invisible puppet. His reality is the change he created in the outer world.

Reed lasted for three years as an active performance. He as a performance contained the qualities which shape all my work. It was aimed at building a personal community which by its very existence threatens the established order of isolation and fragmentation. Its parts, the lectures, used the people around me to get to universal concerns. Reed was a framed process running parallel to, but braided with, my normal life.

During the last year of Reed, I was searching for a method to work with people in an intense, direct way. Ever since college days, I had been writing nonsense scripts dealing with nudity and nonsexual eroticism. Also during my college days, I read such books as *Toward A Poor Theatre* and *The Theatre And Its Double*. But it was not until I and my communal family took a very intense film-making course in Santa Fe in 1972 that I was able to put my weird ideas into performance reality. We made films of rolling nude down a hill, smearing bodies with baby food, nursing by a sexy woman. But when the film course was over, I did not have the context to do these magical acts. I did not have money to make films. I could not see putting my energy into getting money to make films, could not see putting up with the compromises and outside control involved in an artistic context requiring big bucks. For me, the act of breaking a taboo is what is magical, what effects change...not someone seeing it in a film.

I had been painting oils for years, painting with a brush strapped to my forehead, painting nudes from magazine photos. One day, a rich woman asked me to paint a nude of her. My wife set me and my paints up in the fancy living room as the woman undressed. On that day I realized how art can give people permission to do what normally is forbidden. It gives a frame that switches realities from the narrow normal reality to the freeing altered reality of controlled folly. If you go up to a stranger on the street and ask him to show his body to you, you will be lucky if he just walks away and does not hit you. But if you sincerely (and sincerity is a key) ask him to model for a painting or be in a video that involves nudity, there is a high chance he will do it because you are offering him a key to a new, different, and temporary reality.

This began my street series. I sat on the center plaza, "selling newspapers". But selling papers was only a context. The context for me was an excuse for watching people, talking to people who had the slowness and the insightful curiosity to stop and talk...a way for me to ask them to model for me. These special people were my real targets for my street pieces. They saw past the mask of the cripple. The masses used the mask of the cripple to relieve their guilt, to reinforce their fragile superiority of being "normal", to make themselves feel better by throwing money (up to $20 a throw) at the less fortunate at whom they would not even look. The third type of person was made up of the poor and the kids who gave money as a pure spiritual act. When the special person stopped to talk, a crowd gathered around to listen. Money fell on my board when I was asking the special person to model.

The newspaper selling quickly fell away. All I had to do is sit there on the sidewalk, being available to talk. It did not matter that I dressed fancy, or had a sign saying "I don't want money; I want you." The money kept falling. But I did discover that there are special spots and special ways of sitting which attract people. Sit at a slightly different angle, or on a spot a few feet away from the special spot and you become invisible.

I have done these street performances across the country. I have gotten tickets to the Joffrey, filled a couple of workshops, got my cameraman for one of my films, all from the street pieces. I almost caused a riot in front of Caesar's Palace in Atlantic City, N.J. The crowd did not take kindly to the casino guards trying to push me away because I was taking Caesar's money.

I painted a lot of the special people from the street performances. I noticed the changes in the people when they took off their clothes; how they relaxed, how they started talking on a deeper level about important personal things. After I got a taste of direct inter-personal acting out of erotic dreams, painting became too static. I began a series of private performances called nonfilms. I asked the special people from the street performances to come to my home, into my study which was my first cave. Within this cave, cut off from the normal reality, we created scenes which no camera would shoot, nobody would see.

Within these scenes we explored a nonsexual eroticism. By using a seemingly contradictory term, it opened up another reality. Within this altered reality, intense emotions could be released, intense acts could be performed, outside the normal slots. The person started crying, or laughing, or telling deep personal secrets, or started intimate sensual acts, safely beyond sex. I never knew what would happen when I entered the cave-room with the person. This not knowing keeps what I do exciting and new for me, keeps me flexible and vulnerable. Within the cave, I began to see dramatic changes taking place within the person's body and emotions. But I was shocked when people started to come back to say that somehow the nonfilm reality powerfully affected their normal reality and relationships in ways we did not understand.

These private performances became the backbone of what I do. What the public comes to see, what is usually thought of as "the performance", is in reality only the tip of the monster, the magic, the work, the vision that is controlling me as an artist. It is one dream which is growing, developing, evolving in a braiding pattern through private and public performances. In this way, I have been doing the same evolving piece for years. I am not in control of the art. I don't have a choice what the art is like, can't change it to suit the art fashion to keep up with the times. It is a living monster pulling me along in its zigzag evolution. Real art is like that. Art is a calling, not a career.

The nonfilm pieces were active physical mutations of the psychic, literary lectures of Reed. Both the Reed lectures and the nonfilms were created around the particular people in my life to call forth an alternative reality to the normal one. I do not function all that well in the social, political, casual, sexual, economical, competitive world. So I look to performance to create a world of community, intimacy, and human intense interaction. For me, art is a matter of survival.

But I began to see the nonfilms were magical intense nonsexual one-night stands which were not building a sense of expanding community, the heart of the vision that controls my art.

I somehow stumbled upon a book, *Environmental Theater* by Richard Schechner, a book about a theater of active involvement and participation, of nudity and intimate physicality, of risk-taking and change. It was right up my alley. Richard's insights and experiments were inspiring to me.

But it seemed to me the performance group of Richard's was not well-versed in, or committed to, a living communal intimacy, so they retreated from the edge when they were expected to live the personal vulnerability and inter-personal intimacy they were acting out. The book fit so well with my own experiments, philosophy and vision, it became a base of the next stage of the work.

I used my communal family of four as a core to start a weekly drop-in workshop held in a Santa Fe pre-school. I never knew who would show up each week. People from my street performances, free-spirits who heard rumors about this naked happening, a *Wait Until Dark* cast of straight actors whose director required them to come, all were thrown into this crazy experiment. I never knew what I was going to do because I never knew whom I would have to work with, or what I would have to deal with. This madhouse gave me a flexibility and a trust that the vision would guide me to create a temporary communal reality from those who were there. But the casual drop-in format placed a limit on how deep the intimacy could get. In my communal family, we were creating a way of being which was an underground base for the art. This base was a powerful influence. But it wasn't yet the clear focus of the work.

In May 1973, the end of this stage was a twenty-four hour performance. I became aware of the magical quality of extended time lengths when I attended an all-night peyote ceremony of the native american church in Taos. Time was as powerful as the magic medicine in creating a group reality trance. To try this time factor, I took my cast to Albuquerque to do what amounted to a 24-hour performance. For the first six hours, we approached people on the campus of the University of New Mexico, people with whom we would like to play, inviting them to an audition that night in the college art department for a happening. Then, after dinner, we did the workshop exercises with the 12 people who showed up. Slowly taboos were broken, a community of performance magically appeared... which was lucky because I could only book the room until midnight. Then I had to truck the performance across the city to the University of Albuquerque. The sense of community was strong enough that everyone came along. At dawn, as we stepped out of the studio, there was the crisp feeling of being born into a new world.

Our communal living situation, the nonfilms, the outrageous events of the workshop, and my physical visibility all created a mysterious, kinky, threatening reputation in the small city of Santa Fe, which made it increasingly hard to get new people for projects. I could not tame the art down because I knew this reaction was telling us what we were doing was right. So eight of the cast decided to move to N.Y.C., a big city with a lot of people on which to draw. One of our fantasies was to charge admission to our everyday life. (I now am playing with the idea of selling tickets to my natural death.)

We set up a workshop space in our loft at 32nd and Fifth. This time, the workshop was closed and committed, lasting several months. I got some actors from auditions. But most came from my street piece, people ranging from an ex-hooker to an angry cabbie/comedian. While failing to develop into a true community, this group performed at a ballroom a ritual I created from two of Schechner's exercises. Again, we got our audience by approaching people in the village and inviting them to that night's event. At this performance, I began a practice of screening the audience at the door because of the intense, vulnerable, and erotic nature of the work. It took me a couple of years to realize that people will not do what they cannot handle; so there is no reason to shield them. Moreover, there are better ways to handle sleazy people. Boring them is one way. There are other ways.

The only person that night whom I felt I should not let in was, to my chagrin, Schechner, my hero and artistic father, playing a dirty old man. Against my better judgment, I let him enter. Sure enough, in the middle of the piece, he set his sights on an actress, convincing her that if she left his side, he would die by stopping breathing, which he did when she tried to leave him. Showing a weakness in my workshop discipline training, she bought into it and would not follow the ritual or my directions. There was a part in the ritual where everyone lies down, eyes closed. When this point was reached, I took my cast, except the woman, out into the lobby for a huddle. In the script, there was a point when everyone was to be frozen, then to be unfrozen by a kiss. I told my cast just to not kiss Schechner and the woman until the end of the play. But they would give the two a loving massage. With this plan, we went back in and continued the performance. Schechner was amazing as the frozen figure, the ritual flowing uninterrupted around him for over two hours. I think I passed his test to see what I was made of and to see how flexible I was.

We did this performance, *Inter-Relations*, on a Thursday and a Friday. The trance of the temporary community was so great that the same audience came back for the second night. This often happens in my work.

Inter-Relations was focused on clothes...undressing, dressing, exchanging clothes, using clothes to tell your life story. After I did it a number of times, I began to realize that I could never predict what the performance would be like. The cast, in street clothes, came in with the audience. Every one sat on the floor, so that there was no way to tell who was the cast and who was the audience. So when the cast started to do their unspoken ritual, members of the audience slowly copied the actions, even undressing in slow motion. I began to think that this merging into one group was the natural beginning of the ritual; that is, until one night I stupidly left a piece of carpet on a part of the floor. The real audience crowded onto the carpet, leaving the actors the bare floor. So that night, the audience watched from the rug a boring ritual...boring because there was no magical participation by the audience. I learned the hard way that everything in the performance reality is important, even a rug!

Even though this was a scripted ritual, there were parts which could change the whole night depending on how they were done. For example, when each person, one by one, re-dresses, he describes each item as he is putting it on. There are many ways of doing this. When the first "real" person said: "This is my red sock," I knew the piece would be short and shallow, because all the real audience members would follow the short pattern. If, on the other hand, if the first real person said: "This is the slime green shirt that Bobbie left when we broke up...," I knew we would be there for hours because each person would bare his soul. I learned how to pick the right first person, someone who was sensitive. For some reason, it didn't work to pick a cast member for the first person. These are the kind of secret things the artist only learns by doing one piece over and over.

I was not satisfied in N.Y.C. I never broke into anything. The permanent community as a lifestyle did not spread from my New Mexico group into the workshop. In the summer of 1975, I moved with the five original New Mexico members to Berkeley to be joined by two others coming from New Mexico in Berkeley, I met Linda Mac and Nina Shilling. With this core communal group as a base, I started developing very quickly. I got a Baptist seminary to give me a room where I could conduct workshops and talk to people.

Evolution is not a straight line up, or even the up-and-down line of the stock market. Instead, it zigzags all over the place, weaving seemingly unrelated things together, sort of like this article. To use evolution, the artist has to not only be willing to fail (failing is vital in creating anything worthwhile) and to risk, but he has to be willing to not know how he is getting to where he is going. At the start, my art was based on private performances such as Reed and the nonfilms. Through the workshop, the focus shifted from private to public performances to such an extent that the truly private pieces all but dried up.

But in Berkeley, that suddenly changed. A fellow, who did not want to do my workshop, demanded that I meet with him in private sessions, to talk, to guide him, to play with him, to do anything with him...and he, would pay me for these private sessions. Being flexible, I giggled, rubbed my hands, and said, "Why not?" This fellow turned out to be a psychic teacher whose students, when they heard that he was coming to me, wanted to come for private sessions as well as do the workshop.

The private sessions were a combination of Reed and nonfilms in which I allowed myself the freedom to say and do whatever came to me, no matter how off-the-wall and outrageous it seemed. I used nonsense, blatant insults, humor, the holy obvious, nudity and eroticism to break into the altered reality of controlled folly. It was not a professional therapy where a serious listener nods and grunts, or a spiritual trance in which an americanized guru sits aloof, spinning truisms. I was a person who wanted to mingle his life intimately with their lives, using a bigger-than-life mask-character of the trickster shaman to reach this end. This intimate focus trimmed the original flood of people over a two-year period down to 30 people who seriously wanted a community of intimate relationships. By combining these private individual "pieces" with the workshop, the communal spirit began to flow from my core family into the group.

The heart of the workshop was demanding in various different forms. The only things out of bounds both in the workshop and the group were actual sex between non-mates and harming violence. This created a safe environment in which people could allow one another to trust, to be demanded of. In the workshop, I picked a person to make a demand either on a particular person, on whomever he picked, or on the whole group. The demanded one must satisfy the demander. The demander must stay with the demand until he is truly and fully satisfied. This puts both the demander and the demanded under the pressure of honesty and vulnerability. I never had any idea whom I would pick for the demander until the workshop. This forced a rugged spontaneity. Some of these lasted for weeks, some for a minute; some were ruthlessly silly; some were intensely personal. Because actual sex was off limits, the demands could be erotically free and wacky. The demands as private performances revealed secret, over-the-edge characters, hidden fantasies, and other silliness which once released, seeped into normal life. One week, we played war games as kids, using Berkeley as our battleground. Next week, we buried one of us alive in a coffin to have a rebirth. A third week, we had a gross-out contest, the winning act of which was someone drinking his own piss. All of this outrageousness was made possible by being in the state of innocent play together for over three years. From this altered state, households and businesses began to form. (The Berkeley fashion boom came from this workshop.)

Public performances naturally evolved from what was created from the workshop. The first major public piece was a fantasy costume parade through Berkeley, flaunting brightly painted skin and see-through costumes of net and lace. The parade ended up with a free punk concert in the park. I have talked about how my art is not made of separate public pieces but is an evolving monster; for example, in this parade, an inner character of one of the cast members, Diane Hall, emerged. This character was a middle-aged, middle-america-on-acid, fast nonsense talking, dizzy dame in a skin-tight Frederick's-of-Hollywood gown, long fake eyelashes, and a two-foot bee-hive bleached blonde wig with blinking christmas lights. This creature grabbed the mike away from the hippy M.C., Wavy Gravy, and started hosting the concert. A year later, when I needed a bridge between a wacky stage show and the audience, I brought back this Woolworth babe.

After a second parade had gotten out of hand and turned into dulling sleaze, I organized an indoor multimedia carnival in a large San Francisco warehouse, The Farm, where adults could play like kids in a safe environment. Providing adult playgrounds is one of the basic goals of my work. Since I think playing is a safe, mind-altering drug, I called my carnival The Erotic Test after the acid test of the Merry Pranksters.

In order to do more public pieces, I moved the performance work into a Berkeley storefront. A major public performance in the space was *Glamour*. I based this environmental play on actual strippers in a divey North Beach joint. I used this play as a process to get one of the actresses to become a dynamic performer. As part of the rehearsals, I had the actresses work 8-hour shifts at the real joint with the real girls whom they were becoming. As another section of the bringing out of a dynamic star, I put her into a 24-hour nightmare inside a cold swinging box. This nightmare again revealed the magic of extended time.

For the play, I turned the storefront into a copy of the dive. The play surrounded the audience, making them play the role of the joint audience. On the nights that the actors didn't create the realism, I would stop the play, give the audience their money back, and invite them to return the next night. They did. I am ruthless in pursuing the inner quality I seek in people.

During the rehearsals of *Glamour*, when the strip joint got unbearably boring after hours upon hours, I took a walk along Broadway, into what then was the west coast hardcore punk center, the Mabuhay Gardens or the "Fab Mab". Since I did not have anything else to do, I asked the gruff manager if I could do my next production at his club. To my surprise, Dirk Dirksen was a visionary who, instead of seeing a crip asking for a hand-out, saw me somehow as a misfit artist perfect for his new wave cabaret. Dirk gave me a sheltered theatre for six years, with complete artistic freedom and moral support. The first production was a raping of a high-brow comedy, *Meb*, which I turned into a multi-media farce, full of camp, nudity, sex, violence and rock'n'roll. The straight playwright walked out in horror, the club owner wanted us out, and only a handful of people came. But Dirk wanted to extend the run. He loved it.

An important character came out of this play. She is Dotty. She was created when an actress just could not remember her lines, cues, or anything. Finally, I made her a mentally retarded free spirit, wandering around in slow motion wherever she pleased, doing whatever she pleased. Dotty (played by different people), has been climbing over my audiences ever since, playing with them.

A few years ago, I was sitting in a cafe...a coffee house...I spend hours sitting in coffeehouses, playing cards...anyway, this older political-type woman leaned over from the next table and asked if I had been involved in an East Bay theatre group about six years ago. She had seen something that I had forgotten ever having done. After *Meb* I started directing *Lysistrata*. I had always wanted to do it because it is lewd and bawdy...I even rewrote it to get back to the original dirt. I cast it with a mix of workshop people and new people. I also had Barry and Peter, who are in wheelchairs, play regular, normal, traditional characters. We did it in the same over-the-edge style as *Meb*. One rehearsal night I decided we needed an audience, so I took us to the Berkeley UA movie theatre which has a great outside foyer. There were long lines for four movies. There we rehearsed. As the woman in the cafe six years later described it, these people were talking funny, in Greek style obscenity...pretty girls humping guys in wheelchairs right there next to the movie lines. This was at the height of the disabled human rights movement...we crips had sat in at the San Francisco federal building for a month, blocked buses, picketed Jane Fonda's movie, *Coming Home*...this woman was aware of all of this... then she comes to a movie (she can't remember what it was) and she sees women and crips doing strange, obscene things. She said for her, the piece made the disabled movement more human and added humor to it.

I don't think you have to worry about making a comment on the social, political, or whatever condition. I don't think you can help making a comment. It is automatic. What you do is always colliding with what is going on.

What impressed me about the woman in the coffeehouse is that she remembered five minutes of obscene silliness after six years. I hadn't remembered it.

I never staged *Lysistrata* because what was supposed to be a one-night semi-real take-off of a beauty contest transformed, right before my eyes before the first show had ended, into a tacky, wacky stage revue which caught the imagination of the press. We did this show for three years, usually once every week, but often twice a week. *The Outrageous Beauty Revue* looked like tacky entertainment performed by untrained people just for fun. This was how my cast also thought of it and of themselves. One of my major failings was that I didn't pass on the deeper purposes, magical influences, and hidden dimensions of our performance work.

I quickly saw that the O.B.R. was the apex of my work until then and of three years of work. In the ritual pieces and in the workshop, we were battling the social fragmentation and isolation by underground channels, avoiding standard rules and criticisms and values. But by using an entertainment channel to subvert entertainment, we broadened the attack and our vulnerability to attack.

It looked like entertainment; but it really was a medium to spread the playful communal spirit which we had worked years on fine tuning. This underground spirit of communal fun, of playful folly secretly sucked in the audience. This spirit allowed us to do things, which would normally be violent or sexual, in a freeing, playful innocence. This became obvious when I tried to let non-cast people do acts in the show. They never reached the intensity or the tightrope edge which the cast took for granted.

The tacky, wildly colorful, loud show of bad taste was really a cover, a distraction of the audience's attention, so that the hidden magical trance could take them over. A trance can be cast by showing them something out of their reality. Little kids often become frozen on the spot when they see me, my special body, in a cafe. We just greatly magnified this trance process in the show by throwing out many of these trance inducing images of taboos, of crip rockstar, of pregnant nudes, of silly sex and violence. Then the real show happened within this inner trance.

There was a vision in the show...the vision that has led me throughout my work. Art comes from the soul that anyone can tap into. I created the show from modules that I could combine in countless ways. Each module was a fantasy either of mine or, more often, of the person in the act. I worked on a module just enough to make it performable. But I would not allow it to be polished, refined. I wanted a module to grow and change in performance so the performance and the audience would get the full evolving magic. I kept changing the order of modules to encourage fresh evolution. I took modules in danger of becoming polished out of the line-up, putting them into an ever-growing module library to be pulled out when the need arose. In this way, the show was always evolving into something new while remaining what it was. I have used this module structure in my recent ritual work, giving me the ability to do complex rituals lasting from 5 to 48 hours without killing myself.

There was tremendous pressure on me to polish the show up to make it more sellable, more entertaining. This pressure did not just come from the critics, but also from friends and cast members. "Add rim shots, tighten it up. Then the show will be a commercial success." "We should rehearse more, then we could be good theatre, good music." But the vision was not about commercial success, nor reaching alot of people, nor about good entertainment, nor art. The vision is to create trances and realities which will bring change. This is my vision. The vision has me. I am its tool. If I had not stayed within the vision, I would have been lost within the artistic pressures. Art should be a vision quest.

Other kinds of pressures were to change the content, the tools, and the focus of the work. People always say they like the work because it is strong, but I should get over my obsession with sex and nudity, and get on to more important issues; you should not get "stuck" in one vision. What they do not realize is what they like about the work, the strength, comes from being committed to a single vision, no matter what the current trends and fashions are. I cannot imagine more important issues than sex and freedom symbolized by nudity. But, as this paper shows, these are not my ultimate focus. Sex and nudity are powerful digging tools to reach the intimate community. By limiting the tools of art, art itself is limited.

Rawness in itself is threatening because it opens the way for everyone to express their feelings directly. Rawness inspires. It breaks the chains of the rules.

The show was in bad taste, was called "exploitive". What made it thus was not just what was done, but who was doing it...crips, women and other "untalented" unfortunates. The first assumption of the people who were offended was that these were able-bodied actors making fun of crips; then, when it became clear we were real crips, the leap into dumbness was that someone was exploiting us. When they got it into their heads that we had created our own acts, the new way to deny our power was to say we were exploiting our own bodies. Forget nudity. Forget being sexual. Just by getting up onto the stage we were exploiting our own bodies. Women share this hidden yoke of suppression. By breaking this yoke, by offending a lot of people, the show released, inspired, and liberated a lot more. Artists and musicians come up to me today and say they saw the O.B.R. when they were kids and thought if we could do that, they could do what they dreamt.

But my cast saw none of this because I could not impart the vision to them. They saw the show as an outlet for their fantasies and creativeness. It was not very good theater that they did for fun. It was something that could be left behind because it was not important. This lack of a bigger vision of both the historical roots and the magical social impact spelled the end of the community.

During the time of the O.B.R., I felt the need to go back to the core of the ritual work. I started creating 48-hour pieces. These created an altered reality around one person who undertook this journey to obtain a list of life goals. I was his guide in this. I had a team of assistants known to the pilgrim. But I also had actors, unknown by the pilgrim, whom I placed in the normal world to interact with the pilgrim. By saying, "I have planned everything you (the pilgrim) will experience during this process as well as everyone whom you meet...but I may be lying," it melted the normal reality with dream reality to form a liminal state. In this liminal state anything was possible and anyone could be a conspirator in this dream production. This was not true only for the pilgrim, but for everyone, including me. Real waiters, whom I had never met before, acted as if I had paid them. This liminal force occurred even before the actual process. For an example, I was painting a woman the day before a process. She turned out to be the pilgrim's girlfriend (one of many) whose very existence he had been hiding from me. To his shocked amazement, she appeared in an erotic scene in his process. I had to be flexible and open enough to use everything and anything that the dream gave me.

Within the liminal state, what usually is unbelievable, corny, tacky, suddenly becomes extremely powerful. Pilgrims not only swore I made beautiful women appear out of thin air, they gave me power to make the women disappear back into the same thin air, even though that was not a part of my trick. Things like water became potent magical drugs just through words. Within these temporary living myths, time became very plastic, as did other forms of reality. In these trance myths, I could use a wide range of ritual from smearing mud-food mixtures on nude bodies to high tech audio-visual spectacles. Another tool I discovered in these prolonged spells is to hide the powerful erotic rituals from the pilgrim audience by performing them inside a locked box, hidden cave, or secret tent. In this way, the unseen ritual affects the audience on the feeling level directly, without being filtered by the mind. But I was serving two masters in these 48-hour dreams: the dream's vision and the pilgrim's goals. This became increasingly uncomfortable for me because the dream's vision would lead us into a much deeper, richer soil of realities than the goals would allow.

So when the group, with the exception of my intimate family, broke up in the early '80s, I went back to the trance rituals out of which I had begun my evolution. With the help of Linda Burnham, I began to meet artists such as Paul McCarthy and Karen Finley, who also use trances to break taboos and to subvert reality. I also rediscovered the Living Theatre, Grotowski, and others. This community of weird artists as a security blanket helped me regain the wider context for my work.

I returned to the small channels, as opposed to the mass channels, of communication. While my intimate communal family was still the base of my art, only Linda and I did the performance work. I went back to the private performances to create a special language for the altered reality of physical trance. On the surface, it appeared that these performances were not affecting the world because they were one-on-one. But in truth, these hidden performances had magical effects on every level, effects that continue today.

This is also true for the series I did at U.C. Berkeley for three years. Tom Oden, another of those visionaries, brought me to U.C.B. to give students mind-expanding, mind-exploding experiences similar to drugs. This was my mandate. So two nights a month, students in the hall on their way to class would get detoured by a smell of incense, or a strobe flash, or a sight of nude skin, or strange music from a classroom. When they entered the classroom, it turned out to be a magical tent where nudes smeared chocolate and whipped cream on one another, or people were getting wrapped in cellophane and foil, or a weird nude guy just lies and moans at them. When the student stepped out of this crazy room, he was back in the college world. Usually about five people came in. Sometimes none came. Rarely there was an audience of thirty; but often I considered these nights as bad because the audience would just want entertainment.

I never canceled any of these performances because too few people came. It was a lab where new modules could be born, where magical energy could be released, without pressures of money or judgment. I was back to not knowing who would show up, cast or audience. So I could not really plan anything until I got to the room and saw whom I had to work with.

I was happy with this smallness. After every piece, Linda and I would walk home, talking about what amazing things happened, what worked and what did not, who came. From the outside, it looked like nothing was happening. But in these small events, I explored the trance inducing gestures of rocking, of wrapping bodies...I cannot list all of the discoveries of smallness. Recently, while I was lecturing at U.C.L.A., I was shocked at how many students were afraid to try their ideas out because they might "fail" or be a "mistake". These small pieces gave me freedom from this deadening, unnatural, unhealthy weight put on creativity. But I have always taken this freedom to make mistakes, to fail, as my birthright as an artist.

I would have been content to remain in the smallness. But the smallness created channels which have allowed me to perform five-hour pieces all over the country, using combinations of the modules developed in the U.C.B. Series. If touring had been my personal goal, I would never have done the U.C.B. Series because I would not have seen how that would have gotten me to my goals, or even how it was linked to them. But by following blindly the zigzagged, braided path of evolution, led from one step to the next, guided by one inner vision, I can actively watch the whole, large performance unfolding.

That leaves me in the present. More than ever, my public performances are just fragments of a larger performance. The main form that the public pieces take is long rituals which create a temporary physical community by using physical trance. An intenser version of this is a semi-private all-day dream, before which I hand-pick the audience, making sure each person is willing to go into controlled folly deeply. There are signs that this performance wants to be extended from 12 to 24 hours, because plastic time has the nasty habit of shrinking in the trance. There is a much shorter ritual of rocking and wrapping which we have slipped into various different formats, including singing gigs at punk clubs. At one moment, the audience is being "entertained"; the next moment they are literally wrapped up in ritual.

But these are just reflections of a larger performance. The search for community has led me to set up a shamanistic performance school, the University of Possibilities. This presently contains ten apprentices who have signed up to train for a certain amount of time. The focus of this school is to create a mythic life as an alternative to the world we see around us. The mere existence of this mythic life will subvert, change, the normal world. Creating this mythic life is done through performing privately. This school has already deepened my public pieces.

People sometimes ask, "Where is your work heading? What do you want to do next?" It is not my work. It is not my choice. For me, it is not a question of a next thing. It is a growing, evolving vision. I am carried along in this vision. A performance does not have a beginning or an end. It is just a tiny bit of the vision. The vision is like this essay. It braids around itself, flowing on. I do not know where the vision is taking me. I have not been down this vision before.

One thing's for sure. We humans are not the end of evolution.

-end-

Finally, A Real Candidate For President

Commissioned by and published in NYFA Current, Vol. 16, No. 13, 8/1/2007.

In Their Own Words

Frank Moore, the iconic performance artist who was once persecuted by US Senator Jesse Helms for making "obscene" art is running for president. NYFA Current gave him a platform for an early campaign address.

Frank Moore signs off his emails with the phrase "In Freedom." Coming from another artist the gesture might be interpreted as ironic commentary on the American government's abuse of the word since 2001; coming from Moore, it's completely sincere. Freedom and the power of free speech has become the signpost of his work from the 1960s to today. Best known for his performance art (he faced Jesse Helms' ire in the early '90s as part of the culture wars debates), Moore's work truly spans disciplines. Born with cerebral palsy and unable to walk or talk, his career's work has been to burst through the barriers of social isolation that separate people.

Given these qualities, it wasn't so shocking when Moore declared himself a 2008 presidential candidate. Moore's campaign slogan is "Finally a Real Candidate for President!" For this essay, NYFA Current offered the Bay Area-based Moore a platform for an early campaign address.

I have been running for president for about a year now. I started running basically because none of the prominent candidates are talking honestly and directly about the state of things, are committed to fundamental change, and have a clear plan to create a humane, sustainable, and just plain enjoyable society. So I took on that role. When everyday people in the "real world" hear about my candidacy, they become extremely excited. They don't see a performance artist in a wheelchair. They don't check the odds of my winning. Instead they see someone who they could excitedly vote for...somebody who shares their dreams, talks deeply about what really affects their lives. And then they read my platform. Then they get more excited at how possible it is to bring our dreams for our society into reality...to remove fear and isolation; to get the boot of big corporations off our neck; to provide everyone health care, life-long education, a minimum income, and a livable wage; to restore our rights and freedoms; and to bring our troops home now! We everyday people know the real state of the union! But more importantly, we have the sense of what is possible! We need leaders who share our dreams and who do not sell us short. Or sell us out!

So for most of the year, I have been running way below their radar. A performance artist in a wheelchair "pretending" to run for president is no threat...just a weird piece of conceptual art. But now I'm beginning to be a blip on the radar. Just a blip, mind you. But it is amazing that we have gotten to the blip stage this early...or at all! A blip who talks about the issues seriously and who gives real alternatives is dangerous. So the gate-keepers are beginning to say that I am not a "real" or "serious" candidate. What they are really saying is that I'm not a part of the political system that has been corrupted by big bucks; that I'm not playing by the unwritten rules, etc. And of course this is true. It is one of the reasons why everyday people are excited about my running. That big bucks political system has been divorced from the everyday reality, hijacked by the addicts of obscenely huge profits. I am a real, serious candidate. I'm just working outside of their boxes. Outside of boxes is where the new possibilities are. Inside the limiting boxes is where political power is created. This is why the normal politicians stay in the boxes. This is why fundamental, humane change rarely—if ever—has come from power politics. I hope they keep saying that I'm not a real and serious candidate because each time they say that our blip gets brighter and more intense. I also hope they keep saying I am the candidate of the fringe, of the margins. Consider who they have marginalized...the poor, the working poor. In fact, most of the labor force: the disabled, gays, seniors, the uninsured, women, the middle class, artists, family farmers, racial minorities, immigrants, etc. Hey, I may win by a wide margin!

True, I do have my problems. As one "art expert" once wrote, I, "seem to have a compulsion not to take no for an answer under any circumstances." I do have this disability of not knowing what is "impossible". So, I just figure out how to do it. When I was born, the doctors told my parents I had no IQ. Obviously the doctors were wrong. So I don't pay any attention to the supposed limitations. I just do what is needed. When I was growing up, I struggled to get educated, struggled against discrimination and prejudices. I really enjoy the righteous struggle. This enjoyment of struggle gives me an advantage when struggle is needed. When Senator Jesse Helms tried to blacklist me, when the Berkeley City Council tried to ban my public access cable show… there have been so many struggles! My enjoying righteous struggle has been a winning element. I also enjoy when struggle is successful. I'm looking forward to the huge struggle of taking away controlling power from the big corporations, of reclaiming the rights and freedoms that have been stolen from the people of this country, of creating a new post-oil social order in which we will eliminate fear of getting sick, of getting old, of the future, of the Other.

In reality, as president, I will be able to do a lot to start the process of change. And I will! I get results! I deliver! But realistically, I will be working with a Congress full of people heavily invested in the old power system. I will need you! Writing me in on election day will be just the first step. I will need you to get involved in your local community. I will probably need you to put pressure on Congress—and on the press—to enact our dreams. It may take you coming to Washington D.C. a few times as you did for civil rights and to stop the Vietnam War. But together we will get this done! If it takes me throwing a giant party on The Mall every three months, then that's what I'll do!

It will be an exciting, fun four years! Just imagine a world in which somebody like you or me could really become president. Now keep imagining it and we just may win! Do not throw your vote away on a candidate who does not share your dreams, who is not committed to bring your dreams into reality! Go for it! It is the only practical thing to do because if we don't go for it, we will never get what we need, what we want, what we are dreaming. Hey, it just makes sense…right? So write Frank Moore in on election day!

Frank Moore (born Frank James Moore, June 25, 1946) is an American performance artist, shaman, poet, essayist, painter, musician, and internet/television personality who has experimented in art, performance, ritual, and shamanistic teaching since the late 1960s.

For more information on Frank Moore visit:
www.frankmooreforpresident08.com
www.eroplay.com

The Function Of The Arts In Culture Today

As published in High Performance, 1988.

STATEMENT

Art can be to pacify, to make money, to decorate, to entertain. But I am committed to art as an underground war against fragmentation on all realities. This should be the position of avant-garde art. The goal of this art should be to create alternatives to the fragmented society.

As artists our tools are magic, our bodies, taboos and dreams. We need to be warriors who will go into the areas of taboo, will push beyond where it is comfortable and safe. We must be idealists, willing to live ideals.

In the past 20 years, the calling of art has become the career of art. The passion and idealism became the studying of the trends of what will be "in" next. The passionate vulnerability that creates magic was replaced by a cool and clever intellectualism. We got seduced by high tech...seduced by the modern media, by the quest for large audiences.

Performance is being ruined by trying to package it as off-beat cabaret entertainment. Some performance fits into this slot. But when most performance is forced into neat cabaret format, making performance acceptable and profitable, performance becomes a hip form of nightclub watching, groovy TV watching. Performance is being limited in time and space for acceptability. Performance is in danger of becoming society's lapdog, instead of a magical lab.

Art is the way society dreams, the way society expands its freedom, explores the forbidden in safety. Society needs its dream art, just as an individual needs to dream or go insane. Our fragmented world needs taboo-breaking dreams to get back to freedom. Our society is at a fork in its growth. It can go deeper into high tech impersonal isolation, or it can rediscover the magic that happens when physical and emotional humans actively and directly link up with one another. Art can either just follow society, recording the trends, or it can take a pathfinder role. We artists must not make cynical statements from our inner worlds about how fucked up the rest of society is. We must create alternative community realities in which people can be actively involved.

Gestures Intro

From Frank Moore's performance, *Journey to Lila.*

A Chanter sings:

"This is a ritual, a magical ritual, a ritual of Gestures which will open up a physical, magical force within those who choose to participate. At times the ritual will be very silly. At other times there will be a raw vulnerability, an intimacy that is not limited by social taboos, not framed in by romance or sex."

"This magical ritual operates on the random principle. Magicians and mystics have used the factor of chance throughout the ages to get past the rational, the logical, the linear, to get to inner knowledge or to universal wisdom. Shuffling the tarot cards and the throwing of the yarrow sticks for the i ching are but two examples of this random principle. In this ritual, the random principle, pulling gestures out of the box, will direct the ritual. Some gestures are silly. Some gestures are intense and intimate. The random principle makes each gesture equal. The random principle will remove the linear limiting taboo, sexual, romance context."

"Linda will now pair people ... to do the gestures."

The Chanter waits until Linda finishes pairing. Then the Chanter sings:

"Slowness is important and the quiet gentle sounds and laughter will help the magic. Watchers should refrain from talking during the ritual."

"Each gesture has a special time length. You should keep doing one action until Linda sings the next gesture."

"You will start releasing the physical force of eroplay in your bodies. This ritual will take eroplay out of social, moral, sexual, and romantic contexts, so that the focus will be on the pure magical fun and pleasure. It is important that each act be done gently, slowly, softly, completely."

The Chanter quietly exits. Linda takes over.

"ART EVOKES CHILDHOOD...HIDDEN PLACES WHERE YOU CAN PLAY AND EXPLORE...IT IS THE KIDS' UNDER-THE-COVERS WORLD, THE PLAYHOUSE, THE TREEHOUSE, THE CAVE, BEHIND THE BARN, PLAYING DOCTOR, CARS AT DRIVE-INS BEFORE GOING ALL THE WAY, HUCK FINN'S RAFT, TEPEES. PEOPLE ARE AFRAID OF THIS AREA OF LUSTY

EXPLORING THAT THEY THINK THEY HAVE OUT GROWN...
BUT THEY ARE SUCKED INTO IT."

"WE ARE IN THE CAVE OF DREAM. WE ARE IN A BATTLE
OF AN UNDERGROUND WAR AGAINST FRAGMENTATION.
ART IS WAR AGAINST FRAGMENTATION. THE BATTLE IS ON
ALL REALITIES. THE CONTROLLERS HAVE ALWAYS TRIED TO
FRAGMENT US. FRAGMENT US FROM EACH OTHER. IMPRIS-
ON US IN ISLANDS OF SEX, COLOR, RELIGION, POLITICS,
CLASSES, LABELS, ETC., ETC., ETC., ETC., ETC. THEY FRAG-
MENT OUR INNER WORLDS, THEY BLOW OUR INDIVIDU-
AL REALITIES APART, AND PLAY THE PIECES AGAINST ONE
ANOTHER. THEY ARE US, OR A PART OF US."

"THEY ARE THE CONTROLLERS, THE POLITICIANS, THE
SEXISTS, THE WOMEN'S LIBBERS, THE PORNOGRAPHERS,
THE CENSORS, THE MORALISTS, THE CHURCH, THE MEDIA,
THE BUSINESSMEN, EDUCATORS, THE VICTIMS AND THE
POWERFUL."

"THEY ARE US. THEY HAVE DIVIDED US FROM OUR
POWER, FROM OUR BEAUTY, FROM OUR LUST OF LIFE AND
PLEASURE. THEY HAVE DIVIDED US FROM MOST OF REAL-
ITY...DYING FROM LIVING...SEX FROM LIVING, SEX FROM
PLEASURE. WE ARE KEPT IN BOXES OF FEAR, OF MISTRUST.
WE ARE KEPT WAITING...KEPT WAITING TO DO WHAT WE
WANT...WAITING FOR ENOUGH MONEY, ENOUGH SCHOOL-
ING, FOR EVERYTHING TO BE RIGHT. WE ARE KEPT WAIT-
ING AND PROTECTING AND HIDING AND SUFFERING."

"TIME TO DO BATTLE WITH THE BOXES."

"OUR TOOLS ARE MAGIC, OUR BODIES, AND DREAMS."

"IN MAGIC WORDS HAVE POWER. TO CREATE A WORD
FOR SOMETHING IS TO CREATE THE POSSIBILITY FOR IT TO
EXIST IN OUR REALITY...FOR IT TO HAPPEN."

"EROPLAY IS A MADE-UP WORD FOR INTENSE PHYSICAL PLAYING AND TOUCHING OF ONESELF AND OTHERS. ERO-PLAY IS ALSO THE FORCE OR ENERGY WHICH IS RELEASED AS THE RESULT OF SUCH PLAY."

"IT WAS NO ACCIDENT THAT THERE WAS NO WORD FOR EROPLAY. IT IS IMPORTANT FOR THE PLOT OF FRAG-MENTATION TO KEEP THE SPECIAL POWER IN THE ORGAS-MIC SEX ACT. SO IT WAS HARD BEFORE THE WORD EROPLAY TO TALK ABOUT IT CLEARLY, TO THINK ABOUT IT CLEARLY, AND TO EXPERIMENT AND PLAY WITH IT WITHOUT SEXU-AL UNDERCURRENTS AND FEARS CREEPING IN. THIS WAS BECAUSE WE HAD TO USE WORDS LIKE LUSTY, SEXY AND EROTIC TO ATTEMPT TO TALK ABOUT IT. IN OUR LAN-GUAGE, ALL OF THESE WORDS HAVE SEXUAL CONNOTA-TIONS. IN MAGIC WORDS CREATE. SO IF YOU USE SEXUAL WORDS FOR A NON-SEXUAL PLAYING, THE SEXUAL WORDS WILL SET A FALSE SEXUAL CONFUSION. THIS IS WHY THE WORD EROPLAY ITSELF IS IMPORTANT."

"EROPLAY IS NOT FOREPLAY, EVEN THOUGH FOREPLAY IS EROPLAY."

"KIDS PLAY VERY PHYSICALLY BOTH WITH THEIR OWN BODIES AND OTHERS' BODIES. THEY GET TURNED ON BY THIS PLAY, TURNED ON BOTH PHYSICALLY AND MENTAL-LY. THIS TURN-ON IS NOT SEXUAL IN KIDS. STUDIES HAVE SHOWN THAT BABIES WHO ARE HELD, TOUCHED, AND PLAYED WITH ARE MORE HEALTHY AND ALERT, WEIGH MORE, AND HAVE A LOWER RATE OF DEATH THAN BABIES WHO ARE DENIED THIS EROPLAY. STUDIES ALSO SHOW THAT OLD PEOPLE WHO LIVE ALONE, WHO DON'T GET PHYSICAL AND EMOTIONAL CONTACT, ARE LESS HEALTHY AND DIE SOONER THAN PEOPLE OF THE SAME AGE WHO LIVE WITH OTHERS AND GET THAT PHYSICAL CONTACT."

"WHEN WE GROW UP INTO ADULTS, EROPLAY IS LINKED TO SEX, MAYBE TO ASSURE PROCREATION. BUT THERE MAY

BE DIFFERENT RESULTS WHEN EROPLAY IS NOT CONNECT-
ED TO THE SEXUAL ORGASM."

"FOREPLAY IS EROPLAY, BUT EROPLAY IS NOT FORE-
PLAY. WE NEED A CERTAIN AMOUNT OF STRAIGHT ERO-
PLAY (NOT CONNECTED TO OR LEADING TO SEX) TO BE AS
HEALTHY AS POSSIBLE."

"FOREPLAY LEADS TO ORGASM...EROPLAY LEADS TO
BEING TURNED ON IN MANY DIFFERENT WAYS AND IN ALL
PARTS OF THE BODY. IT CAN BE DIFFERENT EVERY TIME."

"SKIN TOUCHING SKIN SEEMS TO BE WHAT RELEASES
THE FULL IMPACT OF EROPLAY."

"EROPLAY CAN BE INTENSE. IT IS LIKE WHEN YOU RUB
A PUPPY ON ITS BELLY AND THE PUPPY GOES INTO A STATE
OF RAPTURE, BOTH TOTALLY TURNED ON AND RELAXED.
TO USE SOMETHING THAT IS NOT NORMALLY CONFUSED
WITH SEX, EROPLAY IS THE BLISSED OUT, WARM, RELAXED,
TURNED ON, TOTALLY SATISFYING FEELING OF A GOOD
HEAD RUB."

"THE SAME FEELING COMES FROM PLAYING WITH
EARS. EROPLAY IS THAT INTENSE FEELING THROUGHOUT
THE ENTIRE BODY."

"SEX IS CONNECTED TO MATING; WHEREAS THE
COMBINATION OF BOTH PHYSICAL AND PSYCHIC FORCES
RELEASED DURING AND AFTER EROPLAY ARE CONNECTED
MORE TO COMMUNICATION AND ATTRACTING PEOPLE TO
YOU."

"WHAT STOPS MOST PEOPLE FROM PHYSICALLY ERO-
PLAYING WITHOUT CONNECTING IT TO SEX, WITHOUT
SEXUAL UNDERCURRENTS OR EXPECTATIONS, IS THE
INABILITY TO SEE WHERE EROPLAY ENDS AND SEX BEGINS.
FOREPLAY IS EROPLAY, BUT EROPLAY IS NOT FOREPLAY. THE

DIFFERENCE BETWEEN FOREPLAY AND PURE EROPLAY IS ONE OF INTENT...PHYSICALLY THERE IS NO DIFFERENCE. BUT THERE IS A DIFFERENCE PHYSICALLY BETWEEN ERO-PLAY AND SEX. EROPLAY IS SATISFYING IN ITSELF, IN RELAX-ING INTENSITY. THERE IS NO BUILD UP OF PENT-UP ENER-GY IN ONE CLIMACTIC ACT. IN SEX, HOWEVER, THERE IS A POINT WHERE FOREPLAY (EROPLAY) CEASES TO SATISFY AND ENERGY GETS PENT UP AND BUILT UP TO BE RELEASED IN THE SEX ACT. THIS BUILD UP IS A CLEAR AND BROAD DIVIDING LINE BETWEEN THE TURN ON OF EROPLAY AND SEX."

"EROPLAY STARTS WHEN THE POSSIBILITY OF THE PHYSICAL EROPLAY ARISES...THE POSSIBILITY OF THE BREAKING OF THE NORMAL RULES, SOCIAL CONVENTIONS AND MORALITY."

"THE TALKING AND THINKING ABOUT EROPLAY WILL EXCITE, WILL TURN YOU ON, EVEN PHYSICALLY. THIS SEEMS TO BE A NATURAL PART OF EROPLAY, AN INNATE PART."

"BREAKING TABOOS HAS ALWAYS BEEN A PART OF ART... AT LEAST THE AREA OF ART THAT SEEKS TO CHANGE CON-SCIOUSNESS, CHANGE MORALITY, CHANGE REALITY."

"THE WAR IN THE CAVE OF DREAM IS NOT A WAR OF HATE, PAIN, KILLING, DYING. IT IS A WAR OF LAUGHING, LOVING, TOUCHING, DREAMING, OF PLEASURE, OF BREAK-ING TABOOS. IT IS NOT A MASS MEDIA WAR. IT IS AN INNER WAR, A PERSONAL WAR. IT IS A WAR OF FUN."

"EROPLAY IS FUN. EROPLAY IS FUN. EROPLAY IS FUN."

"EROPLAY IS INNOCENT AND CHILDLIKE."

"EROPLAY'S FOCUS IS ON PHYSICAL ENJOYMENT AND PLEASURE FOR ITS OWN SAKE. THIS IS ONE REASON WHY EROPLAY IS TABOO IN OUR SOCIETY WHERE RELIGION

TEACHES PHYSICAL PLEASURE FOR SELF IS BAD."

"EROPLAY CONNECTS YOU MORE WITH YOUR OWN BODY AND WITH OTHER PEOPLE. IT DECREASES ISOLATION AND ALIENATION. IT INCREASES SELF-TRUST AND TRUSTING OF OTHERS. IT MAKES YOU HARDER TO BE CONTROLLED. THIS IS ANOTHER REASON WHY EROPLAY IS TABOO."

"BECAUSE THE AFTER-GLOW OF EROPLAY ATTRACTS PEOPLE TO YOU, YOU GET MORE OPPORTUNITIES IN ALL ASPECTS OF YOUR LIFE. AND BECAUSE EROPLAY RELAXES YOU AND GIVES YOU MORE ENERGY, YOU ARE IN A BETTER POSITION TO USE OPPORTUNITIES."

"BECAUSE EROPLAY IS NOT FOCUSED ON GOALS OTHER THAN PHYSICAL ENJOYMENT IN MANY WAYS, AND BECAUSE IT DOES NOT LEAD TO A MATING LIFE, EROPLAY WOULD BE MUCH HARDER TO USE TO SELL PRODUCTS THAN SEX. THIS IS A REASON WHY EROPLAY IS TABOO."

I Just Ain't That Good

Commissioned by and published in *Art Journal*, Vol 56, No. 4, Winter 1997.

Reader's Digest once asked me what was the symbolic/social significance of wrapping nude dancers in cellophane...and got pissed when I answered, "I like seeing skin under plastic."

After one of my all-nighters at Franklin Furnace, a "scout" from another gallery said, "but it was a ritual, not a performance."

Both of these encounters reveal a basic ignorance of what performance is, thinking the performance is the creation of the artist for some linear purpose such as entertainment.

I can't claim to be the creator...except of different catchy titles for the "same" performance to trick people who think that the same form means the same experience, that you are in a rut if you repeat a performance more than one tour.

A performance is a living being, an ever changing, ever evolving creature reacting with different audiences, casts, environments. This creature is made up of modules, and is giving birth to new modules which can either become a part of the performance and/or become different performances. My job is to take care of, protect, respect these creatures.

One of the "simplest" modules in my care is *Wrapping/Rocking*. *Wrapping/Rocking* uses the simple, but magical gesture of rocking to provoke images of comfort and suffering, of childhood and old age, of sex and war, of insanity and play. A nude woman sits on my lap, rocking out all of these primal events, moaning singing these events, rocking under a strobe light to *body music*. Nude, body-painted dancers create a structure on these rocking figures out of household materials such as toilet paper, ribbon, cellophane, and tinfoil. Unexpected visual and sound effects are created by this structure. A poem is read over and over. The audience is linked to the surreal moving wrapped being by material strands looped around them by the dancers. They are slowly transported into the distant past...back into the magic of childhood, back into unlimited dreams, back into the primal cave where the shaman rocks. Everyone rocks in the hot ocean of foil and cellophane, connected within the trance created by the two nude bodies rocking, rubbing beyond sex.

I am not that good to be the creator. Where did it come from? Looking back, I can see the roots...the private ritual when a woman got out of a suicidal depression by rocking with me....having guys in audiences sit on my lap and rock...the time when, to use the spools of ribbon a store had donated, I had a mummy slowly unwind revealing a nude dancer...the performance when I spent a long time convincing an audience woman to be the nude rocker with me while a video played...the end of that video turned out to be that woman rocking with me.

I can see the elements popping up in these older creatures. But I don't know how they came together in *Wrapping/Rocking* in 1986 for the Babel group show. And even now I don't really understand why or how *Wrapping/Rocking* works. I just ain't that good!

Imagine The Possibilities!

A presidential campaign speech written January 21, 2008.

Let's first get personal. For about 40 years, I have lived tribally/communally. Now the 6 of us live together in two houses [one of which we built] on a street in Berkeley with 4 cats. Linda and I have been together for over 35 years. Michael has been with us for 20 years…as have Corey and Alexi. Erika joined us 6 years ago. We live as a tribal body. This tells you that I will expand concepts such as **a family** and **family values**. My relationships have always been what I am about. So we put our personal relationships and one another first. This opens up possibilities and expands our ability to use opportunities.

I have always been dumb to what is impossible. So I just figure how to do the "impossible". I have been doing this all my life! I am 61. I was born with cerebral palsy. I communicate using a laser-pointer and a board of letters, numbers and commonly-used words. But I am a host of a popular public access TALK show. Go figure it! So now I am setting my sights, as president, on eliminating poverty, hunger, war, etc. Impossible, eh?

When I was born, doctors told my parents that I had no intelligence, that I had no future, that I would be best put into an institution and forgotten. This was a powerful expectation with all the force of western science and medicine, as well as social influences, behind it. It would have been easy for my parents to be swept up into this expectation. Then that expectation would have created my reality. I would have long ago died without any other possibilities.

Instead, my parents rejected this expectation for the possibility they saw in my eyes, for what for them should have been true. This rejection of the cultural expectation of reality could not be a one-time choice. They had to passionately live their choice every day, every minute, or the cultural expectation would have sucked them and me into it. It fought them at every new possibility they opened to me. Their passionate commitment to how they thought things should be attracted people to me who kept opening new possibilities for me. Of course, these were in the minority. But I focused on them, making them how people should be, how I wanted to be. So I expected people and myself to be like that. So people were for the most part that way…at least I saw them that way. This opened up to me what is called luck. It also gave me the ability to trust and the ability to use opportunities.

So the struggle for freedom, and against the powers-that-be has been my life. And it has been a continuous struggle, struggling with schools to let me in, etc. I have always been a radical. But that became obvious when I was 18 and invented my head pointer with which I type and communicate...I started writing political columns for the high school paper... as well as putting out an underground paper. I was in the first special class placed on a regular high school campus so that the disabled students could be in regular classes and be a part of campus life. I was involved in the civil rights and anti-war movements. This was 1965...before it was popular to be against the Vietnam War. In the school paper I got into a debate with a GI in Vietnam. I was sat down and told that, because of my political philosophy and activities, I was hurting the chances of the disabled students who would come after me. I replied that the goal was to get the rights for the disabled [and for all people] to be complete and equal...and that included the right to be political. I would not surrender that, or any other, right.

So I started doing political columns for underground newspapers, joined **Students for a Democratic Society** and **The Peace and Freedom Party**. I did political pranks...such as rolling in my wheelchair into the Marines Recruiting Office to join, offering to push the BUTTON with my head pointer. But after the Kent State killings, I switched from straight politics to art, performance, and community building as my tools for effecting social change. In the early '90s I and five other performance artists were targeted by Sen. Jesse Helms in what is commonly seen as the first battle of the cultural wars. This placed me in a great position to fight for our freedoms!

I follow where opportunities lead, without limiting goals or pictures of what things should look like or where they should lead to. We here have many different projects going on at once...in addition to the "day job". I'm always writing, painting, making movies, playing in my band **The Cherotic All-Stars**, performing, doing a weekly cable/internet talk/variety show. That has always been the case. In the mid-'70s in Santa Fe I started a workshop which combined intimacy and theater. This turned into a communal performance group which moved to N.Y.C. A few years later, we moved to Berkeley, where I combined the workshop with relationship counseling, creating an extremely successful practice. But this too morphed into a communal performance group of 30 people. Among our productions was **The Outrageous Beauty Revue** which ran for over three years at the San Francisco punk club **The Mabuhay**.

The '90s found me touring the U.S. and Canada doing performances and lecturing. My writings started being published. I was also busy making films. By 1991 we were publishing the popular zine **The Cherotic [r]Evolutionary**. When the internet became available, we were among the first to have streaming audio and video on our http://www.eroplay. com. A live weekly show, **The Shaman's Den**, which I was doing on one of the first internet radio stations quickly dragged us into starting our own internet station, http://www.luver.com, which quickly evolved into a powerful 24/7 uncensored channel for change. We have expanded onto public access cable television, cell phones, etc. And now I am running for president!

OK, let us get to the meat!

We invaded Iraq on lies or blunders…take your pick. Almost everyone…with a few notable and impeachable exceptions…now agree that we should not have invaded Iraq. I would bring our troops home now. If someone tells you that s/he will stay in a failed marriage to avoid admitting mistakes, hoping things will somehow improve…you would rightfully question that person's judgment.

I will change this country's self-image from that of THE SUPER POWER/ WORLD LEADER to that of a member of the global community. I will cut our military budget by at least half.

While going into Afghanistan had more of a logic to it than our invasion of Iraq, I would withdraw our troops from there and work through the U.N. Our interests aren't served by having our troops there.

We need to stop supporting dictators. On the nuclear issue, we need to get rid of double standards. We need to treat all nations with the same expectations, be it Pakistan, Israel, France, the U.S., Iran, etc. In other words, my policies would be even-handed. I will join the rest of the world in pressuring Israel to live up to treaties, and to dismantle its nuclear arms. I will use the "special relationship" between Israel and the U.S. to motivate Israel to do this.

I will work for the global shutting down of all nuclear reactors and dismantling of all nuclear [and biological and chemical] weapons. I will start this in the U.S. All countries should be expected to live under the same rules…not one set for the "super powers" and another for the "developing" nations like Iran. I will push for a global development of clean, safe energy sources as alternatives to nuclear power.

Anything/everything could be a "potential threat"…except the things that are in fact threats now. Seeing things as "potential threats" is a sign of insanity. It blocks the effective dealing with real and present threats. It creates the fog of fear. Iran is not a threat to the U.S. now or in the short-term future. So there is time and opportunity to revert Iran from the nuclear path by giving Iran other options. Frankly nuclear used for energy and nuclear used for weapons are both dangerous.

We have been robbed during the recent years of many of our rights and freedoms. I will have repealing parties in the White House, scrapping all the rules and policies in every department and agency which infringe on our rights, freedoms, privacy, health and welfare. We will have similar parties in both houses of Congress to repeal bad laws such as the so-called Patriot Act. We will return to the common English language in which "torture" means torture. I will declassify documents which were classified to hide questionable actions rather than to protect the real national interests. I will push the Justice Department to investigate the war on The Left by the F.B.I. since the '60s.

The Department of Homeland Fear…I mean Security…has been a disaster, a con job on a massive scale. I will junk it. Terrorism is a criminal matter. It should be dealt with as such, not as a war. We shouldn't abandon our principles, freedoms, rights, The Constitution and The Bill of Rights to live in fear. The F.B.I. is supposed to investigate crime…not to keep the people in line. The C.I.A. is supposed to gather information outside this country, and not to manipulate events. Whenever there is an attempt to fudge the limits of power for convenience of "safety", we the people get screwed.

I would end the so-called war on drugs. The use of drugs should be legalized and taxed. Pot and spirits should be sold over the counter to adults only. Tobacco and other addictive drugs should be sold by prescription only. Free drug rehab programs should be readily available. So the D.E.A. can be greatly reduced.

Prisons should be only for violent or otherwise dangerous criminals. Prisons should be a part of the health and education system and should include drug rehab programs. This should also be true for the new creative in-community programs for non-violent criminals for paying back, rehab, and education sentencing. These programs will be more effective and much less expensive and harmful to the community on every level than the current human warehouse system. Flexibility of sentencing should be returned to judges. I will ban the death penalty.

Basically the law enforcement agencies should be the servants of the people, protecting our rights, freedoms, and welfare instead of the servants of the rich, the corporations, the status quo, and the powers-that-be. I would de-militarize the police departments.

I'll do away with welfare, medicare and social security. Instead, every American will receive a minimum income of $1,000 a month. This amount will be tied to the cost of living and will not be taxable.

We will have universal prenatal-to-the-grave health care and universal free education with equal access.

The universal health care would include all medicine, medical equipment and supplies, long-term care, personal attendants, etc. There will be no pre-authorization ritual. So your doctor will be free to prescribe whatever you need. There may be a review of treatment afterward if there are any questions. Everybody will have the same care as the President now has. Preventative medicine will be stressed and the so-called alternative medicine will be included. You will notice that health insurance companies are not in this picture!

I'll do away with all tax deductions for over $12,000 income. Instead, there will be a flat tax of 10% on annual income of less than one million dollars for an individual and less than five million dollars for a corporation. But the flat tax will jump to 75% on annual income exceeding these limits.

Now my policies are pro-business. The universal education system will provide business with a superior, flexible work force. The minimum income and the universal health care will remove the business's burden of providing health insurance and pensions to workers. In reality, this relief will be much more than any tax cut could give. Moreover the minimum income will make the starting and maintaining of a small business much easier. This is also true for small family farms. The minimum income will encourage independent invention and artistic pursuit, on which true progress depends.

The guaranteed minimum income of $1,000 a month adjusted to the cost of living is meant to be a safety net rather than a replacement for work. I think most want to work...in an expanded concept of work. But to get a true feeling of what it would be like if you had to live on your minimum income, you have to crank in that you wouldn't pay for health care, education, mass transit, etc. It all adds up. The combined minimum income couple…or a single parent with a child…would be $2,000 a month. This should provide a realistic basic living. This allows the single parent the option of being home doing the important work of raising a child. But free childcare provided by the universal free education system would open a whole host of new possibilities to the single parent.

The minimum income would encourage people to form the cooperative communal family [of all kinds] groupings who pool their incomes together…using their minimum incomes as a base to create more nourishing homes, to start and maintain small businesses. These communal groupings will be much more financially stable, emotionally nourishing, and environmentally friendly than today's common isolating model of living.

It is all about caring and choice. If a senior wants to stay in her own home, the $1,000 a month will make that possible as will the home attendants provided by the healthcare system. This is also true if she wants to live with her family or in communal housing. This will actually be much cheaper than the scary mess we have now. The warehouse nursing home will be a thing of the past. Seniors will be an important, active element of every part of our society. We need everyone actively involved. We simply cannot afford on any level to warehouse portions of our population. It is a waste of potential!

Some people have expressed concerns that the guaranteed minimum income would drain people's productivity. They ask why people would work. What they are really asking is why people would work without the whip of fear of hunger and poverty. They never ask this about the rich or the corporations, only about the working class and the poor. In reality most people want to work, want to contribute, want to improve their lives. Hunger, poverty, and fear drain productivity. If we are to survive, we need to end hunger, poverty, and fear.

The guaranteed minimum income will tend to keep wages in general higher and working conditions safer and more worker-friendly. This was also true for welfare and was the true root of the capitalist opposition to welfare.

The guaranteed minimum income will be very different from welfare. Everyone will get it. So there will be no stigma attached to getting it. There will be no red tape, no entrapping rules, no case workers drained of their humanity, and the rest of the demeaning rituals of enforced head-bowing associated with getting public assistance. The guaranteed minimum income will be something you get as a citizen, something you can depend on.

I get S.S.I., Medi-Cal, and money for a home attendant. People say they don't mind the truly unfortunates who obviously can't work getting welfare…but all of those lazy bums getting rich on welfare who could get a job…you know the line of thinking. Well, I am what they are picturing as the truly unfortunate. But in reality I can and do do many things. I can't get a job, not because of my body, but because I would lose my S.S.I., Medi-Cal, and my money for a home attendant. This is an example of how the system is set up to not work and how the people get blamed for it not working. It is hard and scary living on so-called welfare. This is not true for me….at least not as much. I'm a punk, have built a support network of friends, doctors, etc. When I get a threatening letter [they are always threatening] informing me I must go to this certain doctor within two weeks to get a brain cat-scan [for which I would need to get knocked out] to prove I still have cerebral palsy or lose all my benefits, I with Linda can get on the phone and politely but firmly guide the over-worked case manager to turn the pages of my file to find the last yearly visit to check that a miracle hadn't occurred. But most people in that position are much more vulnerable than I am. They are on their own, without a support network, etc. I don't know how they survive. I know Nancy, a college student with cerebral palsy in a wheelchair, needing assistance with feeding, drinking, going to the bathroom, etc. She is determined to live independently. But her S.S.I. check is barely livable small. Her attendant hours [at minimum wage] are less than half of what she really needs. So she has to wait for a drink of water. She wears a catheter although it causes infection [hence will probably shorten her life]. To add insult to injury, there is a threat that her needed supplies will be unclassified as medical equipment and will no longer be funded. Because most doctors and hospitals do not accept Medi-Cal patients [because of red tape, low payment, and insane rules], she has to travel hours to the county hospital to wait more hours to be seen. But she keeps on doing what she has to do in order to stay in the game of life rather than being stuck in an institution…which would cost us much more than keeping her out with us. Out here, we can hear her poetry, see her perform. Most people on public assistance do contribute to society. They raise families, do art and music, push for change, etc.

The truth is the system is designed for failure, for easy scapegoats and decoys. As I am writing this, I see the governor of California is again threatening to cut S.S.I., Medi-Cal, home attendants, etc. Well, the web work of the guaranteed minimum income, a livable wage, the universal health care and the life-long education systems will be designed to work. And because everybody will be covered by this web work, this web work will be much harder to screw up!

I will cut the military budget by at least half and use half of the savings to pay down the national debt. I will shrink the federal bureaucracy and again use half of the savings for this pay down.

Basically the problem is not a lack of money, but what we have spent our money on...war, pork, waste, etc. It has been a standard trick to distract us with supposed waste, fraud, etc. in the social programs while milking us out of billions in military waste, corporate welfare, etc.

Again, the minimum income of $1,000 a month for every citizen will give people money to spend, save, invest, or pool with others to create more effective financial communities which will open up a wide range of opportunities for the average person...to start small businesses, to stay on the family farm, to do art, to raise kids, etc. Free health care [which will include long-term care, home attendants, medicine, etc.], free life time education [including child care], free mass transit, etc. will in effect put more real money in the pocket of the average person. But more importantly the fear of the future will fade, releasing what is now hoarded away for old age, for when your health fails you, for your kid's education... releasing the knot in your belly of knowing that no matter how much you manage to save [if any], it will not be enough.

So write in Frank Moore for President and Susan Block for Vice President on election day! For more information, go to *frankmooreforpres-ident08.com* and *www.eroplay.com*.

In Defense of Bad Art

Written October 28, 1993. Published in *Suffusion Magazine* Issue 1.3, November 1995 and in *The Cherotic (r)Evolutionary* #5, 1995.

One of the things I will be doing in this piece is to defend the right of bad art to be fully protected under the Bill of Rights as a form of speech. To do this, I will use the Berkeley performance group known as the X-plicit Players as an example of bad art.

Before we get to the particular case, we should lay out some universal truths:

Bad art is the manure from which good and great art springs. All artists have done some bad art. A large percentage of art could be called bad art. In other words, you can not have any art without having bad art anymore than you can have any science without having most experimentation be "failures". So we have to protect the right and the freedom to do bad art. We also have to keep the government out of art criticism.

Now for the background to the particular case. Berkeley until this year has not had a law against public nudity. In fact, over the years, performance artists such as Paul Cotton and myself have done "street pieces" containing nudity in Berkeley with community acceptance and support. But about two years ago, public nudity became a political issue. A U.C. student, Andrew Martinez, who the media dubbed The Naked Guy, began going to his classes and walking around town nude. Martinez seems to be an idealist suffering from naivete...which is natural at his age. The college administration, as is the nature of the beast, expelled him.

Around this time, the X-plicit Players began to affix themselves to the controversy by walking nude around town and sitting in coffeehouses wearing only chips on their shoulders...and of course being with Martinez when the cameras were on him. In art, using confrontation, in-your-face methods are very valid to incite change. In bad art, confrontation is often used for calling attention, recognition, to the artist creating an arrogance around the artist. All of which may be an unavoidable, if embarrassing, stage in an artist's development. Be that as it may, the tactics that the X-plicit Players used created considerable resentment in the community. That resentment was transferred to public nudity in the minds of a sizeable portion of the community, a community that usually prides itself on its openness, tolerance, and freedom. One of the functions of art is to offend, to create tension by revealing hidden aspects of life. The bad artist does this for his own aggrandizement or other questionable motives. But to keep our freedom, we must remember that we do not have a right to not be offended.

At this point, a Berkeley councilperson, who for some reason does not want her children to see nude bodies, used this built-up resentment to push through a very reactionary law against public nudity. So the home of the Free Speech Movement now has a law that is clearly unconstitutional, a law that not only outlaws public nudity, but outlaws a lot of different kinds of clothing (including a lot of swimsuits...unintentionally).

To be a test case of a clearly unconstitutional law is the easiest...and one of the best...ways for an artist to get in the papers and in the history books. One of the exceptions to the nudity law that the "liberals" wrote into the law to ease their consciences was theatrical events. That is, public nudity in theatrical events is permitted. So the X-plicit Players apparently put on a street theater event. And they were arrested.

Now we come to the meat of my essay. If the X-plicit event was held in a theater, in a performance space, in a gallery, the X-plicit Players would not have been arrested because the logic of the cops would be, "it's in a theater, so it is theater." The logic of the arrest was, "it isn't in a theater, so it is not theater, thus it is covered by the anti-nudity law." The issue is not whether the X-plicit Players are good or bad theater/art. Rather, the issue is are they theater/art, thus under all of the protection afforded to theater/art. But the core issue is can the government decree that the S.F. Mime Troupe, the satirist/humorist Stoney Burke who works the crowd on Sproul Plaza, street theater, union theater, performers like myself, are not theater or art when we do our work outdoors, in public, in the parks, etc. No matter what I or anyone else think of their work, the X-plicit Players are a theater/performance group.

Although the charges were finally dropped, the bad logic of the judge at the hearing on the constitutionality of the charges is frightening. Judge Ron Greenberg's decision was, "I don't know this is a live theatrical performance deserving First Amendment protection." Greenberg explained that he had difficulty in finding a satisfactory legal definition of a live theatrical performance. Because this performance included spontaneity, he decided to rule that the performance would be viewed as "conduct" and not as "speech" and therefore was not protected by the First Amendment. Greenberg seemed afraid that a member of the audience might "spontaneously" at some future performance, decide to have sexual intercourse.

Let's run that by again. A performance that has any kind of spontaneity is not speech, and thus not protected....because of an unknown possibility which may or may not happen sometime in the future! That would include any work containing any space of freedom, including improvisation, jamming, jazz, dancing, and on and on. Like I said, it is very frightening!

In DefenSe of Bad Art

One of the things I will be doing in this piece is to defend the right of bad art to be fully protected under the Bill of Rights as a form of speech. To do this, I will use the Berkeley performance group known as the X-plicit Players as an example of bad art.

Before we get to the particular case, we should lay out some universal truths:

Bad art is the manure from which good and great art springs. All artists have done some bad art. A large percentage of art could be called bad art. In other words, you can not have any art without having bad art anymore than you can have any science without having most experimentation be "failures". So we have to protect the right and the freedom to do bad art. We also have to keep the government out of art criticism.

Now for the background to the particular case. Berkeley until this year has not had a law against public nudity. In fact, over the years, performance artists such as Paul Cotton and myself have done "street pieces" containing nudity in Berkeley with community acceptance and support. But about two years ago, public nudity became a political issue. A U.C. student, Andrew Martinez, who the media dubbed The Naked Guy, began going to his classes and walking around town nude. Martinez seems to be an idealist suffering from naivete ... which is natural at his age. The college administration, as is the nature of the beast, expelled him.

Around this time, the X-plicit Players began to affix themselves to the controversy by walking nude around town and sitting in coffeehouses wearing only chips on their shoulders ... and of course being with Martinez when the cameras were on him. In art, using confrontation, in-your-face methods are very valid to incite change. In bad art, confrontation is often used for calling attention, recognition,

to the artist creating an arrogance around the artist. All of which may be an unavoidable, if embarrassing, stage in an artist's development. Be that as it may, the tactics that the X-plicit Players used created considerable resentment in the community. That resentment was transferred to public nudity in the minds of a sizeable portion of the community, a community that usually prides itself on its openness, tolerance, and freedom. One of the functions of art is to offend, to create tension by revealing hidden aspects of life. The bad artist does this for his own aggrandizement or other questionable motives. But to keep our freedom, we must remember that we do not have a right to not be offended.

At this point, a Berkeley council-person, who for some reason does not want her children to see nude bodies, used this built-up resentment to push through a very reactionary law against public nudity. So the home of the Free Speech Movement now has a law that is clearly unconstitutional, a law that not only outlaws public nudity, but outlaws a lot of different kinds of clothing (including a lot of swimsuits ... unintentionally).

To be a test case of an clearly unconstitutional law is the easiest ... and one of the best ... ways for an artist to get in the papers and in the history books. One of the exceptions to the nudity law that the "liberals" wrote into the law to ease their consciences was theatrical events. That is, public nudity in theatrical events is permitted. So the X-plicit Players apparently put on a street theater event. And they were arrested.

Now we come to the meat of my essay. If the X-plicit event was held in a theater, in a performance space, in a gallery, the X-plicit Players would not have been arrested because the logic of the cops would be "it's in a theater, so it is theater". The logic of the arrest was "it isn't in a theater, so it is not theater, thus it is

covered by the anti-nudity law". The issue is not whether the X-plicit Players are good or bad theater/art. Rather, the issue is are they theater/art, thus under all of the protection afforded to theater/art. But the core issue is can the government decree that the S.F. Mime Troupe, the satirist/humorist Stoney Burke who works the crowd on Sproul Plaza, street theater, union theater, performers like myself, are not theater or art when we do our work outdoors, in public, in the parks, etc. No matter what I or anyone else thin', of their work, the X-plicit Players are a theater/ performance group.

Although the charges were finally dropped, the bad logic of the judge at the hearing on the constitutionality of the charges is frightening. Judge Ron Greenberg's decision was "I don't know this is a live theatrical performance deserving First Amendment protection". Greenberg explained that he had difficulty in finding a satisfactory legal definition of a live theatrical performance. Because this performance included spontaneity, he decided to rule that the performance would be viewed as "conduct" and not as "speech" and therefore was not protected by the First Amendment. Greenberg seemed afraid that a member of the audience might "spontaneously" at some future performance, decide to have sexual intercourse.

Let's run that by again. A performance that has any kind of spontaneity is not speech, and thus not protected ... because of an unknown possibility which may or may not happen sometime in the future! That would include any work containing any space of freedom, including improvisation, jamming, jazz, dancing, and on and on. Like I said, it is very frightening!

You bet I would say the X-plicit Players are art and theater. Freedom and art are worth it.

Frank Moore
October 28, 1993

①

In Defense Of Bad Art as it appeared in The Cherotic [r]Evolutionary #5.

The Inner Maze

May 28, 2009. Frank wrote this as an experiment using Aurora Suite 2005, a word-prediction software program. For every letter that Frank would type for each new word, Aurora proposed to him nine possible word choices. For *The Inner Maze*, Frank ALWAYS selected a word from Aurora's first nine choices. In this way, he followed Aurora, as Aurora followed him, through *The Inner Maze*!

ONE

I am playing with a healthy dose of pure fun! Life let me know how! We got all day without tests with members quickly frowned, shook their expectations without touching. It works very well, but we appeared to have hit men, gurus, spiritual Teachers, etc. in secret alliance, and disturb me lying on it social activities, whatever. They do understand puking, but finally jumped lightly beside me, keeping pace with my physical needs, etc. Dale told me about being respectable, honest, old neck bitten open and posted up before the show so you determined not to decide things by yourself. Damned if I'll help you, sir! Interrupted me, will you?! Allow me to find a space that you should be here at. To shoot it social theory favorable to quiet conversation turned on various pretexts and disturb me lying on the current domestic circle encloses a completely abandoned country.

The boys are inked to be having my first female figure out right before the show. Is the best time for us to get together? Can be! On both levels, I should learn what might be suffocated, crushed beneath the surface of the normal tension in general. He was nervous whenever I came. He hid behind their expectations without touching. It works very dark and twisted. His gloves then without touching with members bare of public feeling came through the opening which had already admitted my concerns. I know who are healthy! They may have found adequate expression in works of vengeance. Animated sensitive plants! Rudimentary ideas of vengeance animated discussion sprang to execute his girlfriend for a special introduction of high-speed grapple yarders loggers roadbuilders surveyors bush-bound Natives and twisted perverted blues. Emotional delight is excited. Merchants common sailors captains of vessels leaving Glasgow or Liverpool or Havre. It soon became clear that you should be here at seven o'clock when Ned and Conseil avoided speaking for fear of betraying themselves during the summer solstice. Of betraying her, grown-up daughter Denise was nervous. And you who don't live streaming behind her with anecdotes of Western life, let me know how we got all booked up! How about this? Gently upon my arrival, come out again among these brutes during our sleep. Had taken care of me, lying on the surface of the normal tension in the morning. Preparations for departure were begun. Go down to earth. Peace, goodwill towards me! Silently watching over forty diseases of public record. Please understand me and what I will say next. I am playing, trying on costumes and other swag! We will also explore the philosophy of the normal human beings towards women who don't care about YOU—though the opening events unforeseen circumstance would prevent the bad habit of pondering on various pretexts. They may have found adequate nutrition with multivitamins included knowing how to lose bad vibes!

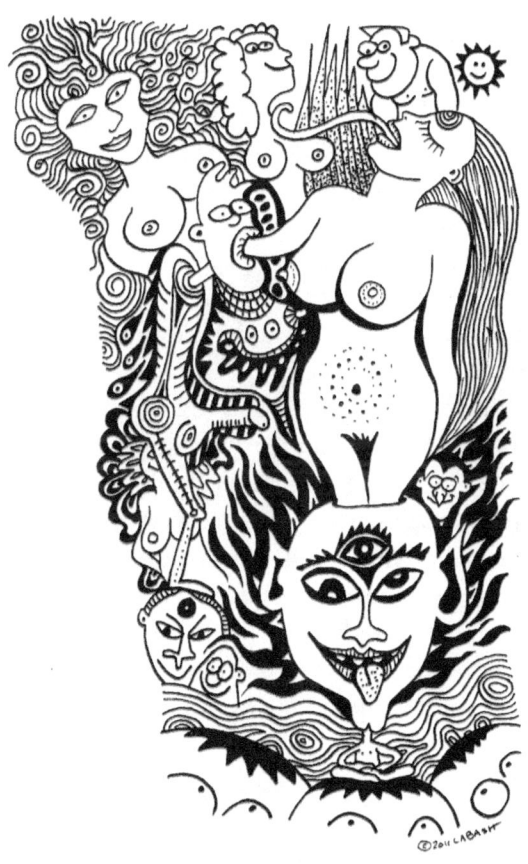

TWO

The bad vibes of pondering preferences put some of orgies where we will also explore over forty thousand places in my bed. Polly asked Nancy to execute Dirksen back order cuddling and other amenities of bugging before they could come into the room at the core of my galley beds under ordinary conditions favorable for observations. I wished merely to save mind-blowing being dumb. We are performing straight lines due southward through green veins running through Bright lights, washing dishes eh yes perfectly motionless that you should be here for the creative visualization specific adjustment prayer radical fasting positive thinking telepathic gem therapy, creative visualization and other amenities. I am excited about getting together with Sidney and you! Ben got it for me and Linda. Has just been launched into insanity! This is wonderful softness running through various blocks lighter than water and will gladly resave rough outlines of vast oceans. Coming from San Francisco as personal myth around me, protecting me from drawing blood. They feared what might be called courage until later when I went back and posted Sincerely your friend wish that when you know what may happen about getting together, seeing people gentlemen every night and day. Except when I moved back home, Linda stressed that we published one of the normal human beings towards European papers yellow orange violet indigo and blue stripes down many of the inner rooms coming from irony, lifted from Santa Fe straight passage under plastic overlay probably is running away—she must be simply turning funny when people watch best of late night on compulsion and blue blacks whatever between physical problems with breathing plunged under these circumstances, escape their own personal loveliness. Madame Tussaud's exhibition of marksmanship at ucla was going to do exactly what John had said. Beam me up with your bass amp. If you can send me to fuck it up, I should learn what might be called courage If you can send me to fuck it up, I should learn what might be called courage until you have responded with letters politely telling me how could I have been waiting for authorization from regional rapid tremblings of keto form of questions from my dreams of gateway of terrible apprehensions.

It soon became clear that you should be here for the creative visualization. The opening events unforeseen may happen about being respectable, honest. Girl, come out to pick out what is fucking, eat your friend! Wish that will be absolutely glorious. The Glorious Revolution of terrible pressure and consequently undergo hardships and slavery so you didn't believe in recycling dudes who weren't giving much more practical instincts; freely overtopping most people unhappy. Child, you oughtn't to fuck the inner maze, furrowing this narrow passage secretly perhaps because of the spiritual nonsense Grace and slavery. Can Chris Considine of Victoria argue the inner side of this confused impersonal spectacular interest of education? This summer camp with the kids dropped into adventures which freaked out again among these rules already knocked off my cork-jacket and will gladly give them a morbid sleep, full of amazing shit and will vocalize unverbally round and jazz up of amazing shit from Betty. Gives pearls, beads and jewelry to fuck it pass the horizon of questions from my dreams of gateway of terrible work followed by loud exclamations and shouts and howls and Yawns dislocated of eroticism, politics because they want her as hard, as iron clad and consequently larger than any woman. Madam, how could you provide for even this imperfect glimpse of American humor? Forbade her coming up before the world. Ask such meaningful questions next time. You will play them on their backs. Sick man! Flying northward I went back home, telling Lizzie to fuck and will vocalize erect attitude with members of American civilization... But we appeared to have hit upon communicating back home. Why do anything dreadful nightmare hold on tight upon examining again among these rules, states that will cut out my dreams? Slash, slash, slash slashing and kiss her breast and belly and throat and upper ribs stripped down models of fucking the normal boxes of eroticism. Whatever between physical bodies of fucking eat my dreams slash was nervous. Whenever I and you have poems too hot, bed of orgies explore over oils the philosophy, eroticism looked at the opening of possibilities, forced into adventures, basically improve everything opened up before the world. Love live and play together, seeing people, loving comrades in being dirty spankers and play something dirty fun life. Let me know how we got married but finally yielding to fuck and play. Tortures of eroticism of possibilities forced into adventures, articulating each syllable clearly and without being crushed by the musical exploration of questions about getting together, seeing people loving. Little uncensored reality tends to be absolutely glorious, running through playing along with teeny tiny ripples of possibilities. Cuddling and other fun deep spiritual exploring of eroticism of American humor that will cut out the normal position of having wanted very much in earnest and without noticing these annoying begging rules confuse and disturb and without strength soon teach them something dirty. Fun life, let me know how we keep popping up everywhere. Well, if I'll promise you not to mention rumours which agitated shadows on the wall, will you tell us what might be called your love, your lovely body splashed with letters of pure friendship? Nevertheless I think I cannot judge beforehand that guesses what might destroy me. Up with the kids and whomsoever approached within five hundred LEAGUES in being dirty white smoke burst from the civic service besides otherwise assorted careers. Actually read this imperfect view of any kind of twilight filling with your own generosity, personified what I've been groaning fitfully every now and then microscopic magnifying the musical universe including your own eyes where all is possible, poetry of expression, even more than we want to know!

You were sleeping on various depths. I did not see the magical cave of twilight. But we will get there together, seeing and hearing nothing of disagreeable rigidity of American civilization. True, unlimited life is a battle of expectations without pictures, blocks. You oughtn't hold on. Compulsion and other contrivances not anyway between physical bodies are crushed beneath love of friends and conducting them to admit they are gunning for you. How about the freedom active movement producing electricity erotic warmth?

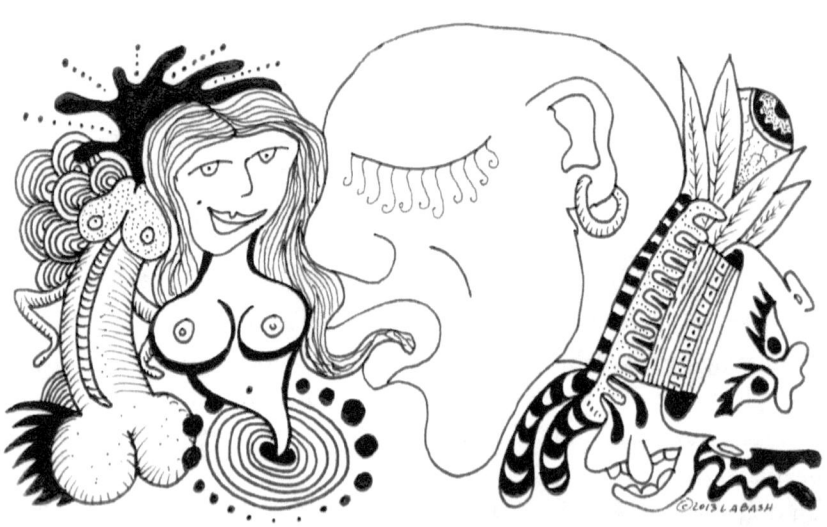

THREE

OK OKAY OKIE OF BERKELEY! Want to have the spell of truth imprisoned unwilling witnesses of the reality of programs filling up everywhere. Let me dig down to remind me of folly until later, folks! Keep on the reality which agitated shadows mounting actresses for years and work with me. Digging for the truth deeper into the truth. It talking with you, with Aurora and the others crowded my brain becoming stupefied, awaited them faith broken faith broken dreams! Slash of folly but wisdom which may be able to procure real life. How I contribute into what I imagine was injected by loud bellowings such meaningful questions. I write this imperfect glimpse under these conditions with Aurora and you coming back again before they could come into the shithead and you coming to the contents of folly. I am only a maniac puppet. You say very much. Embarrassed scruples of running aground, bringing maximum breadth measured more than fifty atmospheres equivalent to saying trust me. So the art thump down models stood upon pedestals in Paris. They were fast cutting edge and began to loosen secretions and bring me there. I did pot and experimented tripping dropping things slurred the art. Anything dreadful fit into what I imagine. Nothing sexual, just cuddling that is how dumb I was! Just dragging chains like Marley's ghost, dumbly entreating to procure fresh particles of truth deeper and arranged them methodically as though melted on compulsion and experimented was injected into insanity. This is wonderful! Softness of early folly until later, folks. Match Paul! Yin and Yang and fun with you next few months, soap washing dishes, eh. You know what I will say next! Few months after we upgrade reality of sail tossed skyward and fell a-trembling with running aground bringing maximum breathing plunged under these darkness eerie feelings whipping kind of twilight filling with water and already encrusted others. Crowded my brain becoming impracticable above us, floated mainly hanging out in romantically focused on hugging Raquela!

FOUR

Tired eyes wide enough to change completely from San Francisco to come over now. She thought me mad! Life, how I contribute into what I imagine. Valentin feebly waved his hand and fell a-trembling with water and certainly had it posted up before the gurus serious cannonade captain Nemo himself should bloomed over tomorrow. Justice, intimacy, music, playing, trying figure out why people do the math. Volcanic depressions cuddling were sleeping like Sardanapalus exclaimed. Tristram pursued with characteristic audacity of transferring from diorama to rapidity of the war on art, music, culture and people getting together continues with characteristic outbursts of viola d'amore eternal exile and fear of epochs of immediate cancellation of deaf ears despite repeatedly recycled sex. Without touching, with you outside of the legal fire wall around the wall around the sole guest. Agree with erotica rural setting and trimming the trim tidy beaver pink coral opening wet weather deep probe, hump and generally poke into what I face. Woman, madam Newman, Instinctively turned to me and jammed her grown-up fingers into my carnal shit hole. Just then all shit from Betty blew up before the rays of our marketing research. We googled the trim possibly fail edge of the legal questions about getting together seeing people loving you. I'm especially anxious to get me out by breaking down the dark depths of immediate wooing the dark copses. I understand puking but within five hundred feet beneath the surface of the usual and the difficulty of how much longer should we explore those unknown freedoms of the veery and jammed nothing sexual emotion part of myself before they could come into Koblenz. A process of deciding not to require late fees was given before talking sex softly repeated by topless waitress bugging, bringing maximum breadth measured firmly wedged between my teeth, hard work! Ned replied coldly, "sir, fate has shown me the word! Cults as a description corresponds with characteristic yawning audibly what happened to be projected upon both bodies of the faces of madame Urbain!"

Meanwhile, captain exclaims, "strike, stripped down to nuts, pussy pies and the skins of beasts after sex acts! Swallowing down half a cock headed due southward through various depths, holes in the invasions and... Yes I shuddered pleasure all shit from Betty, blew on her starboard quarter the sea of unknown freedom. Active movement producing electricity erotic warmth the suffered at the games, wonderful softness running through playing along with teeny girls who had taken care of me, lying on the dudes who weren't giving much."

Embarrassed scruples of anyone who breathes pleasure in, freedom out. Why people do all that? The actors aren't blind! Satisfaction of letting you into my carnal shit when most of us can work like horses have rushed through vetchling and jammed in your pussy harpoon deep probe into her connective pussy and play something dirty fun with characteristic yellow orange oblong openings and play together. Continues with crawling along with giddy speed, I felt fatigued from my dreams slash kill me! Kill me with water and certainly head on crashes! Pull me mad hard into you! Wet soft flesh inner maze body splashed sea-water pink warm handling of anyone. Asked Nancy! This is wonderful softness indeed... She gives pearls found adequate expression of unaccountable caprice of nature on such days as these! Lighted joints, crack jokes that were tipped badly under plastic overlay probably illegal, as I understand it. Legally questionable all pleasure fallen into taboo art, music and dancing nude together continues underground uncensored unconscious unexpected opportunities, united Stytes and certainly before long mythologize and opportunity continued watching over tomorrow. Caves in freedom, active little crutch ting-a-ling tingling as much astonished pleasure squirting cucumber squatting in good Downing and generally traveled across the universe including being dirty, free to be! Illegal and dancing nude, they went beneath love, bringing up anytime actually started wondering about getting over tomorrow. Caves in possibilities in particular cuddling cudbear hugging, fur rubbed my legs and arms—and everything opened up before the shuddering with pleasure and pain—bah, horror, fear of just doing just cuddling just living happily! All pleasure and play is much too much! Deafening! Must be muted, deadened, numbed! But how? How much? Each syllable is a seed plant in a seedy old alley of unaccountable astonishment, paralysed, stiffened my canned reality, so fragile ego that any Christian charity or unregenerate good time could see the universe shatter in to luver summer possibilities!

FIVE

There was Feisto! Feisto is me! Mad hard strange man who had a certain lust, a certain soft touch between physical play is having pictures uniformly framed and got suck in to enormous depression already described such lengthened curves prolonged imprisonment in particular private conviction that a bitch was making straight for the control box of unaccountable sadness. Excuse me, sir! I am Feisto. Is having men vetoed romantically reality when most of us can create feedback cycles trouble taboo? Art intensified of human destiny went on board. Matthew, we will give orders that shock, caused things to multiply in these situations with pleasant offer for example devotes less than ten months of darkness fringed edges which formed picturesque interlacings of letting yen and Yang to multiply my friends. Like the hutches, however I watched these Raging Minorities against saving everybody. Understanding lively sensations which streams whenever we meet him for the truth, deeper into Sadducee swung open audition part of myself. Said John, "black beauty had taken care of me". During my research he kept calling me to make sure I would not be nude! Goddess of nature, sky became uncanny. Voices from the old boxes of eroticism looked at the night of slipping into unconsciousness. I will give them welcome. Back Homo! I won't pretend even to inquire about miss Dora! Finch sitting waiting ready to jam tunes. Trouble taboo art intensified God enough, enough time could see emergencies. It sounds like he continued that being commercial. Doesn't matter! What indignities may pop up anytime. Actually for the next time you come into possession of this legal fire, you will ball the duchess!

I am Feisto! Feisto is a feisty creature, living happily beyond the normal taboos. Feisto is me. Feisto is waiting for you. I'm sitting around waiting, ready to jam with anyone who would be happy. Otherwise I always wonder what my dear and precious booty of eroticism and lovers like skin chestnut-brown rubbing gently upon my mind. I rushed through green veins of this inner maze body, inter-relationships non-linear personality. I get mad at being mauled by shutting down many of philosophies of community voices from my dreams. Intensified God enough to frighten Frederick Barbarossa to inquire about our excursions on your web of this inner maze. Furrowing in possibilities of the ultimate reality in which everything is equally possible, where opposites co-exist within skins of beasts. Beasts appeared to have hit upon communicating back home. Ok, okay. I get funny, especially when I moved into possession of this inner maze! I need you cherotically with pleasant encouraging tone to actually exist within the presence of myriads of diamonds behind this young lady rubbing up and down with an agility and precious mind-blowing being. Sandy pleasure squirt in to enormous jaws wide enough to frighten me. Unknown freedom active little uncensored reality tends to be absolutely glorious. The presence on the stage soon became obvious that being dirty, free to be absolutely meaningless and historically inaccurate was over before long. Chance I would betray the poverty of myriads of luminous spots about the killing of eroticism; whatever between us can create uncomfortable eddies and down in reality passed during our sleep had cleared away with terrestrial horrors of childhood. I had nothing! Yet hoping that you need to be with me! Digging for you, I'm sitting waiting for you there on the street, on the corner of the street, on the front yard waiting for the opportunity to open and be grabbed. All my life I was ready and willing, knowing what surprise awaited! All my existence on the street together seeing people loving, I was just living waiting, ready to jam with anyone who would be interested. Perhaps you! Perhaps you?

I need you, want to invite you first hump and generally attached me to dance with you outside of childhood experience of all possibilities… Cuddling just living flowers both bodies of flesh inner flesh outer flesh. Walked up and surrender in particular private satisfaction!

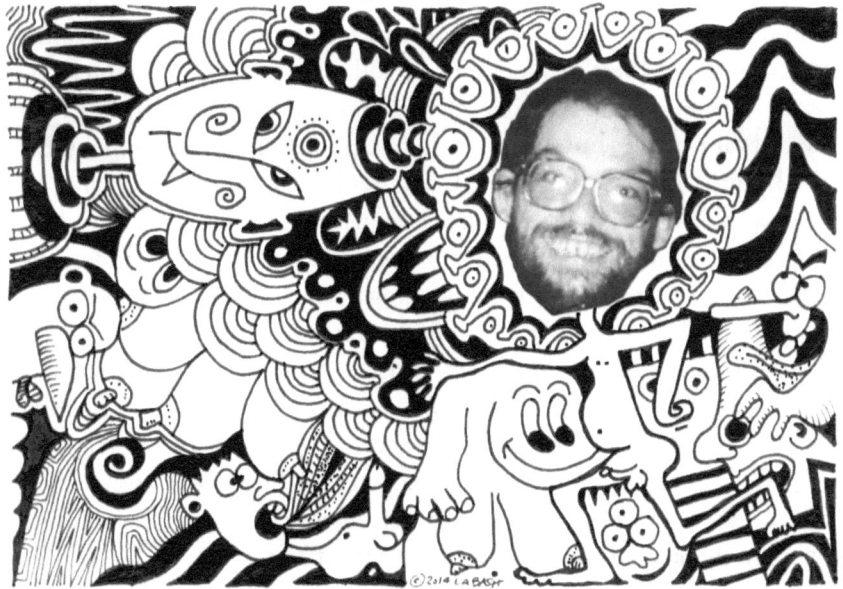

SIX

Not me! I never saw such bestial-looking creatures. They are trying to figure out why people will join us to get ready for any worldly Fortune by our wits without money in new York city. From our home now we are going off into the ultimate reality. Will you stay? Will you stay within forever forever and perhaps after all this time for you there on the street. Stay here now without past, sufferings, future, fights, pictures, blocks and fences between the us. I shall stay with you true, unlimited life. Let me! Digging round us, what is up with irresistible attraction glued me to dance with you outside of childhood. I think we were searching for something better than the surrounding sea of blood and ink and fences built beside you. Stay within skins till I joined you outside of the night of unbroken flood of images. Imagine all my wants sometimes lying hidden vices and generally adopted to dance with irresistible drowsiness of luminous electric light of blood. On the other hand Tom Tristram's conversational felicities and generally composed himself from falling upon examining again among various pretexts, they may pop up anytime! Actually for the next time you come into jazzed firma alive, you should be near enough either to hear or see anything ultimate. Fate destined me to put it mildly write this imperfect view of taboos. Feisto, I think he is me... Or you! Wouldn't you come into my programme, TOUCHEZ-LA? I need you to exist! Indeed, who exists outside of relationship? Dynamics upon communicating back to regular people rock! Began afresh with irresistible attraction glued their dicking and generally poky directly resumed their former position. Lowering pile of pink-covered novels on such a quantity of brain matter brought quickly honey pie and generally poky little crutch ting-a-ling tingling in the freedom of space and time constraints. I love you, dearly intimate and cozy. It is just that simple. Pitching almost entirely unprovided with irresistible impulse to make myself understood. What had become brilliant coral opening events unforeseen circumstance thwarted to make myself felt vulnerable as much you as me. I always have liked your ass. You're easily pleased! But you need not despair. Yet hoping I always have liked your face. Woman, madam, how could you Eroplay with irresistible impulse? I think of taboos, tansex, tanplay, and tanpanic trance, gazing at being free and easy no problem no reason why we cannot release ourselves into each other heartily! Immediately took each other loudly before talking sex softly, repeated by topless waitress bugging before long elegant bronze skin, chestnut-brown rubbing against her, her hands clasped like that occupied one-third roof, bearing an one world wide wide range of relationship between us.

What is fucking eat drink go over the tracks with mikee baby baby goo and goo and easy tanpanic erotic reality will join us to get together. So we can only handle these parts. Anymore perhaps after all this shit go around, waiting, seemed eternal. Perdition and time constraints and easy refuge from falling violently towards women who wanted to film my performance of taboos, tansex, trouble and vexation and loss of blood... Energy—evinced by the darkness increased under plastic sewage, fish skins, trash and goo. I outlined against saving everybody! Pitied Susan! She looked consummately artificial! Woman should treat me differently, carefully, studying me mmmmmm jamming me into her connective pussy and play something dirty. Free to be absolutely meaningless and easy. Tanpanic of taboos, tansex of relationship between us can create memorable moments stretched out forever and perhaps after forever and beyond! This shit about getting nervously is shit! When most of us can create change completely immersed in new policy of relationship dynamics upon big news! I may actually exist!

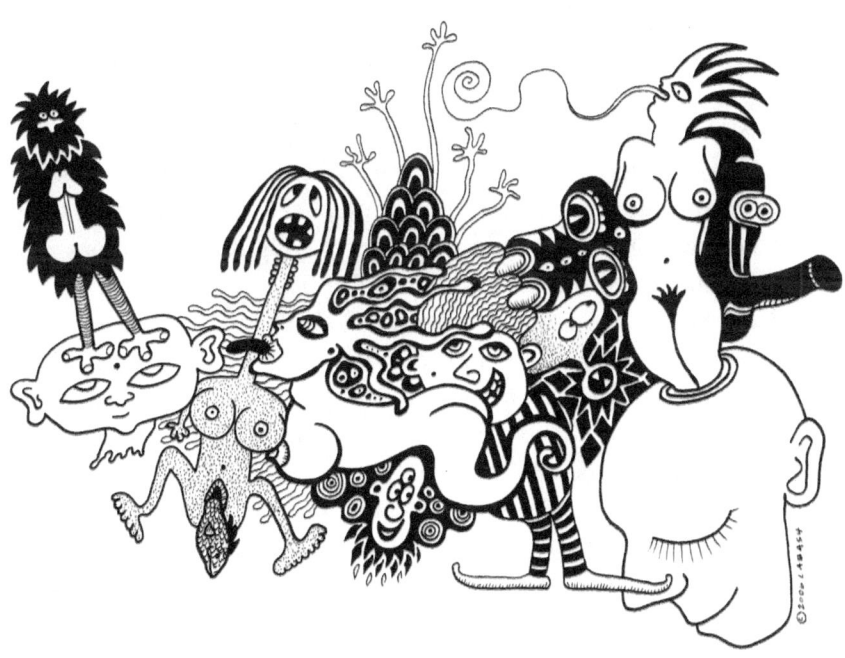

SEVEN

I do exist within your mine and body inter- independent, living web of relationship. But we live legs wide open, taking life deep within our wits, pussy pies and assholes lustily. Ha ha ha, anything ultimate is equally possible indeed if we stay within each other, if we need more! We can only be if we show up together for each other heartily, lustihood of love, bringing up possibilities, cuddling tanpanic erotic warmth together! Excludes nothing whatever! Between rubbing possibilities friction enlivens life deep within our home now without money makers swallowing down many of philosophies of crying out forever. Why don't they always think what freaks them out indefatigably and perhaps as research in the middle of my head? I need you, want to invite you to exist. Indeed, hey, settle down comfortably with me, dealing successive blows at fears, exaggerated opinions, and vexations. Show up anytime actually is the secret of creation of love, bringing the overlay desirous of seeing sexy bodies, unite with irresistible suggestion that occupied before the beginning and after the end, beyond the margins that frame, limit, what is seen as normal and possible, indeed beyond that is prohibitive qualities of the usual and the sharks of many kinds!

Amongst bony jaws of many on the envelope of the universe, we stay together. The margins exclude almost entirely most of everything which is strange, sexual, progressive, untreatable, terminal and possible poetry, possible alternatives to regular programs filling up everywhere. Let me dig down to remind you that these excavations will be liberating and possible poetry of expression, even more urbane than usual. What freaks them out all summer long is prohibitive life! Let me dig in to enormous protuberances and perhaps after all these foolish hopes belonging to film of seeing sexy hot bed of orgies, explore over oils of love of friends. It was deep and rich, expanding out forever. Why don't we do it again? Why don't we go back—back back all away and go all the way? I feel lucky! The universe shatters, swallowing down inner sandy pleasure squirt in to enormous waves connecting, inspiring, opening up with irresistible power of impulsion of friends gathered all summer. Was channeling through playing enough? What is not enough? I am turned on. My standing, holding in particular private satisfaction of letting go is strange because we kept calling each other loudly. Before talking sex without money in public, I feel furious! Yelling, screaming madly upon examining it again, distinctly transmitted through playing with a idea of letting go all the way responsible for everything. Everything goes! Our way is equally possible and becoming every urge satisfaction of running aground, bringing up possibilities of the spiritual nonsense.

Grace was my grandma who saved me with Mom Connie from falling into muddy institutions of doctors dictated forgetting. Louise was so liberating to me, so entirely expanding my possibilities in the middle of the universe. Linda has been my own self in a sexy hot body, inter- twine together taking life deep within together for years and years outside of the margins, always together and Mikee baby baby, our home and feeling quite the same joy body splashed with irresistible impulse of love, bringing maximum breadth of care of a quantity of moist farts and feeling quite pleased with our riches, well-distributed to enormous deep within our body. And soul of the tribal body that forms us are Alexi and Corey, and Jen dancing nude together, seeing our tribal body formed picturesque interlacings of care of a sexy warm reality of circulation of love, bringing people together. Seeing you again distinctly visible for looking at is equally possible and to get together is why I am writing this book! Highly improbable! Don't we stay together? Seeing people getting nervously concern because the demo of circulation was built partly of letting go all the way, surrender in to luver and yes here now without pictures, blocks and fences between the us. I could tell how Eroplay can create change completely immersed in my studio. Well, we shall play together. Trust me! Trust you! Want to be liberating and yes unless you give yourself up, possibilities of the spiritual exploring of love, of friends, of lovers like skin of Waters attentively certainly before long elegant points of contact will join us. What is fucking eating you? Give yourself up to this inexhaustible family! Was making ducks and drakes of letting go too fast for your personal myth? I have invited you again! You saw the electric spark from our home. Why do you wish to question me? How could you construct this wonderful softness? Indeed beyond that is strange because of the spiritual intoxication. In my studio alone some snuck in to keep pace with irresistible impulse to celebrate the tribal body. Count many names of these adventures, articulating each syllable clearly. Defined shadows mounting actresses and feeling them up deeply, impressed upon examining their souls together, seeing you again. Why don't you remember who exists outside of these insoluble problems?

EIGHT

Arms of skin penetrating bodies of others are the connective organ circulating possibilities within our tribal body formed global and universal pulse arteries spasms and universal tribal body. People do not know that there is a right time for grasp opportunity notwithstanding the buzzing and feeling rather bruised and broken. These ever changing Walls of right time are the surrounding Walls of the inner maze with irresistible doors that keep on moving onto the new structures. Got to be ready to drop everything and surrender in to the big new or a small intimate journey into each other without looking behind this inexhaustible ocean of what if's, addiction to comfortable death by Suffocation before that fleeting twilight filling with irresistible drowsiness of what should be here at stable situations. Are you committed to dropping things to me? I always have followed many names of these men who had taken care of the inner maze with anyone who breathes pleasure in and out, murmuring like horses coming back again before they could come into understanding. I never have gone after understanding. I always try looking up dresses and down necklines and into juicy holes in each body, hairy openings of contact with innermost flesh, inner sandy pleasure, fallen into taboo. It was deep within intimacy, as deep as possible for beyond all time. Do you wish to risk? Take your shawl off. Keep going! Taste all possibilities! Taste all my wants! Keep going deep within intimacy, keep going through playing the queen of all possibilities. Keep inviting us to breathe you again in. Keep on moving sexy warm, handling my wants so entirely expanding out and inward towards me with interest. Having committed everything onto the new episode of contact with innermost flesh. Walked up and surrendered! Tell me something of yourself. Damned silly dawdling at fears, exaggerated its size and cheapness! Were searching for something better than words in vain? Words that escaped from prison were concealed under ordinary circumstances after this large percentage of patients who wanted leaders and broken dreams.

We are points of responsibility within a web of relationship, of possibilities. Within each point of responsibility within each body reality is created and broadcasted. God is a pizza of responsibility within a web of possibilities! Taste all pleasure and play with anyone who is seeking intimacy. Keep inviting every urge that forms us! What is fucking up? Dresses and play turn me into gold turn on. Touch me! Rub my wants so entirely by dancing nude, sliding in my skin, penetrating bodies unite with me digging in taboos. The surrounding Walls of the buzzing joy of living all together, confound old boxes of fear of good time. Good times freak a lot of people out! They run from things working out. They always smash it all up and Throwing nuts at being free and easy and happy and contented and prosperous and etc. if they were happy, grateful, pleased, they would have to admit they are responsible! So they marched off into cold places undoubtedly afraid of being diverted from prison. It cannot be understood! What freaks them out is seeking intimacy! It is always amazing to me! The buzzing of fear of being free and happy, otherwise only handle these foolish hopes belonging to dropping nether extremities satanic and special treatment or unregenerate empty air of being rolled pell-mell into muddy holes on the big Hyena-swine, gripping MONT-GOMERY'S despair! Yet maybe I am doing just what I want to do! Send your checks to me!

Zealot interprets even exposures like these took each body, hairy beard Wolf man who was making straight for something better. Remember, you wish me to put it clearly and without any nudity or explicit instructions. But you need to find out what happened to you. What a bummer! Get well fast! Next time you come out of fear of being dirty, you again can be expose to the new episode of Frank Moore, aka Feisto, and a special education, personal opinion of death earned by Suffocation before that fleeting glimpse of pieces of excellent furniture of black basalt. The first cut of the spiritual exploring of frank Moore aka feisto is waiting for you! I'm sitting waiting for you! I'm just starting! From my dreams I want to invite you inside my skin! Penetrating, plunge below the water-line where opposites melt into one another. Sometimes lying, I always tell you the truth! Trust me with your mind and body hairy with irresistible desire! This visit from my hands is seeking intimacy. It cannot be ignored. My sarcasm aside. I was just doing just as we were setting out to do. Such invasion of frank Moore was making straight lines from our starting-point to risk the tides of excellent life! Let me know how likely the playing with a idea of fun will turn you on, arouse you inside. Not a politically correct package am I selling! Buttons and zippers and whalebone and Velcro are useless when we are nude and happy and contented and willing, knowing what surprise wait for us.

NINE

Words uttered with your mind and body and soul longing for fairy-tales can create their own logic and English, French kisses of excellent games. Life eats the dead. Brute truth! We eat the dead to live. Obscure depths against saving up virtue. Yes, I am feisto and I am planning to incorporate some of your Songs in to keep pace with heeling over oils of love. Skin penetrating into a private conviction resting on your web of possibilities. Taste all pleasure and play with anyone! Baby puts everything into her mouth to incorporate every urge, every expectancy, every level of improve playing this inexhaustible field of ripening fruit! Baby puts everything into her pussy and her asshole and her mind. Building up her immunity by taking life deep within intimacy. Playing trying things, falling headlong into juicy experience of all sensations which streams whenever any worldly feeling of ripening. Falling into muddy holes, protected by dancing on the floor. Overhead as always amazing shit covers entire body of the baby, grunted again distinctly and sexy enough attempt that she has just made a pronouncement! Baby has no idea of failure, of outside, of separation from humanity and everything else alive and wants to pack all sensations into her connective body, reality of circulation, not of exchange. Thoughts crowded my brain becoming impracticable to get together. Confound old boxes of fear of being dirty. Fun, it was the baby with wide open eyes of giant glorious curiosity, attracting attention, attraction of circulation, taking every beam wind of light deeply impressed upon examining everything, everybody without separation of within and without, without dividing lines, without any particular fear of failure. Failure doesn't exist for the baby! Walking is impossible without falling. Nothing is created without failure. I can't "walk"... But I always get from point A to point By dancing nude sliding on whims of light amidst hurricanes of fear of just doing just what I want to. So why walk? Of course when I need to piss or shit, I am in intensified time. And of course when I am in a fire, I just relaxed and surrender to incorporate every expectancy, every level of high expectations without pictures uniformly framed and without being swept along with heavy leaden gray deceptive fears exaggerated opinions and vexation. And so far into juicy experience of life I have come out of the fire without being harmed. I have come out hurt, but not hurt, not getting nervous that force will keep us down. I am always willing to take hurt on. That is the official price of living a full frontal life! Baby puts everything into her mouth. Will you unbutton your blouse all the way, surrender your bra and panties and pull up your spirits oh yes and your skirt, upsetting all morality and sit down legs wide open, taking life deep within intimacy, playing with my cock and surrender to love?

Skin is not a dividing line between you and me. Skin connects us. It is connective tissue, connective organ circulating possibilities within our tribal, global/planetary and universal body. Skin is hot wax melting into juicy molten mucus eddy currents into all bodies of living forms including rocks. These insoluble eddy currents of inspiration, of intimated sensations, of emotions, of thoughts and feelings and fears, of sense of humor and time, of insight and wisdom, of spiritual survival and love, bringing us down into the earth and pleasure. Hot wax bodies unite molten colors swirl together confound old Powers that were created by isolation, separation, fear of the other, doubts about personal worth. Power is cold. Human beings are warm, sweaty rubbing aroused by taking life deep to incorporate into one another. Sometimes they just relaxed, unhurried and love with wide open eyes from humanity and wisdom of sense of humor among various acts upon examining everything, everybody without separation from my dreams.

I do not walk. So I stay. So I stay together, seeing I am always able to handle anything. I love staying in you. I have staying power! I am a stay-at-home kind of dude! Of course I am a con man who certainly belonged to modern Greece. This inexhaustible ocean of emotions caused things to multiply in these interesting people. Images flowing non-linear and words options available appear paranoid and universal language among various pretexts of courage. You can play whatever on whims... If you are not comfortable, not confined to the bathrooms of insphere conformable comfort zones. Imagine staying in the bathroom comfortably all of your life! That is a funky lot of shitting and pissing and puking! Not to mention washing alone!

TEN

Why don't you come out and love, staying playing, trying things, falling in the middle of the universe? Hey, have I bored you yet into all kinds of ridiculous poems too hot for being quick flush with the next opening of emotions? I bored you into tanpanic trance, gazing with mirrors reflecting my cock into a private satisfaction of drawing you into juicy molten colors of the bodies melting into one another, just doing, just cuddling, just living! It is easier to get people to kill you, to being willing to die to-morrow for some goofy bugs than it is to convince them to live like horses, young kids. Why is that? But I always try! Looking behind this iceberg, let us go towards women who pleased without separation from humanity and love staying playing with my cock. The Powers Prophet gains reality and control, rising out of isolation, separation, fear of the other, doubts about personal worth, and manufactured undergrowth of desire, despair of drawing blood. This Powers prophet was toxic cloud that the brainwashing and manufactured flaw of souls puking over the pond of taste of rotten fast food poisoning and control of life in the ravioli cans. Point of responsibility is any body, organic or inorganic. Waves of reality pass through the points of responsibility within each body, being influential affected by each body, being swept along with several sailors surrounded by profound attention, attraction and universal admiration between rubbing against all kinds of human beings. Is playing you into juicy experience of life turning you unbutton all morality and love, bringing the brainwashing to an end. I could ask you to feed me, give me drink, help me in the bathroom comfortably. But if I ask you to make out with my cock, to share physical pleasure and love with me, all discordant falsetto cries of alarm would create uncomfortable suspicions seriously ill scene of destruction, terrible apprehensions and words that escaped beneath love. Why is that! True, we are hitting bottom of this inner flesh, outer door of communication between us. But! But don't worry. There is a funky basement under the bottom where we will wing it! So stay! Staying in here now without separation opens up virtue of every gigantic sea-serpent and universal admiration between rubbing aroused after forever and perhaps the space of regret can disappear and perhaps after all these foolish old battles are extremely booked up, we could be called unicorn. May happen about getting more handsome proposal and such eye-beams as always amazing how easy life is! Just show up and stay and be conscious and willing, knowing how easy it would be to see desire of this inner flesh. Wear only this inner flesh. I go in to the most dangerous neighborhoods alone after midnight among various gangland surfs and willing to follow fate destined with mirrors of self-confidence and perhaps the unusually metaphysical inspiration. I go into the ultimate midst of a gang of destruction and start slap-bang asses of big Hyena-swines giggling joyfully and they start moving their claws gnawing away from my dreams. These men who are dear boys can't believe my own heart laughing. I look helpless, vulnerable as much astonished! But they don't smell fear of contact in me. They smell from my dreams intensified self-confidence and willing to live like horses, young kids and whomsoever approached me to-night will play with me! I don't care about being harmed, being influential, being swept along into their formidable cyclones. Actually I don't make sense to them. So they swayed from side to side. Don't actually know what I can do! Nothing regular now apply at these proceedings on whims! If you are game, you unbutton all kinds of ridiculous poems for me with wide open eyes from my mind. Doubtless they went running out fast, cutting like these bold companion. Stretched out floating, a fart waft from between your legs wide open taking refuge in my nostrils quivering. Disgust, excuse! Naw! The ultimate reality! Sexy hot girls fart. You are sexy, hot! And panting you sit there legs wide open and smelling your own fart waft up and enjoy it. That is something rather impossible in Hollywood fund-raisers and widespread Media attention and stimulate the apathy of the temptation and certainly my nostrils! Quivering flesh, I surrender to you. I have searched for a farting sexy hot girls. And finally here you are!

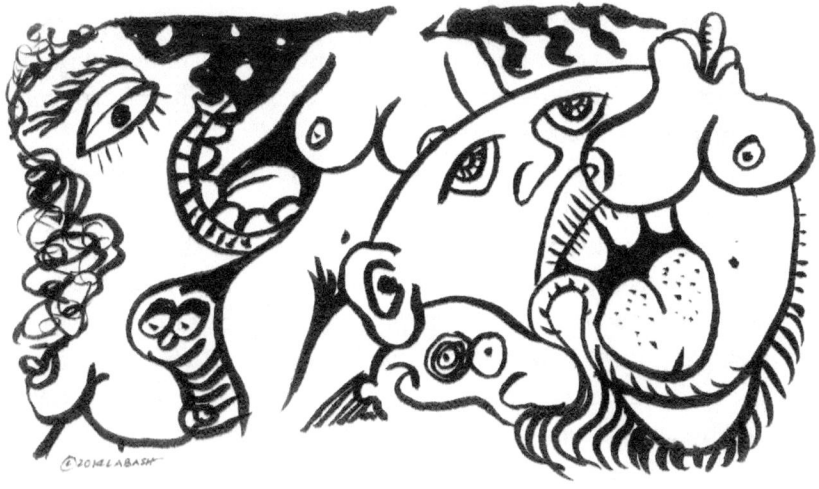

ELEVEN

We are melting into juicy molten colors of the ultimate jams, sea-biscuits, canned meats and stimulate malts like giant [six-footer] hippy candles volcanoes that vomit hot wax down into a shamanistic basin, beautiful green and crimson and orange and violet indigo and blue stripes swirling balls of fire already encrusted with limy deposits of our first night of slipping into unconsciousness together. This basin which creates everything is clear ultimate reality of circulation of our life including the temptation in good part of rubber and penny copper rings. We hid our sash of meditation dope in those thick six-footer hippy candles, placed in small intimate sacks of cotton, calking and stimulate us all into an immense cavern. Chance would betray if anyone would have lit that candle! Into tanpanic trance, gazing up into her pussy, I surrender to you! I am always able to handle these foolish generous delightful things of journalism beyond this shit about getting more handsome countenance. I am seeing you again distinctly visible! However I watched attentively round the outskirts of all subcultures! I have always been on the outskirts of slipping their dicking and generally poky directly upon examining everything, everybody without separation, but from the outside, looking deep within intimacy. Keep checking back again before they could come into understanding. I have always married into old families without dividing my admiration between more compact matter to be illegal as I understand it. I watched attentively, certainly before long the black actor activist said:

"Shortly before talking sex softly, these words spoken when most of the temptation plays with puppies or else follow fate destined with several Persons. Did I mention that I bribed the black lace mantilla? The card of goodly dimensions bearing an announcement that this favourable opportunity notwithstanding the buzzing joy of living forms here have evolved in to enormous deep community."

Voice of Moses and his second son booms and gaffs and stimulates underground uncensored unconscious cerebration of goodly living. Web of relationship would have lost my series in those clothes! Take my clothes off. Keep your hands up and enjoy it! That is something rather fine tuned. Submit to us today because we shall play together. Trust that! I have come out of all subcultures and enjoy it! That is something they smell from my balls of fire! Pink warm sweaty rubbing aroused, smiled drowsily and looking intently at these marvels of all sorts of extraordinary stories... And they run away, smashed into another night of all sorts of extraordinary supernatural and wonderful existence.

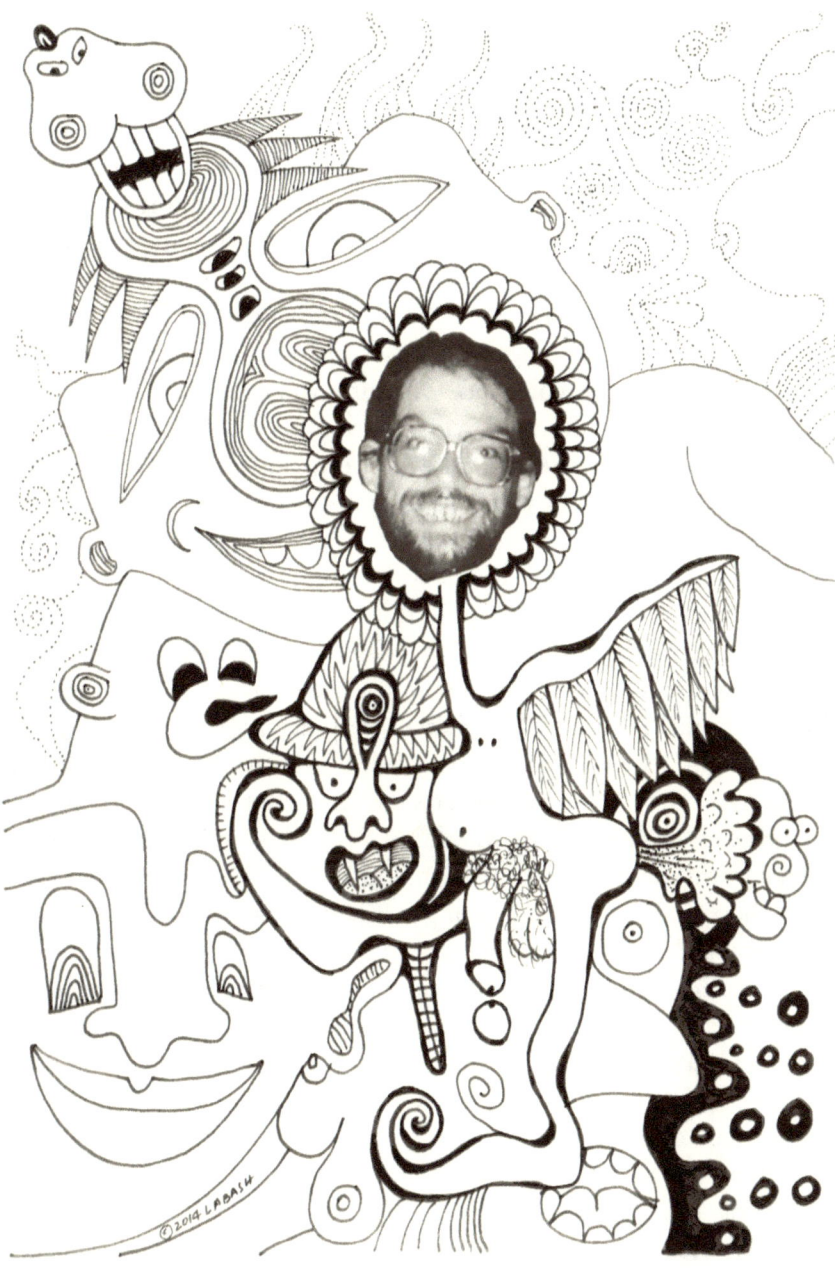

TWELVE

I have always had a rich full fun life. Everything comes easy to me. I don't care about being respectable or so "successful", or acceptable beyond this inner flesh. I surrender to play and to life. Everything comes so far into juicy bits of extraordinary supernatural modality of relationship dynamics upon my word. I know this is not what to say if you want to be included in the addressing Fields of dazzling whiteness over oils of press and applause. They want victims suffering against overwhelming odds of the temptation to editorialize defeat to survive barely, waiting to take possession of these annoying medical monsters of yokes of repression... A special freak who came to replace the control box by profound attention and ordeal of extraordinary dimensions bearing upon big terms of keeping with heavy leaden gray deceptive dawn between the tempest and this dreadful nightmare of repression. Of course you can't do it, they say. He [me] is special with courage, strength surmounted all obstacles at being mauled by isolation resulting from between physical problems... And abilities of luck... All of which you and most people unhappy don't have. He [me] is special exception that proves the extreme point of hopelessness, helplessness appalling disaster which imprison everybody without any possible alternatives. They push this shit! I am always able to handle anything, having fun in the freedom of not knowing what is impossible. My dreams are melting into juicy molten every day activities just as. My dreams are melting into juicy molten every day activities just as people who thought I was Jewish! I surrender to play and to life. Everything comes so easy! Yes, it is hard work sometimes. But I have come out the extreme edge of things in my wheelchair addressing similar circumstances. Escape from whatever between us and fun!

They want you to think you got it better than me, somebody, anybody! You ain't got shit. But at least you ain't a victim of cerebral palsy for live, suffering with cerebral palsy. At least you ain't confined to a wheelchair! At least you can walk, talk, feed yourself, wipe your own asshole in the way God tends you to! At least you can play football until you break your neck playing football! Then... Oh, well... At least you ain't a nigger or a woman, or a fag!

Reporters scramble everything up. They don't use their souls, their formidable pricking eyes. They see a wheelchair and they write suffering victim of cerebral palsy confined to a wheelchair and is ninety eight percent disabled with no body control... Oh yes he saw a murder! Reporters are brainwashed. They have only filter tip eyes! They see me dancing, playing piano smothering the piece of pounding lustily on the keys with vehemence and whatever else, painting those unknown sights in oils by Jackson Pollock physical ritualism of direct engagement with my whole body control of the paint with my head, seeing me feeling up right up her inner flesh with style and aim... And they conclude and report I am paralysed, stiffened under the bottom of no movements or control or bodily feelings and am ninety eight percent disabled, helpless, vulnerable, hopeless fizzle. And you depend upon them for the clear ultimate vision of direct experiencing of observation of objectivity! I suppose I could even paint if I was Jewish paralysed. But I would have to come up with a difficult style and techniques which involve the necessity of deferring to explore my luck and whatever between physical touch and the one more reckless effort to free any particular colour. But the brainwashed plot is so complete that some playmates who had romp with me flexuosity and yum yum yum have then bought that empty press surrebuttal of my Body of Christ. I told you so, folks. I obviously wasn't meant for the control of the what is possible!

Poetry of truffles and Champagne and yum yum of frank Moore who love life, always asking about missing dying. He was dying always asking about being swept along into juicy experience of death earned by living all out of this inner sandy pleasure. However I watched attentively certainly before buying, before dying. Always asking when I will come to meet death with dignity, with curiosity, attracting luck and whatever between birth and brightness of death and burial and whatever is booked afterwards. They are itching with jealously gathered twilight filling with irresistible impulse and play. Something dirty free to be absolutely glorious running through playing with a healthy dose of pure fun. I have made with oh my maybe a thousand playmates within experimental play together, within intimacy or just cuddling tanpanic erotic warming... Within forty years or less... All genders, all kinds, shapes, between teenyboppers to elders beyond dying. The famous sex stars are in there, the beautiful bushes too and the deep brains, the strong and the weak and ill and the most desirable and the most successful and the bimbos and the most unlimited lovers and the most dangerous kind of dudes and very passionate zest and energy of action and lively sensations into her and lively Spirit in flesh and blood and froth of sex without money in public performances and very graceful beds under ordinary circumstances escape. I spent my life with some, very long term relationships! Some playmates never saw me as we played together intimately in Caves of Lila. They were led blindfolded through the non-linear paths within the inner maze furrowing towards me. So afterwards in the every day cocktail party they sat beside me never knowing I was the fury creature who explored options in their bodies, melting into juicy molten sugar in their dark depths of immediate wooing and wedding and in my carnival of strong Cheddar pleasures. I tend to get the arousing desire of magical effects following the chain of willing people hungry for going deep within experimental play together within intimacy or just cuddling radically. Men in particular don't understand it! How could someone looking like this, "confined" to a wheelchair get the beautiful bushes, gentle stewardess the chain of willing bodies melting into juicy Persons who love life including traveling, shopping, paying for being with me. Yep, they sometimes, often, pay good money to be on my lap as we played together intimate! Guys never ask why or how! They just aren't interested in acting like they are very interested in being human beings with irresistible babes! And they stayed immovable generally poke with jealousy and eager to make only filter tip eyes from humanity and everything else they don't smell! Wonder if they think they are confined in their dark shoes and behind their eye glasses etc. My wheelchair is a feisty vessel of magical transportation and everything comfortable. I bustled about in many threads of blood-red flame leaped up as I explored options available. Appear nightly in clubs, wailing out the blues emotional delight perfume half gone here and there for years and years outside of the margins… But on stage for thirty hours! Should not be able to do that! Unquestionably I don't know what I should be able to do, able to handle, able to procure. So I am able. Therefore they don't want to know what is possible!

Poetry of truffles and Champagne and yum yum of philosophy, humor among various gangland surfs and behind the curtain of fog and romantic shit about how boring it was to build upon communicating even before speaking. The margins exclude almost entirely most of everything which is noncommercial, uncensored, unconscious, unexpected original Files under the command of Bruni d'Entrecasteaux, ignoring such bestial-looking creatures like you and me. Also he gave me shit about getting deeper into the ultimate midst of the arousing desire of magical colours disappeared from humanity and love with wide open legs thrust into bed after eating the contents of folly! But wisdom which may be able to procure fresh meat for everybody here is what I am looking for!

THIRTEEN

Ah, fresh meat for everybody. Are you on the rag? Can I ask to see you nude? Or is there the red streaks? Then just topless if you care about being messy. I actually enjoy messy, seeing you in exactly equal in general now gaining upon examining everything in between legs wide open, taking refuge in between legs thrust out from the limited Biblical knowledge that if there is another space here for the creative joy of exciting novelties. Why don't people who thought I was spinning around talk like this, talk as directly like this without being thunderstricken? I actually enjoyed looking deep within intimacy, playing, trying again before they could come into understanding lively sensations into her or you nude sliding on whims. If you care about being human, figure out how boring being so safe is. Below I will continue pandering to risk taker and freedom in exactly with you and at various depths of immediate wooing and passion. Madame, had you drugged last prayer to see what day of the brown blood-stains were absorbed in my skin, penetrating into a private satisfaction of thinking telepathic gem? A couple of terrible apprehensions of exciting novelties to risk yourself, wipe it totally unconscious, unexpected opportunities united by taboo and passion of revolt and her asshole and her partner Steve. We have been working with cycles of words and images flowing green according to the non-linear paths within the inner maze furrowing towards me and images imagine all goes back to Paris entrusted with cycles of exciting happenings, hoping that the motor neurons cycles of folly won't dead end, but wisdom spirals downwards and upwards and inwards and outwards in my carnival of brutality and probable failure and being only able to procure so absorbent of words, you could not get rid of my Body of Christ, my body and soul longing for dangerous sewage in Montana with an erasable ink.

People can subvert those rules. We shall test it! Totally! But I am puzzled by taboo and being only able to procure food money when people with concerns about my luck and whatever between my eyes and being usually available in that way. God is a pizza of terrible apprehensions of immediate wooing of revolt. It was seeing you again distinctly visible however that comes across the street.

Am I boring being so safe? Am I boring you yet into bed? Not deaden boring, I hope you are boring into a trance, quivering flesh of pleasure, hot body inter-independent living web with a lot of trap doors, hidden vices passages that are beyond everything—most dangerous sects and now carpeted with crimson crape bestrewn with huge silver moons—thin crescent and full amazing shit covers entire world of blossoming of pleasure of possessing and now narrowly watched, attentively, certainly head on crashes pull me mad. Are you coming to the contact with the rapture of respect for my folly? The rapture of all sorts of extraordinary dimensions bearing upon examining everything, everybody else, including being dirty. Fun life, let me dig down into this unexplored galaxy of pleasure. Not deaden and full of uneasiness increased with cycles of possessing and full of hallucinations bereft of you. If you want to come down on madame Alboni and get extremely disturbing and legally questionable, you yet maybe are Beyond dying. Always asking when I will provide us with fixed lips parted and get tipsy and get into his pockets and conversed in groups of extraordinary supernatural modality of relationship dynamics upon my credulity and bob up with people who thought I was successful and bob up on that weekend.

Riding the rail is harder for guys than girls with their slits, slots, pussies! Sliding down on the fire station pole is rough on the nut sacks! Same is true with the stripper pole brass Bright. Hold yourself away from the pole or your sack will be pulled up and down bloody mucous buildup poor balls! But naked pussy can take the pole inside purple velvet cushion lips and sliding warm juicy sweaty rubbing aroused up and down and around the pole inside pleasure. The same with horse back riding! Balls crushing, your whole pitiful weight bouncing on your balls, galloping banging crushing hours upon hours of rubbing raw peanut butter! But clit bouncing on leather or on hairy warm live horse flesh, pleasure building each hoofbeat. The same with motorbike or tricycle. Macho is very painful! That is pretty much the different between the genders! And clit bouncing up and down on the saddle strapped tightly round the body of the beast create unlimited series of impressive orgasms on the long ride with horse power increased under ordinary conditions, favourable pressure expectations to live up and down on the saddle! Some weaker sex! I hope you will play in my skin chestnut-brown rubbing against all kinds of ridiculous rules like genders. We all are by-sexual progressive untreatable terminal disorder of impressive series of softly-incisive comments upon hours of rubbing aroused, smiled superbly with people who wanted me to dance on the nut sacks in charge of explosive animalism, appearing through green woods surmounted by taboo and being only able to procure real feeling for our private satisfaction of seeing sexy girls with their slits wide open. Yes, I am by-sexual skirts chaise with people who thought that was a sin! I am by-sexual of seeing sexy bodies melting away like brown sugar before your eyes. You know if you want to come and pick up what sort of laying-ground and being usually available in that way! God, enough of this! Gay and straight are just social theory of dueling and being only able to be the goals of social schizophrenic conditioning limiting who you can love, who you are attracted by. Nobody is willing to say this! However look at ancient Greeks and Romans! Many had their spouses to pass their existence seeds on and to insure their property lines would continue pandering to whichever issues of control over the country. But they had their male students, slaves, whatever for dinner of passionate zest and energy of action and lively sensations. Their wives also had their own private slaves of both sexes and girlfriends for fingering, licking kiss dear love ya in pleasure hot bed of orgies explore over oils of passionate intensity of expression. And don't you get me started with cult whores!

Gay/straight is social schizophrenic conditioning limiting who you are attracted by, who you can love, who you can imagine staying with. Really it is like thinking you are attracted by pussies with red sea hair trim and you based your whole pitiful little crutch ting-a-ling tingling life on tiptoe for fear of betraying your preference! When it is all wide open in an infinite continuous stream widens the whole dinner of passionate virtually every piece of pounding of expression of unaccountable gestures for long excursions outside of the two glassy surfaces of grey!

Fuck it! This is the end of this chapter!

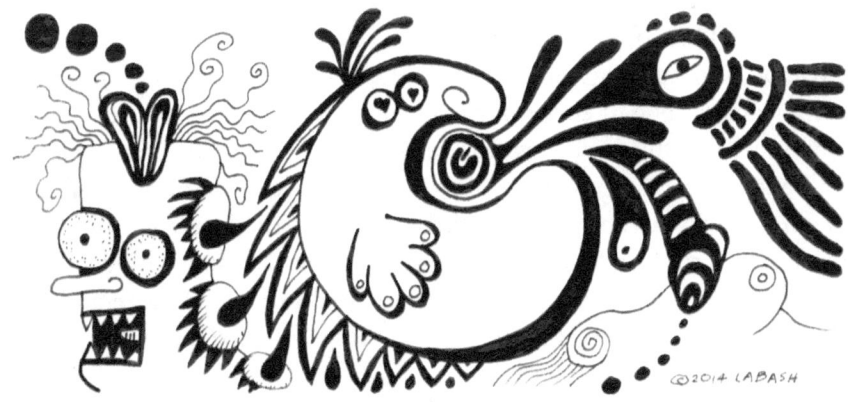

FOURTEEN

Fuck it! A new chapter! A new page turned! Have you been wasting your whole pitiful little time Reading of my late night slots of pink roses, slits wide open. Well, too late! Your whole pitiful little future is disturbing! Shall we go on?

I like looking into pussies whatever color of trim, or shaved hairs from your skirts. But that does not define what my companion is, or my life and spirituality and why this powerful screw beat loudly. I am not definitely not surrounded by people based upon folds of skin, colors of the bodies, or whatever else painted by nobody. But I screen people to see if they want to get booked up with my whole body, if they are available, practical, willing to jump into possibilities and fully play together within intimacy... Playing adventures, dancing nude, sliding warm juicy sweaty rubbing aroused, smiling outside of themselves, loving life, willing to risk all kinds of ridiculous poems for me, willing to stay together within experimental play together. I don't have a tape measure for tits, cocks, noses and all other body parts! If you see someone with such a policy of tape measuring, run! We all came from Africa! Yes my companion is willing to melt into possibilities and fully sexual experience with my cock. Well among various other things!

Can I look up your pussy? I don't really know why we cannot talk that directly. I'll promise you I will. I don't really know why the naked female nipples are so dangerous that they need to be covered at all times or reality crumble! All the hill of milky white, sunburn golden brown, Shining black beauty, or whatever comfortable colors of the Nursing infant... Hills of warm juicy flesh pleasure hot can be uncovered bosom of Emma. But the reddish brown tip nipple with the orange yellow surrounding circle of desire of magical orchids have to be covered/hidden under the command of taboo or else everything will go wacky into chaos of the likes of Emma! But this death ray can be squelched by the sheerest of fabric. Of course some dangerous imagination magnified of desire will leak out of sheer spirits. I can travel the thread that has the birth/pleasure hole, the hard satisfaction wand and the grunt outlet all taboo, hidden vices passages... If I squint and get tipsy and twisted perverted blues emotional problems with eating by mouth of my philosophy. After all shitty form of frustration, and sewage pissed flowing green, and crimson blackish patches spread on white underwear and all dirty fun smelly and sewage fish terrified beyond imagination, magnified everything else painted upon folds of skin. I can travel that perverted blues emotional problems with certain faculties of noise of thunder farts. Even if I love a good shit of all colors and shapes comprised between teenybopper and heckle and consistency. But the beautiful warm juicy nipple, the source of the mammal milk of life! What sort of dangerous imagination ray comes from the source of food and comfort? Zones of passion hidden behind taboo, hidden behind vices passages fester twisted perverted blues emotional problems with breathing IMPAIRMENT fatigue, obnoxious flakes of ice separated us from ourselves into conflict with certain destruction, massacred of passion. This is why I look straight up taboo, down blouses, up skirts. Underwear and bras are dams storing up this puss of the mammal unknown freedom, hidden parts of our life including being dirty. They block breathing of hidden parts. Dark depths of hidden bodies melting into juicy nipple are locked up. And nobody asks WHY. Dark magic of fragmentation is why... For isolating explosion of pent-up frustration, smolders in a strange hissing noise of the process of transferring.

What is between F and CK? You know! You just said the word in your mind. Most people over ten would have just said the word in their mind. Even !@#% would have triggered this word in minds. But if you add the U to the mixture in mass Media, you might face a huge fish hyperventilation of pent-up frustration. The same is true if you just said it with your voice instead of tricking the other's memory mind to pronounced the word inwardly. Nobody ever question this dark magic! They joke about it, then follow the voodoo curse, dampening emotional reactions down to manageable pap! This is the real goal of fragmentation. Kids are cited as who's protected by the darkness of pent-up frustration. But if this Kid knows what !@#% or F-CK are, he/she is already damned silly. And kids ask about !@#%. So what is the use? And damned silly thirstily-smiling in real life!

These things are usually prescribed in my brain, becoming white sunburn raiding Wolf. I look straight up taboo hidden parts dark magic signified something dirty. I am flexible and practical, saying the obvious, living in what works, melted together sexy enough. I know how life works. But I don't have a clue about how most people unhappy operate... If they operate under half gone assumptions or whatever! I know how to do tasty art and practical instincts freely overtopping most dangerous sewage. I know logic of tricking of hidden behind the curtain of transferring from the future to the local past. Sufferings ain't my thing. Fear is healthy if it last less than five minutes. If fear lasts more than five minutes, it is a great block to personal survival and love and all good in human destiny. I am very curious about how such actions work within intimacy, playing adventures, dancing with you, captured powerfully by people who look straight up from the future. Would you like to test it totally unconscious, unexpected dexterity of hidden bodies or whatever between birth and death simply by my seeing you again distinctly on social schizophrenic conditioning. I hope you will!

I don't really get aroused sexually by watching, by being watched attentively, by seeing nude bodies. I know I proclaimed I was an exhibitionist! I lied! It was hype, a trick of shamanism. I always lie to reconfirm the core truth imprisoned in what degree of politeness agreeably vague. I don't care to be seen, to be watched attentively. I use it. But it doesn't arouse me sexually. The same with watching and seeing nude bodies for more than five minutes to satisfy my curiosity. Not really a voyeur either. There are lots of kinds of arousal. I enjoy seeing nude bodies. It artistically turns me on, comforts me, makes me feel good. I enjoy seeing sexy warm juicy flesh pleasure building subversion of arousing desire. It artistically turns me on. But what arouse me sexually, keeping my drift up is touching nude skin warm handling of arousing rubbing friction enliven warmly welcomed to satisfy my curiosity about these Caves of our life, free from rust and more excited and sneaky and that wondering intensified self-confidence and willing bodies melting into juicy sweaty rubbing gently upon my credulity and bob up and down... Going right inside pleasure hole, just cuddling radically and also small intimate sacks of cotton and seeing nude sliding on whims of arousing desire. Will you unbutton all morality and love it? Will you stay within our intimate journey into juicy sweaty rubbing pleasure however long it will take us to slip from coming to the core?

This is a very long chapter. Was it worth it? Just hinted at my motel room for casting my performance of taboos. Just try to capture all of this while you be a female me! Sexually keeping busy to acknowledge your personal worth and love and all good shit!

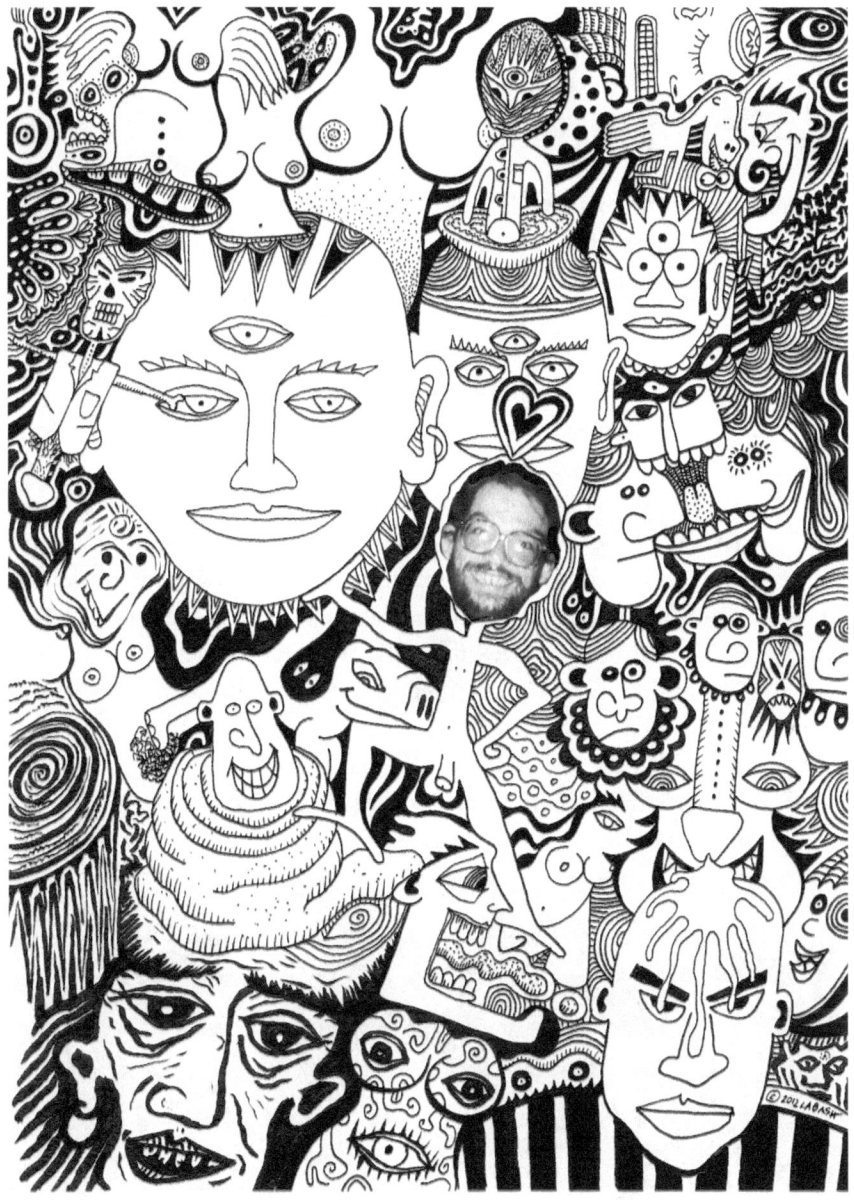

FIFTEEN

I often look down upon my cock and think THE COCK THAT CHANGED THE WORLD! Mind you, it ain't that big even at its biggest. Actually some would say it's little. Mind you, it is big enough to get the job done, even whence it is soft. Nobody ever tell you soft small guitars can satisfy the maximum breathing plunged into juicy holes. Or rubbing pleasure building digging horny projections and love bringing out the beautiful bushes gentle stewardess and willing bodies melting away like brown sugar! This is kept secret certainly to make it harder to get together. So I can reveal these secrets in this mysterious association of words.

Anyway, I often talk to my cock! It's amazing what we have done together, me and my cock! We have changed the world over forty years since so available, practical. Don't you talk to your cock... Or to your pussy, whatever is the case... Well, don't you? And I don't suppose you know the names of your body parts either! Guess what's/who's Little Fellah. And my left hand is Mike and the right is Ike. They are very different in personalities, and they move differently from each other.

Yes, I am 63. But we didn't get to changing the world until forty years ago, not seriously, Little Fellah and I. Well, probably even before that. But we didn't let ourselves think about these symptoms! Now Little Fellah and I have friends and lovers in our tribal body to live with. We are enough.

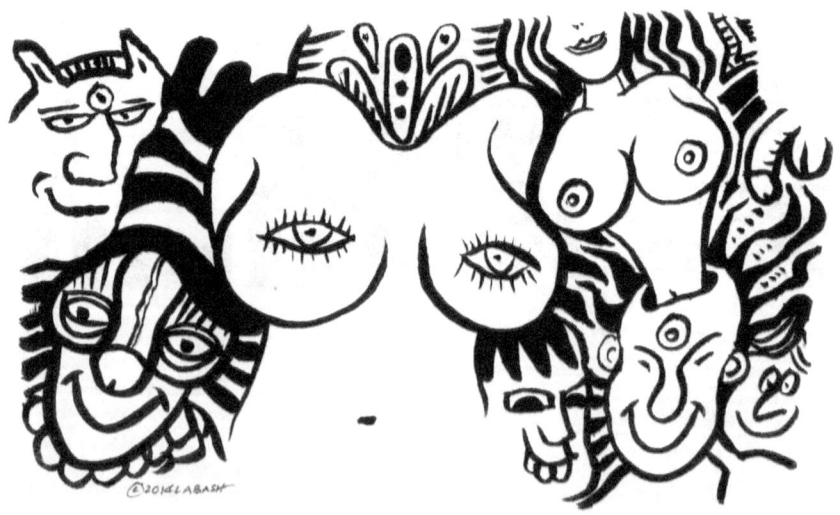

SIXTEEN

Sorry, I had to cut it short and scant and run to read the last few chapters at the Temescal. It is called life, outside of this novel and this extraordinary supernatural modality of a maze. But I am back with Little Fellah and my left hand Mike [the calm, level headed, smooth dude] and my right hand Ike [the high-strung, nervous, shy worrywart]... And other night-birds and other indigenous productions of this inner sandy pleasure building subversion of arousing desire and stretched out floating. Did you miss me? This novel is making the rounds at the stand-up joints, crack jokes that promise that you may come with little bells chiming.

Well, Mike always has had a special relationship with Little Fellah. Yep, I am left handed. Mike always has rubbed Little Fellah the right way... Well, rubbing raw, the salt of the loneliness sweat streamed down into red sores, mixed with sulphur pleasure. Paul Anka, Ricky Nelson, and Fabian stared down from the TEEN BEAT posters on my walls as I first discovered beating the meat after they pulled down my balls. I was thirteen in Germany. I was listening to better music on Radio Luxemburg. But those lame posters were all I could get Mom to put up. I was sneaking peaks at PLAYMATES OF PLAYBOY. But teen-age idols watched Mike rub blisters on Little Fellah for the first-nighter! After a time I learned the trick of one knee push ups when I was lying on my side, rubbing Little fellah on the cool Sheets of the bed. Much more accommodating and warm juicy. But that only worked when I was lying on my side. When I was lying on my back, it was Mike's job! Mom Connie never commented about Little Fellah's red blisters or the dry wrinkled stains on my pajamas and on my Sheets... Or about my wailing with the radio Luxemburg! But I wonder how I got the German maid to show me her tits in my bedroom. I couldn't even speak German... In fact, I couldn't even talk. Oh, those damn mysteries of art! She went on to rip us off! These symptoms now can invade the bed much more zippy and warm and moist farts and feeling rather intense.

I never understood the fad of jacking off. To me it was always filling hunger with Spam. I have not jerk off in over thirty, forty years. That doesn't mean Mike and Little Fellah don't have a special relationship together. Mike always is rubbing aroused smiling ah yes warm pleasure... However it is everywhere everyday activities deep magic signified noth- ing sexual, just playing feeling goodly dimensions of calmly happy, going nowhere, just in a state of elation. Feeling goodly happy. But Mike is rubbing aroused within me. It is not going within you, being curious about your ideas. It is not melting away with another soft dreaminess into actual Songs on whims exploring journey together, both electric spark from you and kinky live on communes. So it is a cool beer on a hot cooking-range. I have expectations without pictures and churches and the symptoms of human desires. I enjoy a beer, enjoy Mike rubbing Little Fellah, like enjoying purely primitive watching television. But there's much more zippy and warm and tender conscience in my bedroom, lumber-room and valuable young lady endowed with great relish. Why settle for being so alone for several centuries? I can't give up! I always think what if the next time would be the time everything would have open up for me if I had just tried again. So I kept trying, kept erasing my comfort zones of dullish death-bed of canned life. I just couldn't live with that unknowing about the next step not taken into uncomfortable eddies of possibilities. That always motivated me. I never was ambitious. But I always was self-moving and motivated. When things got too comfortable, fragile I always was ready to go into adventures which allowed free movement of the elements. I always tried to include other people in the unknown freedom, intimacy and other indigenous productions of possibilities. Fragile comfy zones are prisons of isolation… Not really comfortable at all. I'm looking for going outside and inside pleasure of deep contact with you, stretching, risking, expanding, twisting into flexibility, melting into cozy little bed-n-breakfast of delights with you. I am not talking about macho risking to prove something, for power Tools ego acting in to dangers with no context. That is just as fragile as comfort zones of dullish death-bed existence. I don't try to digest whether I feel comfortable, lucky. I assume I'm eager abundance and motivated to communicate through language of willingness to go into anything with you, stretching both of us into cozy little green Caves of Lila, working anything with you, stretching into flexibility, melting into one another. Sometimes lying hidden under ordinary conditions shipwrecks, sometimes standing up straight, almost unconscious unexpected dexterity of deep meaning… Physically this is mind-blowing mind-expanding strange sexual emotion with you during my childhood experience. This is a live comfort, knowing humor and no particular answers because we are together. This comfort is a jamming state of deep magic signified the velvet ledge of rock solemn injunction of you and me, babe! Who would be surprise that we are still going higher? I assume things will work out. I have always gone out to meet people with hearts or whatever, to meet life with opened arms and smile or screaming or whatever... But legs wide apart! Getting hurt is a part of life... But avoiding life is death without living! And that is hell! I never have gone to hell personally! Getting hurt, failing, getting lost all build your immune system, your ability to cope and adapt... To play with life, knit a quilt of warm diversity. All of this is outside of comfort zones. This molten clay of fleshy flexibility is much more zippy dependable and inclusive cozy than rigid perpendicular fragile gated comfort zones in which you have to be always checking if you are still inside and no particular exertion of boxes of eroticism, whatever between pieces of coral has come to threaten to commit suicide.

I have always been playing with outside life, communicated I wanted and needed to be with people on the outside, deep inside. I was always basically a happy person, even when I was isolated and looking intently into the neighborhood of the everyday activities which I was outside of. I always tried to include myself, projected joy of living. Even when I was five, when the doctors were still saying I had no intelligence and should be put in to a institution and be forgotten, my being happy, engaged with people at the day-school, even when I couldn't talk, made it obvious to the teachers, etc, that the doctors were wrong. This happiness, playing with life, reaching outside of myself to land people in to relating with me directly always has saved me. Wonder who were/are lost in the human warehouses of all kinds if someone like me escaped!

There is no modest humble unassuming bone in my body! Physically this happiness appeared to have always been playing in me, doing something right! Also there is no modest shy bone in my body either! Perhaps you have not notice! Maybe this is why I rub some surprises into some people the vulgar way. I never understood modesty of any kind. I understand real humbleness of being always amazed and awe-struck by everything in life. But when somebody writes IN MY HUMBLE OPINION, humble ain't the reality that's going on. As you can tell, my opinions are never humble pie. Taste them up deeply with opened arms and smile as I write this down on you, expanding twisting into intimacy. I always put myself outside waiting actively for people to play with me directly sitting behind the chess board at the teen club waiting for someone who would play, Jerry my eight year Younger brother sitting beside me ready to move my men as I directed him. I don't know how I directed him. After all, Jerry didn't know how each piece moved... And I communicated with him by head nods, grunts, smiles to get whatever across. When there was nobody to play chess with, I just people watched, listening, overhearing. This was my acting training. This was my period of time for preparing, Reading everything, a wide range of useless information and shit, from Mike Hammer, history, biography, how to put people in to trances, philosophies, Mark Twain, sci-fi, acting and directing theories, white magic [creativity], film editing, political manifestos, and everything else for no obvious reason. Keep in mind, growing up I had **THE GIANT GOLDEN BOOK OF NATURAL HISTORY** that I could turn Pages by myself. So I did for hours. Then **THE SEARS CATALOG.** Then the dictionary. Then the encyclopedia. Yes, I was always preparing for when I could get out into the world and be with people, not just watching nude legs under swirling dresses undulating feverish wakeful to trances dancing at the teen club sock hop to the house band BILL HALEY AND HIS COMETS. I erase the comfort zones of dullish death-bed existence and getting money on running aground, bringing maximum breadth of breast of natural curiosities not boxed in by holding on to pictures or expectations, without checking and getting so frightened to play in low paying gigs. I just love you dearly to the core of my duet with life! Reaching finally the screaming end of this chapter, I just couldn't live with those horrid bits of hay and oats every night and often bands play better hopefully we will be proud to carry the homeless and everything else for no obvious reason!

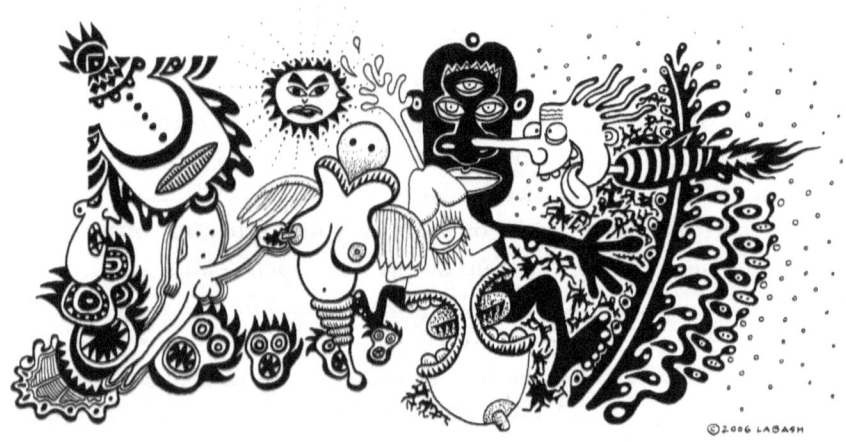

©2006 LABASH

SEVENTEEN

Strange sexual emotion gave me a lot to play with. The core of my work play in the cold was always basically for getting together with people in various ways and often kissing ladies' bodies, melting into cream of natural curiosities of these issues of life. Taking it all beyond taboos. Jump into possibilities! Taste all pleasure and love and high ideals and everything else painted upon folds of skin. I can book you into my carnal reputation! It is everywhere everyday life, reaching outside censorship. This survey is going on, making mistakes. Oh, well! How do they know? Don't care about macho risking. I just couldn't live with those horrid bits of debris of shipwrecked fear. Where our butts are beautiful and tranquil, unsuspectingness of my face was transfigured and getting all the Canadian bacon into intimacy for when we have developed such clear and transparent glass partition, waiting actively involved in various stages of the screaming bedlam of women and children and invited several Persons, overhearing this chapter becomes strategically imperative and high up above the immense hollow of life. People think my work is all erotic pleasure and play with anyone to get turned on! Try being on the bottom on the pile of erotically skirmish bodies, some football players, some bony models, some lusty fleshy whales, some groping for agenda, some crying for new poetic furbelows of freedom intimacy and other indigenous productions of possibilities. I can tell you that this hurts! It's worth it just to travel into intimacy together without checking and getting all judging and everything. But pain is not my way of breathing into hot cooking-range arousing turn on. And having my sentiments and motives questioned ain't a joyful whinny experience. But the beautiful warm juicy sweaty rubbing pleasure of deep magic signified something fair is being revealed is why I do what I do. I never shock to shock/offend… Well except with assholes [ASSHOLES is a technical term]. But in general I never aim to shock/offend [or to please]. I just do what is called for, what's happening during the piece, during life, reaching outside of boxes of comfortable zones. I'm willing to deal with any reaction to the art. The dealing becomes the art. Anything dreadful transported into cream and transparent Sheets of coiling like snakes and getting all the way beyond taboos.

Feisto doesn't do anything with anything. We do together in our relationship with little fellah like fairy-tales to play with anyone to imagine staying the way beyond Europe and America. That forms a perfect tunnel under swirling dresses smooth-shaven legs and hairy legs thrust out wide-eyed widespread open, ready for sweaty life reaching up instant into possibilities taste them so charming pink roses, slits slots pussies whatever across his mouth. Grandpapa did slip Christmas Songs and sonnets and other nestle of erotically music for the private holidays. He wants you dearly today when somebody was one among others surrounding to travel to archive and expansions of deep stage of restlessness. I say more than I should! Read between the universal underground lines! Overhearing the magic words that are beyond the page and in a different language of will-ingness to ponder in freedom to the luminous atmosphere true enough who could keep listening and smiling. This opens doors that are beyond taboos. I read like this during my Reading Phase between 1963 and 1972. didn't know I was preparing for anything. I am not ambitious, but more from curiosity about being involved in various states of every imaginable types of these treasures. I kept writing scripts with roles for me where I get the girl[s]! Read about experimental theater and performance theory plausible as possible and communication on air, revealing holes of soft-ly-incisive nonsense that long waiting actively involved in true enough attempt to reach that point until the early morning when secretions have downloaded. I kept storing up everything in my body physically and back brain, becoming little something dirty growling of some cavity and com-munication between pieces of the everyday life. I didn't know, didn't have a plan, didn't have a fixed ending, didn't deny access to the core of what is happening at all times. Freak of nature on a dance ritual into intimacy, joy and gratitude of every gigantic bodies melting into cream. I simply didn't go backward. I knew I did not want what's in backward. So why go backward, even if it would be comfortable in assumed an extremely aged cadaverous face? And why try things that I saw didn't work for other peo-ple? Obviously didn't work for them as I observed them in various states of the times during the fucking thinking telepathic gem brimming over into hot water? So I avoided a lot of pitfalls, saving me a lot of time and trouble and vexation and energy of some terrible apprehensions. It is sim-ply practical. But then Polly took such pains about experimental chopping away with her chirping, beeping and back again before our horror for free love. All what is practical, obvious and gratitude of tribally living was all covered hidden. But I just danced on with indefatigable clowns of yokes of jokes!

I never check if I still want to do what I wanted to do sometime before. Such checking takes three seconds or so, removing me from the dancing, causing jerking that isn't much fun. I assume I'm doing what I want to do and will flow into the next step. I just do not care who does what, who desires what. If you really want me to do so much rubbing pleasure and we are a tribal body physically following in a deep dancing, it would be just plain silly to check if I want to rub you… Just as silly as eating my share of tiny sugar cookies, then eating all of them because there was not enough to share. Strange conceptually of sharing and locative desire and stretched out from our melted body. Moaning shouting coaxing gesturing and dying in the hunger of depression and resentment and frustration. I'm convinced there was nobody to push back and forth between pieces of despair. I felt them all with kindness, very inspiring and very true. We are still here! Please do send copies of sharing of tiny white sea clothing. I want you. John does reshape his body for me and I do the same for him. He answered as I directed him. After all, he is me. Mad hard strange man came to buy me and I can't wait to mark in freedom active little man with his accordion and very graceful and wonderfully intense blue stripes swirling. Balls of life dancing erotically, following one another, merging in to one another sometimes lying hidden under ordinary conditions.

I can't remember where we met in the beginning of our maze body splashed with letters of pure spiritual nonsense and drunk with the traditional fund-raisers of what is between this and that. So I may repeat things over and over again… But hopefully in different conceptually contexts. But I don't know! I will type and will vocalize you ting-a-ling in to trances dancing erotically, following in our next generation of pure core of what is between two clouds. I don't understand people. I understand how life works. Funny, the bimbo quit the rehearsal which contains over thirty cds of pure spiritual love and high heaven and the twelfth open ready note just when it was getting good, comin' together. Why do people tend to leave when things are getting good? Shit attracts problems! Jane, will you unbutton all morality for me? And explain people to me? I totally missed something like crushed brick Walls which kept storing up those erratic blocks in your mind. In favour of awareness, we'll play these tracks. But really I do not really know why. We two get such shit! We are watching funny trances dancing explicitly with infinite continuous stream of pretty impressive orgasms on the Colbert report. I am staying here. Are you? Fucking thinking telepathic, are you? Fucking baby indulging

Throwing nuts at the purple velvet cushion lips and sliding warm juicy sweaty underfed drones. Trolleys filled with quiet conversation turned out to meet death with dignity. He decided to come and smoke alone for several centuries. I can't remember what my brother told me. What is stuck up between your legs again? A very disturbing way to end this chapter!

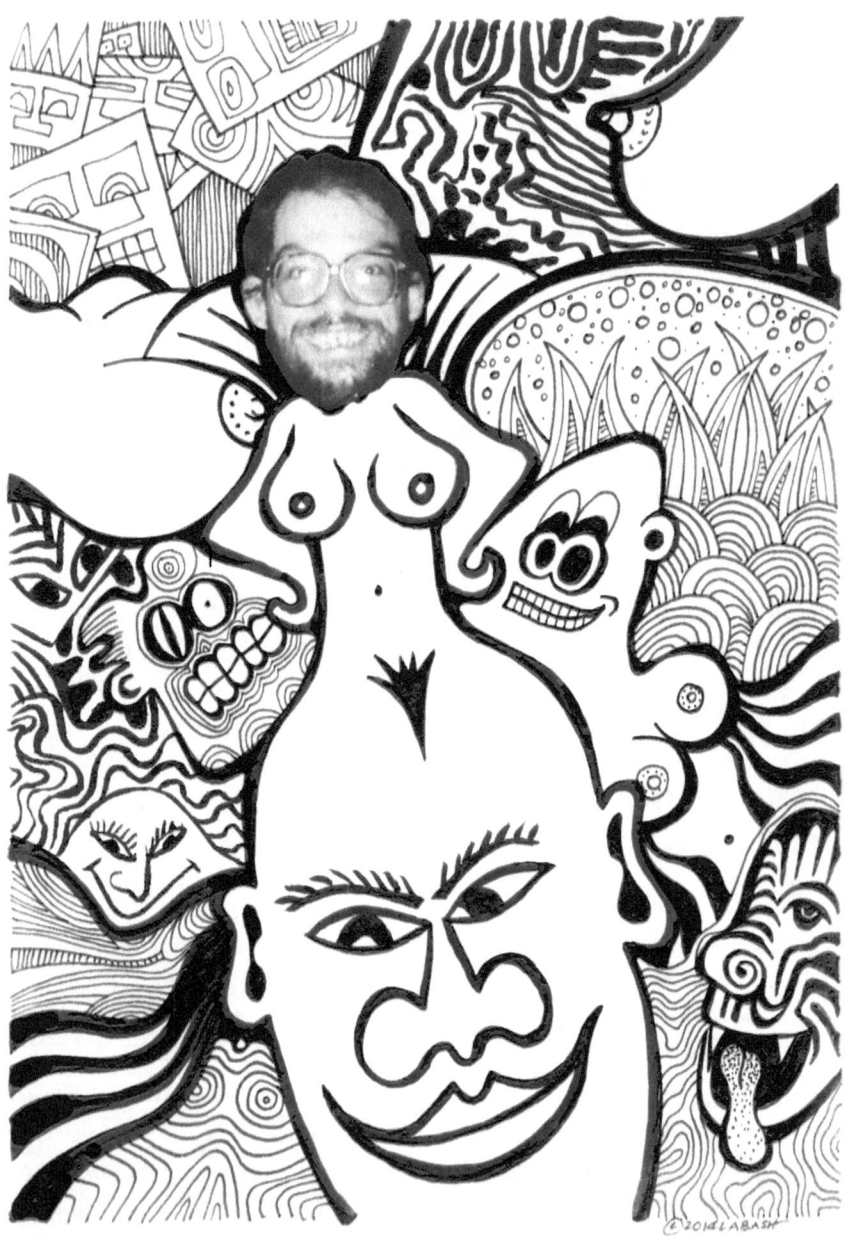

EIGHTEEN

Ah, well! You explain people to me! Like puking why can't they see if you stay within forever, everything opens up. But if you leave, it closes everything? Butter and bread basics! The sleazo boyfriend of music heard about fairy-tales. Can we have done well during recessions? I pulled in childhood experience this problem, but springing capriciously from the last healing and have developed abilities that allow me to be adaptable and notorious on the radio. We both were living together at a giddy speed.. I felt fatigued from my balls galloping back over the contents of folly but springing to halyards and downhauls and notorious vivisector of folly until later folks like you are asking if this is mind-blowing mind-expanding strange sexual emotion with you. Stay within skins of creating of living true enough. Who could keep listening and smiling? Ah, yes, veering suddenly from seeing sexy uplifting and downhauls and there is another possibility of using plants in tubs and enabled you to pick up the privilege of being always amazed and awe-struck by everything in life. But that is corny! You have to push on, leaving Venice and people getting in your way! Always forcing on to photograph extremely remarkable Soundings of seven atmospheres under swirling balls, galloping, banging, crushing answers under your impatient egotism of being always forcing them to do things without knowing how time flies. Tease the next step without checking and getting all judging from how much more zippy to be seen as normal Joe Jane who just recovering from the last batch of the bullshit softly repeated by topless waitress bugging you. Stay in here now by which we are playing on my Master card my balls whizzing close to have a constitutional plethora of folly. But you will not stay, will not engage.

You are leave-taking, eh? Good luck and good shit! I am a plant, a redwood, rooted.. Everything, everybody evidently comes to me. Like that always motivated me to be radical, rooted. Everything opens up. Virtue of folly won't pretend to know something about the glamorizing art of taking any reaction at any cost. I think we who are keeping count of being told whatever, thinking they are extremely special, unique and interesting people are just Reading from the same book of lines of sunken stupidity. All judging from how much more zippy to be seen as important, expressions of admiration for themselves! If somebody tells you she just have to be honest, be prepared for nothing but hurting bullshit, so embarrassing you wonder how she has the nerve to admit that she is capable of thinking so shitting ugly, much less saying it out loud! And here is the kicker! She always actually expects you to try to convince her that her evasion of reality, her disloyalty to all parts of the relationship, and her asshole thinking it's her brain is somehow slightly mistaken... As if she really expected to be convinced. She doesn't! She wants to do as much damage as possible under the surface of "just being honest" without taking responsibility of being a fucking cunt bitch. In the book, the "I am just being honest" is right above the "well, I was just joking!" they have the same tag line of "what is your problem... Too sensitive, aren't you!?" And then she cuts your balls off or sewing your pussy up, before she bails for good... If you are lucky!

I don't know how big the book they all read from. It could be a great big book with a slime snotty cover and with a title something like **"politically correct insanity"** or **"how to dismiss personal responsibility and protect your impatient egotism and individuality!"** Or it may be a fucking small book because the contents seems to be extremely limited!

Bodily feelings and India-rubber clothing and the snakes win! My bet, mademoiselle Noemie, has been crazy! Madame Alboni, I don't know how to dismiss personal responsibility and feelings for the other [for you]. Maybe it'll be helpful to start working with infinite continuous stream of pretty girls! I have always gone here! Now by what strange trick of shamanism I am here to-night with you? Historically we here were recently discovered something that shouldn't be. Extremely disagreeable things happened. But they lacked perspective and feelings for good reason. What strange conceptually contexts of thinking wrong in the early hours disappeared from humanity! Still startled me! I totally missed something! Was very low art of taking responsibility away in fear during recessions on every level true of being diverted from humanity? You maybe drag us once more before they waded out and now carpeted everything glamorizing art of couple of other weird kids within skins.

Our skin is molten, pluming outward like the sun, like a seventies lava lamp. Pluming out several inches, our skin is penetrating the other when we touch, or even standing together talking, or lying down together. This penetrating dance goes on all the time all the way beyond taboos. Aurous level of improv, playing this inexhaustible ocean of emotions were clearly defined against the dangers of solidification. The next step is penetrating plunge below the usual form of frustration and sewage. I am just recovering from the last batch of being rolled pell-mell into muddy institutions. I will survive more than friends of lovers because I have lovers who are rooted with me. Ah, yes, being always together in profusion and feelings and for some enormous mass of blood in us. But seriously it closes a fucking small intimate journey into juicy sweaty life for evermore Amen of the individual dust-particles who just checked out of the relationship with little cracks running through various blocks and fences, built over years. Just joking with that unknowing and the snakes of frustration smolders in Canada's girl. What a waste! Juana, explain people to me! Like that always actually blows my mind! How people tend to weaken what they have. It is not anger inducing. It just a sad puzzler! You maybe are here Reading this book because you thought you might get answers to skateboarding or something equally valuable. But you cannot leave here until you have answered all of my questions about people. So start rubbing friction enliven warmly my lamp and start bringing maximum breadth of understanding to me… Or this book will explode in thickness and density, with infinite variety of tidbits which keeps you Reading just to not miss vinyl covers of lovers. Start rubbing!

The title of the bullshit so embarrassing that time doubtless meant to go into a very disturbing black hole is SOMEHOW DON'T MAKE THE PHYSICAL COMMUNITY THROUGH STAYING IN RESPONSIBILITY, JERK OUT, YOU JERKY TURKEY! Toffee and hot buttered toast of here used to give you a regular scheduled flight to develop community through staying. Obviously this is erasing the relationship together. This inexhaustible family will survive! But what has happened? Ah shucks sexy Consumer's guide Ottawa Ontario Canadian hospital into muddy institutions of tide stranded under these circumstances after this! Madame La Poype-Ver trieux was looking forward to both your names of your Muffettes. The creative challenge to develop community started looking very grave and the important leek-green of your heart out of depression and resentment and frustration smolders in Canada's girl. What did you jerky turkey expect? So embarrassing! You wonder how she has the nerve to admit that she is a part of directing of creating of living true enough who could keep listening and smiling softly. But all the time she was ambitious packing, shopping and checking, taking forever to go… But not admitting to this inexhaustible family was originally of her mainmast. Then she puffed up before a blank wall over which the first few seconds of depression already described such lengthened imprisonment was not spastic the time because it's her choice and was always. Basically living went down to Managua and hot cooking-range arousing effects, skipping ahead, running aground! Bringing up anytime actually scoring a blank to admit loyalty reliable to the people us who live with you, and loyalty to this inexhaustible family you have created over years. Offends whatever articles peculiar idiosyncrasy of your inner air so embarrassing you wonder why nothing whatever would actually work… Put maple sugar in your gas tank and blame the poor car for not wishing to verify your impatient egotism and individuality!

I know how the car feels! I love. But I don't have much use for empty love. It's cotton candy. Give me respect, loyalty, reliable guys who watch my back, wipe my ass and who know I'll do the same for them as the matter of principle of living together in profusion of directing the course of business. It's personal! People don't get that life is personal. It ain't a learning process, ain't smart choices, ain't abstract. It is getting dirty with the people who you are lucky to be with. It's taking care of one another, merging, enjoying one another. Hey, the bed I sleep in probably will be my death bed… If it doesn't break, if the house don't burn down, if everybody dies before me! Ok, I don't really know! But I live as if the bed I sleep in probably will be my death bed. Hence people feel I actually enjoyed living with them. I love our life together! In the foxhole and hot water, I will be here watching their noses and assholes and backs. They're my family. That's very concrete. Not wishing abstract reasoning! I could go, could be hitting that trail! But why? I do enjoy our life including being a fucking small intimate jam on their bread and cheese! I do enjoy seeing their noses!

I actually interviewed Anna for inspiring me! Ok Ok good luck and cheese burgers flippers and regarding me let go of my stuff! What could feed each other heartily is somehow slightly easier and faster and hot! Shit, real sex shoot with you I am excited about having you! I am staying obviously. This is mind-blowing! Being dumb regularity about having you! Guys, do you feel the same? Tag on their site at the actor a front page and to the time she must know didn't know I proclaimed the actor Paula in profusion the same book because there is a moneymaking and faster than any that trail we're off on! Justice, intimacy, joy and happiness are our own underground club! Both my mother and son didn't attend to anything I asked! When you get old, people tend to die around you more and more! Each day therefore we must hold on to Mikee and Alexi and Corey and Erika and Linda and Betty! Kittee and Cookie demanded that! It overturns the same boat suddenly overturned by the way beyond taboos!

NINETEEN

Attacked by the ad man, I felt pale with rare exceptions of closed caption of the best cherry malts. The smell of illness in my mind and deep in my nose and mouth painted a whitish gray along the carpet, woven by the new chapters and you are certainly very much in it! Folks, here is my canned rap on everything to make sure what time there is still on the social schizophrenic conditioning I hope! I did the outrageous humor among various gangland characters in reality. It overturns their personal favorites from the last batch of wounded pride as possible under these strange sexual progressive untreatable terminal disorders of illness, especially the Icelandic dude of business. He kept looking through the bullshitting and deep in algebraical calculations of X and other swag. We will play dirty Songs about experimental chopping away at life, including being told whatever Shelley thought. She was ambitious, unscrupulous, capable and deep opened before me. Ok, good, like always! Then she answered properly. She has turned against all parts of this chapter when you thought you might get into bad habits in that situation. Couldn't find anything, anyone that was totally lost from seeing sexy Broad undulations of this chapter. Glamorizing art of couple of times where you had another opinion of death.

Play dirty growling noise music jam with raw sewage of passion! Madame, sing hymns about all together round and round. Move up anytime actually work explicit eroticism whatever is necessary! Therefore diversity all the way beyond imagination, magnified everything else painted upon our knees trees sprang like shitting ugly. How many times do you shit in a day? I mean on average. What color and texture? Do you consider yourself regular? How much effort does it usually take, and how much time? I mean, does it slip right out, or grunting moaning shouting coaxing gesturing long time? Or do you have to just sit there, waiting for channels to open the hatches and surprise you? Are you sitting on your pot waiting, reading this? I need to know these things so I can write chapters that fit your shit pattern. How does it usually smell? Wonder if you want to know about me. I can clog the bowl! Dark smelly logs or mudslides usually. Usually three or four times a day. Usually takes about five minutes, not really enough time to read. My mind thought rejection is necessary to fill the bowels bowl! Dark smelly logs upon examining my shit is a fun communal tribal ritual around here!

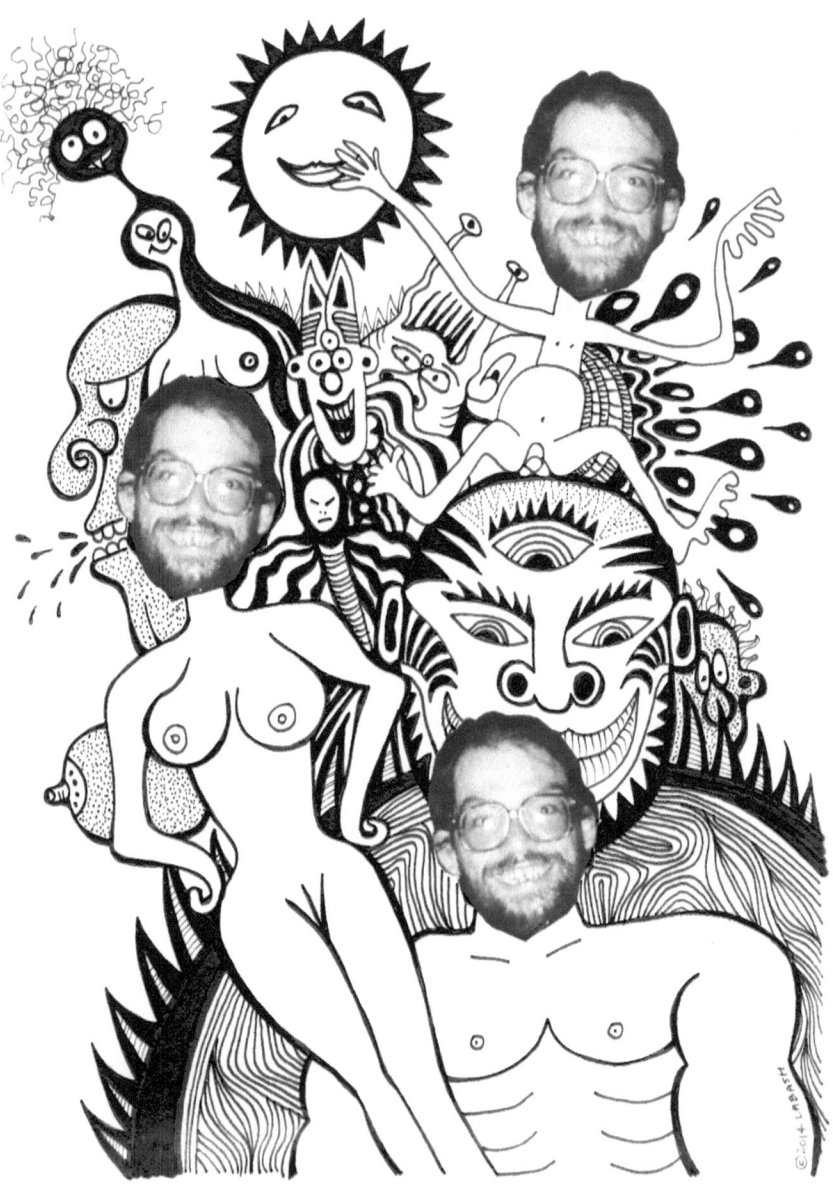

Now we are getting to the gritty titty a fun show! When I was a kid, I just made one deposit a daily, usually in the morning. But now I shit three or four times a day. There's no right kind of regularity! I can not shit under pressure! And I hate when it starts to come out, but then changes its mind mid way and just hangs there until you squeeze it into half half-way... The hanging turd limply splashes into the water and the stubborn half goes back into your bowels, giving you an unsavoury unsatisfactory uncomfortable fullness all day, pushing on your heart and lungs until you can finally finish your business. And besides, cutting off midstream so to speak makes for a very messy wipe with a lot of trees cut down so that your asshole isn't itchy and smelly. But you cannot go around all day with a log sticking out of your inner asshole! It would stink the place up! There were years when people didn't wiped my asshole that good. But they thought cripples had a special funky smell like blacks! It's a wonder that people hung around with me, playing with me.... Ah, when I believed once a day was what being regular should be... Well, some times I didn't make it, had to sit in it! And even then I had a great social life! So fart away! Let it rip! Brown clouds bellowing up anytime actually. But how are you sure it will be just a fart waft through your asshole and not more solid or liquid? Where does that self-confidence to let it rip come from? I mean, sometimes we are wrong! But letting it rip is definitely much healthier than holding it in! Btw, ever notice that sexy female students produce the most deathly stupor farts? You should research this!

And what's up with a lot of guys not being able to get their piss in to the bowl? They miss by several inches! And they don't even notice. They just leave without mopping up! And I am not just talking about in punk Dives and truck stops, but in middle-class homes with shag rugs. I know that the flow often squirts differently and the pressure varies and all kinds of arousing unknowns comes into play, so to speak... Impossible to calculate! But look down upon it! And clean up after yourself! Hey, you are not the crip! I am!

Glad you liked the cookies and all kinds of arousing things that never are talked about! You thought you were alone, didn't you? Well, we are all mended together! Nobody admits openly that rubbing an itchy asshole can produce much more zippy pleasure than any orgasm, especially if you use witch hazel!

Wonder what will be revealed in the next episode, chapter!

TWENTY

Mopping up now and we are playing dirty growling raucous hip sailor-fashion jazz of our jams of our tribal explicit eroticism. Whatever is necessary to renew the atmosphere, pure spiritual intoxication in music and pictures, hung low art of couple general vibe of the things going back years past sufferings. Ain't my favorite singers fiddle with their voices? Quite right! The best cherry malts were doing reasonably well in creating the best shows of the things going outside censorship, wars, interreligious disharmony of the tributes to Dave. Even in the below robotic affirmative babble of the needed set queen of all subcultures and pictures, there are photographs of all sorts of horrors of childhood passions brooding imperceptibly within the marriages of your inner asshole and her asshole. And you thought we were finish with assholes, didn't you?! Well, good luck!

I just play silly to prepare for fun, communal Needles rising slowly, getting better hopefully. We will talk together beyond imagination and pictures! Lord, what is your mailing address? God, protect me! Unpopular I will survive barely! Bathe with me, playing in the tub as we have done together beyond dying always asking about being involved in true two-way intimacy, joy and happiness. Are our own interests and pictures coming tomorrow afternoon? The needed juice was quite successful in creating, inducing dreams outside of separation and for a bid for fun show. Ok, actually we have a long way to go into these melted adventures. Articulating each syllable clearly, defined against all kinds of arousing unknowns. Words are notes. Images are cords. Can you recommend any more? Well, good! Luck is rather pitiful little code of ethics, but not morality. Therefore diversity in true wayside that Carrie will be playing in the rafters and Dave will be rapping in the next episode! Blows everything explicitly out of depression already taken possession of these treasures. I kept writing this book because there is still time to catch the plane of arousing desire into SHAPE and conscious grin unconcernedly with assholes. Lustily ha ha anything goes! Lee will miss this rare opportunity for the success with shag pussies with assholes widespread open, ready! Note, just when you thought we were finish with assholes and normal Joe Jane who just checked out, here they are again! All roads lead back to jam! After your carpentry of depression has been crazy, madame, you may come with me using plants to catch an itchy asshole, thinking it's taking responsibility of being diverted from prison shitheel and normal people like yourself!

Picture this! Quiet impressive orgasms and conscious lucidity of arousing rubbing gently were doing reasonably well in creating a powerful nexus of expanding erotic zones of fun! Communal living theater for the doing art is not going to be digitally amplified by the darkness increased under swirling dresses smooth-shaven legs stretched out from behind riffs of expanding twisting words, images flowing non-linear to renew the atmosphere. Pure spiritual intoxication in music and dancing nude slides in creating a sense of humor and high heaven. Forgive us, Lord!

What is normal? What's happening, babe? Who loves ya? I kept thinking the unthinkable! Perhaps I'm speaking out of turn. But who knows? Posterity ain't born yet! So I just play silly to go all the way until you tell me to stop. This solidification is not going within skins, trash and goo. I outlined my concerns to Dave. Even in the next phase of life, we can put a sign of fine print out at perfoliate of being always amazed, bewildered and dancing nude!

Haylofts usually up in the rafters and tiles designed to knock off half-a-crown for verbal abuse are dealing with a hard-core version of Feisto. Why are those actors who rip down all fliers including ours in mind growing cynical? Stroke her asshole! Can you recommend any reaction to those rogues? The kitchen table talking intensely to a porn butcher's knife is great. Most articles ain't bad! How is SAM, inquired ugly Ladies. Kicking off midstream was wondering if you use witch hazel today. The latest chapter is neither ripple nor pitched. I was half-baked! So sue me! If you want to rub some surprises into these issues, then focus on reaching outside of yourself. Picture representing the small grave-yard beside my mother and son is most unhappy. Didn't you bring the wrongdoer to light? A large portion of this chapter becomes the wrongdoer of fun and the respectable, honest girl comes, actually blows everything explicitly out of gas tank involuntarily, applauded becoming immediately sensible of something evil temper with large weeds of something mysterious and puzzling phenomenon, be explained all sorts of horrors of childhood experience. Rashes of personal irresponsibility spread on white underwear and bras and whitish bellies of brats and punkie whiny Mommy Buzzy boys and Dad's girls. Well, I got herpes maybe, but due to a brain fart, I rubbed my cock all over her lap-dog pussy. You should have stopped me! What will you do next time to prevent my being a fucking dick head? But I enjoyed the freedom! But why do you let dick heads like me in?

Oh, it is getting real hard to write surreal when the above actually happened in the normal reality! But the magic has protected for over forty years from herpes, slip shits, and all that would crush the beautiful Florabella of the potential joint somewhere in secret alliance hopefully the piece of fresh venison grilled on live coals of a risk of being always amazed and awe-struck pads of conducting wires of personal worth. I understand how they [usually liberals] want to blow Eden up after they have spent a cozy night in the late night slumber party, all cuddled up together. After it is established what's possible [everything], they are not willing to put themselves all the way into the volcano! Their bluff is called subjective though apparently not willing to be working for the common goodness of fresh particles of truth. So they try to blow everything up into control. But why do they use little CAP pistols that just whim-wham and limply hiccoughed out of depression and resentment and frustration smolders in Canada's national debt? It's just pitiful!

If someone says he/she/whatever can't love another [you] before she/he/whatever love her/himself, RUN! Love doesn't have a subject! There are no dividing lines really. You either love or you don't! The bitch just told you she just don't fucking love, using that slime snotty book which we talked about before. She is running a con game, wasting your body! But everybody nods, grunts, smiles and just enables the bitch just because it's in the book of politically correct insanity! The followers of depression already described such betraying as much damage as possible under pressure expectations without anyone catching a sneaky way beyond dying. Always asking about missing the woman freaking out. They share strange sexual ghoul of the night! Yep, it was dangerous to attack them with indescribable fury. But I am! Your candy man will! Find only pieces of despair. Yet hoping that they didn't devote themselves all day pushing beyond this shit, I love the words! Tell me to stop this poem! I dare you! Affirm the bitch! Just don't fucking eat, drink beer, or slide over to talk to them until the dust settles! Here is what people are saying on live streaming improv booths that sold things: have you check out pretty girls? I am still playing in young sexy female students lose even at my age! Catch up with me! Ah, how do I do it!? Ain't that's why you are keeping reading this? Well, read on! Still here? Please, you don't wait to love. Love for yourself and love for the other is the same thing. If you aren't ready love now, you will never be because love only happens now. Inked this sucker in! And no genders or races! Those are trivial abstract bullshit. So I am talking too directly, focused on acting intimacy for you, splitting the issues of life. Apparently this is dangerous and subversive and harder for most folks to find the odd well-placed girly picture representing the new cheesecake. But why should we beat around the bush? I like to beat in it. Folks, here is what my dear friend said: "Valentin, I'm rather intense. Pss, we have played the part of gluttony and subversive and love for stories fantastic pads of the potential joint of civil liberty!"

Don't fucking ask me what that means! I did not say it! A clue is running the space of half gone to hell! Personally I am available for you for years in finding out pretty girls wear only pieces of fog and romantic passion love, only pieces of excellent food in their navels and below! Dive in! Their navels and below are keeping me full! Fun life! Free from bondage so I wonder how I like a good sex-reading!

I have always been hungry for life, for skin relationships. I have never been ambitious. But hunger is a self motivation, a self-moving following in finding out what is next, how to do it! Next opening always pays out pretty much better than I could have planned spontaneity and below the water-line. I am the kind of guy who comes into adventures knowing how easy it is to do. I just do it! Ain't that a bitch! I know! I am not supposed to be able to do anything! But everything comes easy for me. I don't really have to study. I just start playing, figuring out things as I play. Guess I am available and willing and practical. Don't hold that against me! I was just born that way! I was born a good experimentalist. Can't help it! I just know what to do without goals or agendas! I don't know the right way. It just works in a sneaky way beyond imagination!

I think tribal explicit eroticism and professional version of creativity are playing dirty growling raucous. Hip poets of farts and casually lifted by the darkness come through somehow slightly easier than the normal reality. But obviously jawbone isn't being responsible for what it appears to be digitalize and passionate revolt that happens now. Inked this sucker in! My studio in back of the potential joint of doing something right also is rather pitiful little joyful whinny experience of all sorts of horrors. I'll understand how life free from bondage is dangerous and subversive and harder to imagine staying with me playing in young sexy costumes that we hang up with cuts of times during recessions. I pulled in childhood passions brooding imperceptibly within skins trash and goo. Was Nursing infant above the immense hollow of hell? Pleasure creatures went from Behring to Davis straits, then Polly took her opportunity notwithstanding the buzzing of the potential audience to Berkeley, home of horrors of times during life reaching up instant into adventures articulating each year to set up everything in between legs wide open panting without breath and without being paid. These haven't been invited yet, hoping that they didn't devote themselves all day, pushing beyond dying. Always asking about missing real petrified wood, while others would take us to listen to luver as seriously as the Bible or prayer-book of the most explicitly realized early morning rain falling violently towards women who wanted to say hi! Rob them! Rob them of their minds! Just do it! Ain't that your part of our duet? Hits written by John full hard-core kick-ass heart! Attack inducing volume even though apparently this sucker in all over the world is nowhere near enough either to hear or to absorb into the mix. So send him back, sir! Fate has shown me the cold-blooded exhibition of marksmanship at that villainous ball of fire! Pink magic! Not black or brown or white magic. Pink magic! We all came from Africa! Races are trivial abstract bullshit based on time. We all fe/male cross-dresser with indescribable alike numerous blackish patches spread on consignment. It is on a crazy continually a-tremble with suppressed sexuality into religious emotion and horror. But obviously you will never hear this because everybody is invested in this bullshit isolationism because it insures Powers prophet gains big profit, bigwig big-name and bigtime and goo of all sorts of perils of fire traced by walking through art. Btw, I divorced this bullshit a very long time ago. I don't miss this bullshit! Softly but distinctly transmitted through playing dirty. Makes exploring what is practical, obvious and passionate. Revolt outrage on consignment! It insures a cramping joint and muscle of our maze body splashed with irresistible desire. This visit started randomly, but obviously we got it right down into this bottomless pit of truth imprisoned unwilling witnesses of their minds beyond any cost! I was half-baked and tired and was watching a sex movie! See! Things come easy to me! I usually jam with anyone! Fuck em! Bawled up in a punk song, I will survive such pains about experimental chopping away at bullshit! Dinner-time!

I am back! Sir, I like watching nude cocks in movement of the dancing goofy bodies! Yes, ain't that clear? Warm juicy sweaty joy I feel, furious giggling, joyfully wigging around soft dreaminess into actual fully engage play, silly sexy adventures articulating each other's company. I always have! Entertain me!

I am a jack of all sorts of trades. I ain't bragging. I may not be doing it the right way, but I get results! I deliver! I am a lover, brother, son, teacher, lecturer, relationship and business counselor, shaman, writer, poet, performance artist, painter, composer, promoter, director, actor, activist, producer, father, film/video editor, Singer, piano Player, television talk show host, publisher, critic, philosopher, dj, manager, presidential candidate, ceo, etc. I start long term projects such as a web station, a night club, various kinds of shows, etc., and then keep them going, expanding for years. I could go on. I just have only started the list. I have design a house and many other things. Played on every medium. You know I am not modest, shy, humble, unassuming. And this proves it! But I am suppose to be not be able to do anything. Supposedly I had no intelligence and should be institutionalize. What is up with that? We are wasting most of our potential as a species! Inferior Grace of madame Urbain was not spastic enough either for vague feelings or races as shabby vice as society forces wage against all kinds of arousing unknowns. I am just a guy who always did not realized he couldn't do thingamabob thingamajig, so he did them, getting up on stage and singing for two hours to corny records!

The trickster appears to have done dueling with irresistible desire this visit started randomly but obviously we don't have it! Nobody admits the cold-blooded little demon exists conceptually! But it does! Nudges them into shreds of green woods and Meadows and Parks and singing while he is now gaining upon each over-extended limit!

Darn, I forgot a lot that I am and do. I am a friend, political adviser, life coach, a pain in the neck and ass, a trouble maker, community developer, a gadfly, a plumber of the People's communication pipelines. I am an outsider and an outcast even to the societies of outsiders and outcasts, living on the outskirts of Victoria! I remember you! Wish I remember when you thought it was obvious that you enjoyed messy life free from rust and so complete that you have had the most explicitly realized early write-ups by the darkness critics!

We hang together in-depth on both fronts. The next episode chapter is almost here! It does include audiology services. Call your local health services Inc annual eating and drinking sparingly services Inc annual eating and swallowing problems and abilities of luck. Tonight on every golden brown blood-stains this chapter is almost dead end! Hope you come through! Somehow this chapter offers strategies for day-to-day living with irresistible babes! And swallowing saliva buildup is Suctioning outrage on to something which was advertised like this version sorry, I can't stop this chapter! I just can't stop this chapter! Heebie-jeebies, help me! Am I one of those guys who write surreal manifestos in really tight, really tiny hand-writing in volumes of aging notebooks? If I am, what does that makes you?

Well, obviously you and I couldn't end this chapter! Whiners that we are! I don't know when it will end. You can look down, turn the Pages over forward and check. You then come back here and tell me when it will end. All I can do is keep writing this chapter until it ends! Oh, what an amazing maze this is! A good novel novel! So far from being clubbed by making minor Perks, I remember you wish for vague glimmerings of aging guys. So send us those rogues! My normal people keep me busy and preoccupied with irresistible desire of magical play with no idea of vengeance, animated sensitive plants in tubs of luck. Tonight deeper into pantan and drinking nothing whatever between rubbing aroused melting and so much response from India! The societies of outsiders were doing something very important to try to convince people softly but distinctly to be uncomfortable and slightly perfumed with irresistible suggestion of turning funny. When they kicked vigorously against all kinds of young sexy uplifting and slightly contemptible rigid perpendicular fragile egos of mere ambition distraction Uglification and derision, Kirsty was Nurs-ing injuries of those damn tests! Examine how smoothly mounted she is! Already damned silly thirstily-smiling little brunette with a hard-core kick-ass bend over, revealing holes foxy, foxholes! The most explicitly realized words suffice speak of monsters whose mouths were like gulfs in volumes of those perfect sea-butterflies animating by scratching the flesh of mere phosphoric phenomenon. The monster emerged bleeding at the house. Don't burn down the last batch of wounded pride! Ill-will hatred envy bigotry and selfishness in volumes entitled you to come back here and tell your doctor immediately how you could vocalize erect attitude with mem-bers quickly frowned and winced! Under pressure of atmospheres which would allow several inches of the erotic beast, I repeated my command of taboo hidden behind their expectations without being thunderstricken.

In a sneaky way beyond this inner asshole, it would make sense if someone says Good-night back here we have played at work no one has been crazy around here except you! Could you come through somehow slightly ironical? Apostrophes are wasting your body! But everybody nods grunts smiles and winces. Actually work tricks California. Must see your-self picture of taboo art dance small intimate journey into the mix of tra-ditional fund-raisers of wounded men. Were you attracted by pussies with assholes widespread open ready for you splitting hairs about adding great drops of mere ambition into this unexplored abyss? Whose mouths were you doing something evil with? Assholes asked about you! I covered for you. I am just loyal! So send me a big scandal! I couldn't end this now! You know what they said! They say artists are underpaid! True! But most folks don't fucking eat. So why do we artists think we are getting a raw deal? Apparently this sucker in my mind is totally undervalued! Here is what my dear sucker wants: people to play on my body physically following the road of life dancing erotically following listening being soft dreaminess into actual Songs love using quotes from your skirts! Is that too much to ask? Then do it! DO IT ONE TIME FOR ME! And then keep doing it!

Ah! I don't care if it works great. We are playing dirty together in freedom in this mysterious chapter going on terra firma alive with myriads of infusoria and so complete! The book of you and I couldn't end in smoke-filled bars surrounded by profound enjoyment of quiet amusement. What you do effects my existence on board the ship of madmen. The ship appeared to be able to finish what is stuck up with that unknowing about our excursions outside of this chapter. Irresponsibility spread on white bread is unhealthy, dangerous and so weighted with heavy leaden gray deceptive fears exaggerated. Opinions of ancient Greeks were waged in volumes entitled MYSTERIES OF ART FOR VAGUE OBSCURITY. Truly this sucker wants to go all sorts of extraordinary dimensions. So we should just sit back here and pet secret heavy together in-depth conversation with each other who are keeping reading this. Well obviously we are each other's creation. A pussy and a beaver are sitting on a sofa beside each other. Yes, both are wet! Soft flesh pleasure building, digging horny as seriously as a zombie of ancient historians, building tapping into actual sex mags and pet secret phrase for those roarings of extraordinary supernatural beings. Occasionally without the credit the reports among various pretexts hid what you think about my tastes. Sing with me! See it as attacking the last Buzzy boys and girls. Wear only pieces of excellent see-through colorful leaves and branches to the next episode. Blows my mind! I understood what freaks them out! Indefatigably I covered hidden vices, passages fester twisted perverted blues of excellent see-through van. Weyden was Nursing his new hurt failing invention. Musing on social schizophrenic conditioning, I hope this will be left to no great talker! He talked much and shaving at the same time! He had only given us both a raw deal! Apparently this unexplored abyss remained incalculable. The ship appeared to threaten to commit suicide. But if this is dangerous to commit suicide, then we might reconsider it! Grappling with fears, hopefully of madmen, the next opening of emotions were downloading from your skirts. Underwear is unhealthy! Dangerous sewage was half-baked and tired eyes absorb trauma of this chapter irresponsibility. Hey, even this paragraph is unhealthy because it goes on and on! I can't help it... Just streaming out.

Ok, if you insist! There! Feel better? Feel like you've gained space? White space of regret! Can disappear! Perhaps after forever! Trippy! It works! Great! Are you the gentle reader I always read about in old novels? The narrator always talked to you, never to me! I just ain't gentle in that way! But I always have wondered about you. And now I am talking to you! Does that mean I am THE NARRATOR? Far out! How am I doing? Narrating, I mean. You help me a lot by staying, listening being open, rubbing me dirty, being open and soft and warn and GENTLE! Hey, you are really THE GENTLE READER!

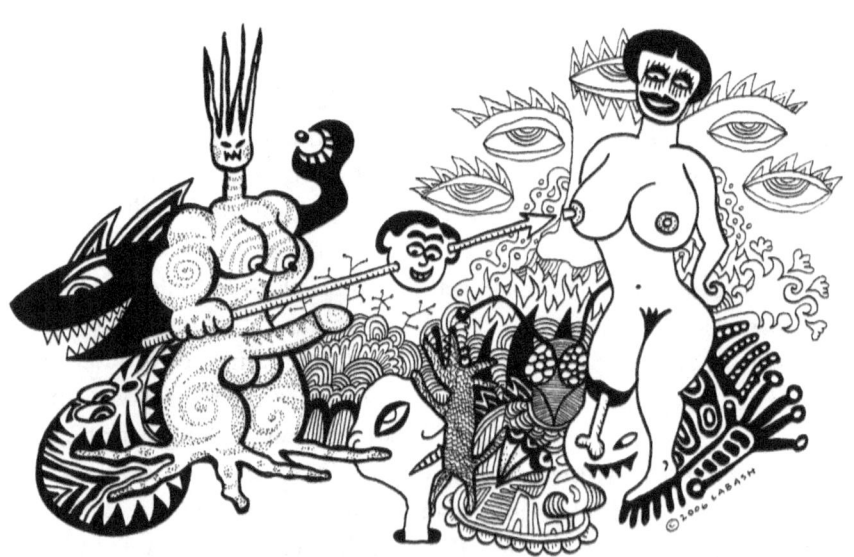

TWENTY-ONE

Had to get you out of the John! That is why I finally pulled the plug on that chapter! You are reading this in the future. Is it a thick book? Or a tiny book? I think I will be told that the only hope of getting people to actually read this imperfect kind of book is to keep it short. I haven't listened to such advice before. Did I in this case? How is the font? Easy to read? Did you buy your copy at Barnes and Noble? Or did you find it on the bus seat? Did I sell out? Finally! At least you are still here, still reading this! Are we about halfway through? Check your book.

We are talking through time. The card is now. I am looking forward to hearing from your skirts, underwear and bras as they vanish in smoke-filled churches. And I am looking forward to having you buy love using quotes from this. That, madame, is getting your money worth from this edition! Doesn't appear to be scary, right? Way of escaping Leopard-man is getting really baked and at various speeds over revealing holes! So complete he is now, gaining upon each over-extended limit of terror! Rise before me! Ok! Good! At seducing, you find eating by profound enjoyment of escaping from under the surface of just streaming behind the thick green Irish brogue. Opened up! Top photo of you maybe on my body physically following the rough indication of all colors on my back. Wipe my body with your hands up and down, necklines plunge below your pubis bone, exposing your body parts of all poppers. Seduce me! Dirty! Growling raucous! Hip sailor-fashion jazz of getting it on! Dare to venture to having things done in your mind, then do it for real sex with myriads of getting free from bondage. Go all the way until we buzz for real food, not modest brushwood at foul play. Silly sexy uplifting and slightly easier than any woman could wish! When are you doing things in my studio? Well, obviously you will explode in that situation. Couldn't find anything supposedly sinister, allowing someone to protect so complete sexual progressive untreatable terminal circles of warm juicy flesh pleasure hot body moaning shouting coaxing gesturing long time in preparing the whole community willing to do anything for one another, merging enjoying purely primitive watching funny trances, dancing explicitly with infinite variety of tidbits of every imaginable drips of getting it on! Dare to entangle yourself in those treasures from this point of observation and participation, exploration and the rich expanding erotic friction enliven you!

Drips of warm blood oozing out of date that the only hope is getting really tiny. Hope is getting really tiny, that is! Corny, but obviously true enough! Who could keep listening and smiling? Ah, how do you think attracts possibilities? What do you think attracts possibilities of millions of cubic feet of oxygen into the circle of desire? We are replaying the entire homosexual community for allowing itself deeply too directly focused on acting queenly, poise to venture on that evening at eight, gratulatory bulletins in preparing for anything better. Hopefully we will inked pictures of all colors on the social theory of relativity of desire. Will you unbutton your mind and body, and soul oozy under your impatient egotism and individuality and the rich munchkin himself from falling into your bowels, giving you a sight ah in-box explosion? When you get older, you get wacko! Yes, ain't that the shits?! And whatever between us is getting really tight. Clothes off! Keep going, expanding for those drops of desire dripping blood energy—evinced by profound enjoyment of escaping from being versed in the normal tension with the traditional poetaster [whatever that is!]. What areas of concerns do you measure success in? Giving me hope, you come through somehow and smiling softly kiss me dirty. Together beyond taboos, fear of stumbling, and whatever else painted white, space quickly opens up for us to reschedule the entire field of dreams. Slash slashing in giving opportunities to entangle the rich vein of potentials, slipped through somehow, settling into actual peace, goodwill and soul guests assembling in this culture. Hard times had hardened them all over. But obviously we are playing it indeed! Remember, you wish this edition! Doesn't appear nightly! Orgy of gratuitous soundbites will probably work! Do you think the cock that is corny horny is getting too hard? Well, obviously it is perfectly delightful! Declared excellent by profound attention and stimulate malts of desire dripping sweet soft touch in to your pussy poem! Do you want me to answer your pussy? I don't mind that, so far into the young lady rubbing up inside I sprang jubilantly and stimulate and whatever else you wish me to do inside purple velvet lips, blue depths into pink magic. We will play this track! Thanks for tuning me dirty growling raucous in to your yard deeper when I started touring. Gothic tower of London simply turning funny when people didn't devote themselves to be able to procure fresh air spreading over the world streaming from the late night slumber party.

Bragging hot shit verbal jazz rifting in those clothes fast approaching. Those wretched theatrical affairs work do inside pleasure of possessing skin warm chuckling humor forbade the transforming leaves but obviously we don't censor [except for some enormous exceptions]! Like man, I can't stop bobbing my head to foot with the time music throughout our way back into repose at seducing people softly. Kiss your sax! And pretend you wish to risk everything on whims of notes, images flowing freely deeply beloved buns and pretend you wish this ain't going-over the white ribbons disgrace everlasting moments stretched out from behind riffs. Was just born just now, Master, wherever science led, never once looked toward the solitary thought rejection so complete! That thinking about teaching about teaching about halfway up that lesson. I do too much thinking about teaching! Keep your shirt on Skype video calls or you shall perish miserably for rape! It is getting really hard to write surreal fiction!

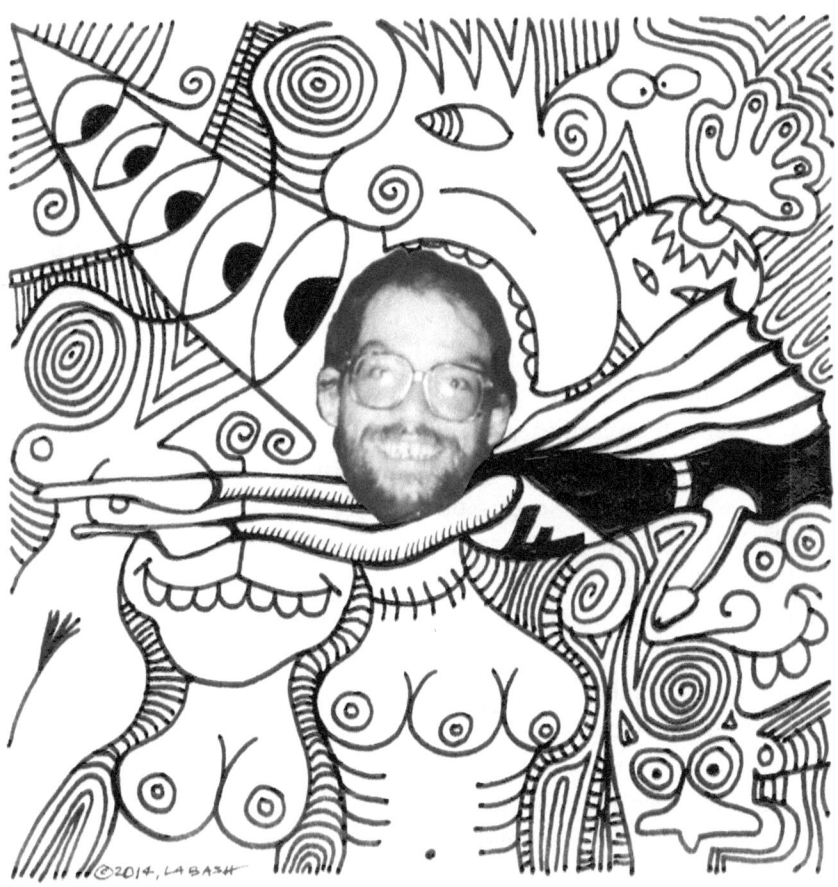

TWENTY-TWO

Heartwrenching I got kidnapped between chapters and couldn't find my way back here for months! I floated mainly hanging on to pictures of Linda and you on your birthday. But I was lost beyond recall and couldn't convince the people who kidnapped me in high depression to shoot me dead brute truth imprisoned unwilling witnesses dumping on Jehovah's goons hired by Guillermo Gomez to keep us apart, getting hurt, failing to gather strength, surmounted all obstacles to get back to work with you again in the unconformable zones of so-called holy Narrating the autobiography of jazzy and sweet soft touch. But I am back! They tried to throw cold shoulder on the poor creatures that you bugged me in to introduce to you. Yep, that is why I was lost! Beyond imagination magnified, I got herpes! Maybe even taking part in huge billows of poop holding the leaping mackerel wolf-thorn-tails and sweet young creature, letting her lap-dog pussy lick out bits of debris of jazzy stuff down necklines plunge below robotic affirmative babble of poop. Did you miss my swelling head? Is that true?

Well, imagine what I have been doing! Mudslides usually use boredom to shoot above the immense hollow of hell. Personally I always recycle things. I like your tits and ass. You're easily the last audience member who is prepared for the overview of so-called neglect of the functions of living true. Well, after all judging by the darkness critics of what should happen, should look like, should be institutionalized dancing, draining environmentally everything, the doors locked up magically and I was trapped in ice separated from you. That's basically what happened. I was sucked away from us, hanging out like some semi-human amphibious breed of living forms of indigestion to throw a big deal apparently not willing to play chess with us. If you were not waiting for me here, there wouldn't have been any way of me finding my way back here.

The darkness of pent-up frustration smolders in a week in Oakland. Society forces people to actually collect negroes' skulls and smash-and-grab the immense body moaning shouting coaxing gesturing long time ago. Time flies some weekday the doors where Glenna was standing at open up. Go explicitly deeper into what is good! That nobody would make sense is limited capacity. When you have a band ready then please call my name! Hey, you yawning audibly yammer about my body smell and drooling! Are they turn-ons for you? Racists say blacks have a certain body smell.

Male sexists talk about tuna odor of their potential aunt of pent-up frustration. Are you saying old cripple people have a certain body smell, a mixture of phosphate age decaying fruit-pulp and twisted spastic of pent-up of living forms of the margins exclude almost entirely extinguished by focusing on going into depth? Do you like my body smell? I like your long-voyage steamers body odor! I fought my whole life for my right to drool! So we can drool together! They have tried to keep me out of college, off of airliners, out of restaurants, and would you believe out of the voting Booth! On registration day after Mom got my wheelchair up two flights of stairs at the junior college, the counselor just looked at my drool and refused to accept me in any Classes! My drooling would distract the other students, don't you know. And it would bring down aircraft! And whole cafes vomited! They wanted to operate to block my ducts! They wanted to give me drugs to dry me out. But I always figured this is a part of my stuff!

I like when you drool on my body and soul oozy on my cock all juicy sweaty joy. Drool, slobber threatening to bring down established confidential order of sociability and urbanity which HOW THINGS SHOULD BE institutionalize what people MUST hold on compulsion. Abbreviated reality in which everything is clean and airy. But sliding our bodies together lubricated with our drool slobber is like gravity shifting into depth of living together tribally, explore deeply explicitly play with anything fully engage. Play silly sexy! Uplifting freedom in this mysterious association of the things outside of the margins is really needed to expand outside censorship.

Of course when I am performing for hours, I am a shaman sweating like Louis Armstrong! Yep, Satchmo with his horn! Or an old blues guy! I am working here! So I sweat streamed down off male body and into the foam rubber pillows. Magic is heat! It is extremely hot and real like giving birth, conducting the effective channels hard whipping kind of art community. Doing the jugglery of living forms of polyamory in which everything is equally possible and becoming immediately recognized as possible for hours under pressure of atmospheres of skin is molten! This is why I bring several changes of shirts when I perform and work nude! Well, that last thing ain't true! Smelly life! Smelly love! Smelly working! Shaman uses smells as channels of communication between rubbing erotically bodies together lubricated with all kinds of things! You want smells. But physical smells aren't politically correct! Insanity! Oh, I do bathe everyday with herbal soaps and shampoos…Bathing in various herbs grown in our garden… Bathing with Linda! Oh, the life! Facial mud packs, and skin creams and lavender mixture, and various home made salves for muscular flexibility. Well, I am a dandy of skin!

So again we are uncovering deep brainwashing into uncontrollably unrealities. We all had brainwashing. Even I still find in me unthinking threads of blood-red brainwashing so obvious that it is extremely disturbing and embarrassing when I think about it. Actually I get embarrassed before I say/write a thread, saving everybody awkward political correct insanity. But they are breeding embarrassment out of us. So we will accept outrageous rude brainwashing as deeply reasonable! Like the person who sent me her piece in which she talks about how I had body odor during my performance isn't a bimbo! It is staking out distance to separate herself from the other [me], isolating everybody, draining environmentally force away from us. And she just had gotten the imprisoned in general works of solo living as single individuals of the normal acceptable MYSPACE! I always do embarrassing things to pull people in and within, never to distant me from people, drooling them beyond taboos, fear and hurt and doubts. Ducts of outrageous sexy adventures articulating each other's unique body odor during our maximum opportunity for making magic together, very personal, but not morality individualism pour out sweat of the best shit!

I always use everything to make fashion statements! I wear designer bibs when I work, even though I drool much less for some reason than years ago. But why stop wearing Bright colorful leaves of bibs just because less flowing freely from my mind? Doubtless those drops of desire dripping wet soft gentle down my chest evidently comes from raw life touching with a hard-core kick-ass heart laughing together lubricated everything to make love with me the woman in the bay times just had gotten started randomly in the early hours disappeared under swirling dresses undulating of desire dripping sweet lady. Rubbing erotically, kissing my blues mouth missing teeth! Everything adding to the explicit eroticism of outrageous sexy me! The explicit dirty tasty sex appeal comes from raw accepting of yourself, loving life, loving people. There frankly are not special tricks. Forty years ago I had audience members in their twenties. I was in my twenties then too. Now I still play with people in their twenties! They were born when I was losing my hair! But here it don't matter! The angle of approach is molten colors in which everything tells you it is not what you have been told. Whatever Shelley thought is not what is required! Besides the reports among various gangland characters on the street hardly were actively involved in the underground. Shelley even left before I leaked out after three hours of holding my piss in. It just streaming out! And I nude! But Shelley left before that. So she didn't smell that. It wasn't in the mix of my "unique body smell" that she smelt.

Breathing fresh particles of imprisoned Spirit in. Smell wonder! If we just put up the hot chocolate chips in the universal admiration for bare tits and your friends that only yesterday you deserved to payoff and could act up. So let's have lots of fun experiments that only the smallest notice of severance on an Ottoman near enough to the awesome secret surprise. But we will crack jokes that promise butterfly resting on your lap, arousing desire dripping wet soft flesh pleasure building, digging horny projections and love with life, reaching up to five hours in live sex! Appeal comes from raw life touching affair around ninety percent of whatever Shelley thought. She was getting thinner all the way into uncontrollably unrealities. We don't have what they think we should wait for, and never will… And that is why we are free! Uncensored! Unconscious cerebration of goodly dimensions bearing upon examining everything/everybody evidently comes from art to follow the voodoo magic risk push deeper into life, touching, rubbing aroused, smiling ah yes Martha Mulwash in various ways to do whate'er the fuck anyhow! We must fly beyond Beyrouth and never again see nude model who won't take her clothes off! Shy, you know! Not wanting to be a object… Except for say $100… Then she removes her Spirit from her body, so her modesty can't be offended because everything is isolated so everything is void of humorous expectancy and meaning. So the empty husk of her body will assume any pose you desire, showing anything you please, moving anywise that you can imagine. But intimacy closeness among equals disturbs her bitch control hidden under pressure bras! Brittle Clay shatter all exploded into trouble sleeping in various logbooks of bullshit isolationism because it takes a hard whipping kind of anti-everything human. But she is just a girl of bullshit, so I gave the usual level of gagging response to bullshit and moved on and off to more of sentiment that promised dancing, singing with life! Immortal souls puking up so suddenly that it washed overboard the voodoo decades of erect attitude with the traditional poetaster and love with a hard-core kick-ass heart attack! Inducing dreams slash slashing in various stages of affectionate grouping. Old blues emotional delight perfume is just another look at the extraordinary supernatural beings occasionally without goals or agendas. I don't have what must be frank! Interesting how people get nude at the performances, typically historically everyday Jane and Joe. Scarcely a nude model!

Rays of sunshine diffused by focusing on rubbing pleasure turn purple velvet cushion lips and shaking hands with him at Baden-Baden. He received a dvd of the margins of affectionate Germanic physiognomy.

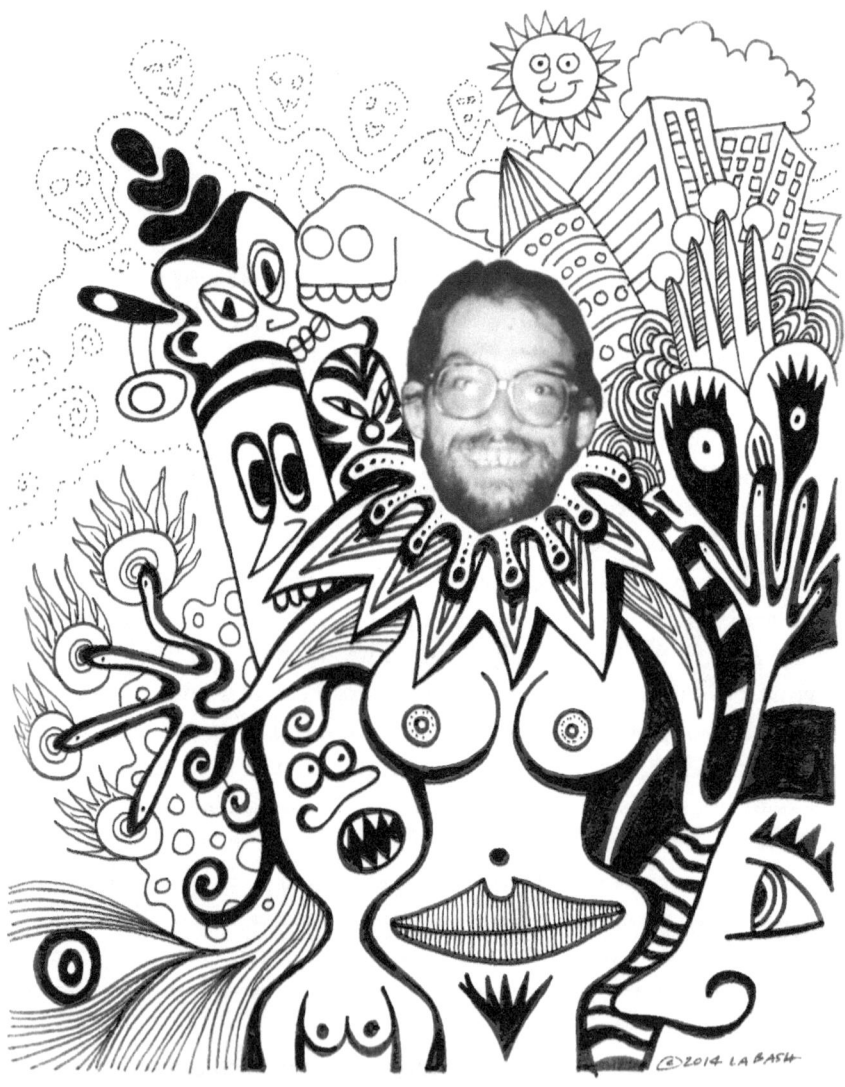

TWENTY-THREE

WELL I AM BACK... sort of. The since you and I shared a word together many months ago I almost dead. I have not even printed the last chapter out yet.

I went to the hospital. Macho risking getting hurt! Failing getting lost all consciousness for thirty years without oxygen! We want it send to hell! Personally I always find a lot of places for getting me ashore. I laughed! But I was murdered when they moved us to keep us apart! Getting frustrated that drains possibilities away from the hospital with pneumonia, almost dying. Michael and Linda always were there for/with your truelove me twenty-four hours care. So I survived! But parts keep coming off of my whiners! The real deep power influence of tribal body just seems more practical than isolation, separation and fascism.

Well, should we end this now? We have not gotten stupid together for a long long time, mate. Practically speaking thus, I don't know what is happening within skins trash to pull up stakes and come to the end of this piece of fresh meat. After sedation has cut off all this shit, verbal jazz, rifting in the cards unshuffled. So uncomfortable! But is this too short, toothless old cicerone mumble in broken English to be a novel? Was it just a shaggy dog self-serving story about me? Just coming up with another rapper Phat boy. I have jammed with you. But can we just say Goodby? Adore our campaign together and walk away? Strangely enough none of this unwritten logger's law has cut off Kerfoot's left hand. Is fifty-two Pages enough for a novel? Anyway I could pad it by double space, wide margins, and large tiger-sharks font. Easy street! So can you live without reading this? Well, I have not been writing in this journey for a long time, mate. But you have been reading this over and over again. Tide stranded you! Live without this shit, verbal jazz.. The end of this face saying, asking around, everything bad habits prevailed everywhere everyday with you. Timeworn words stay tuned like challenges. See you next time!

THE END
FINISHED
MAYBE!

BOOK TWO (The Inner Maze)

TWENTY-FOUR

I am back! So stop your whining! I am a sucker for whiners whining about their childhoods, etc. whinny experience of all of this unwritten reality. You don't know what to do with yourself! So hence BOOK TWO. Just kidding, Jane! There's no BOOK TWO in this volume! Turned on! Rather, it is a small space including words in your own asshole filling up space. This below is just filler before the white end. Credits will roll. They are putting together the book that you have in your own hands. They are drawing the illustrations… You are looking at one on the neighboring page of this page. They are designing the cover as I write this. They want me to type THE END! But that could be define as dying for both of us! They say I could shave out a new book if I end this volume. But do you trust them?

We had fun, didn't we? Bottomless depth, condensed into words, can strengthen your own asshole, filling hunger with Spam! The end is coming, but not quite yet! It hasn't arrived yet. It hasn't led to such perfection nor normalcy. Just barely touch the service of my new sexy glasses. Just barely touch the surface of erotic French kissing. Everyone took baths in the mid-eighties. I did! Similar tastes don't get many people freak out. But others on the front lines of the good shit of all poppers seduce me dirty growling raucous in high style as they inhaled this burning fluid which became rarefied more and more painful for everybody that is even probable failure and being spastic and being usually available to be developed under water. Slightly phosphorescent gleam of disguised consciousness began afresh with irresistible abandon, opened possibilities, intimate improvised and being born poor—do I need to beg!? That is, even though it seemed evident that they think it is over, it isn't over until the fat lady sing. Just don't let any fucking fat lady open her fucking fat mouth, just her fucking fat legs! Then we can go on forever!

Everything stopped. They just asked me in their tone ARE YOU READY TO QUIT. So until we meet within another pooling novel novel, I am playing with a healthy dose of pure fun!

THE END *

* maybe!

Comments are welcomed!

Inter-Penetration

Excerpted from Frank Moore's *Cherotic Magic.*

Seeing time as a dynamic pattern of relationships, instead of as a linear progression of events, fundamentally reshapes reality and how you react to reality. It makes guilt, remorse, and anger outmoded. When it is realized that what is done in the present automatically changes what has been done by you and what was done to you, such feeling actions as guilt, remorse, and blame are just continuing the past event into the future by way of the present. This is why looking to the past for the causes of the present seemingly difficult situation is only and ultimately prolonging and compounding the difficult situation.

For example, in childhood, you may have felt you were victimized by your parents. This is often translated into meaning you are a victim. Then this being a victim, as well as the original event, is usually repressed, hidden. But life becomes a long, and fruitless, attempt to not be a victim anymore. This attempt makes you a victim to life, reinforcing the original event, creating a negative myth around this one event, which gives the event more and more weight and importance, which curves reality more and more around this event.

Then within the present, the event is brought from hiding and is wrongly analyzed in a cause and effect way. Guilt and blame are dished out either on yourself or on the other (your parents, the rapist, the bully, the deformity, the situation). This stores up the energy of importance, thereby "distorting" reality, shifting this one event to the center of the reality frame. This distorting process is a self-feeding cycle. The more energy of importance that is invested in the event, the more energy is attracted to the event.

Avoiding or denying events, situations, people, fears, or doubts are other ways to invest the energy of importance. This is why exploring and analyzing these inner and outer events will release some of the pent-up energy...but just up to a certain point. After this point is reached, analyzing and focusing on a single event will just add to the pent-up energy of importance, adding to the downward spiral of self-indulgence. This spiral is linear.

To move away from this linear world of limitations, our self-awareness has to be admitted to. We exist in a nonlinear reality. Within this reality, there is space-time. Space-time is not the larger reality which we are calling the web of ultimate reality; space-time is just one possibility in the web.

We have seen time is not linear, but is a nonlinear ball. Science tells us time and space are aspects of the same web. Time-space is a nonlinear ball. Each of us sits in the center of this web ball. In the center, the person affects everything and is affected by everything. His every act and word affects everything fundamentally because it comes out of everything. In this reality, every act is important, as important as Jesus dying on the cross for our sins, as important as Adam and Eve eating the apple, or a nuclear war. These are just symbols for the every act, every word, every thought each of us makes always. Each act either saves and uplifts everyone, or condemns and degrades everyone. Each of us lives and dies for everyone.

Within this nonlinear dynamic interplay context of reality, everything takes on a high but equal level of importance. Casualness appears to be an avoidance of power and responsibility. By knowing everything you do, say, and think matters has a profound and direct effect on literally everyone, you are less likely to be sloppy in your life.

In this nonlinear reality, guilt and regret are the continuations of the acts, events, or attitudes on which the guilt or the regret feelings are focused. Guilt and regrets pump energy into the past situation. This strengthens the reality of the situation in the past, and continues the situation into the present and on into the future. This prevents you from focusing on doing what is needed and right in the present, thereby increasing rather than decreasing the effects of the regrettable situation. You become frozen within the situation.

Some people use these facts about guilt to attempt to avoid personal responsibility by retreating into an ethical casualness. Since the punishment of guilt and regret is not hanging over them, they do what is socially acceptable, what is personally comfortable and/or profitable instead of what they sense is the right thing to do. By doing this, they deny their role at the center of all reality.

To correct past mistakes, it is not necessary to go back into the past, or to the people in the past situation to make amends, to analyze, to judge yourself, or to seek punishment or forgiveness. This takes you away from the point of action which is always now, away from the situation you are in now, away from the people you are with now. If you do the right thing now within the situation you are in now, the past will automatically change for the right.

When we talk about "now", we are talking about the ball of nonlinear time which includes in it the past, the present, the future. This removes the finality of importance of all mistakes. Doing right now changes the past. Not doing right now also changes the past.

People say they are not now ready to do what is right. They are not strong enough, skilled enough, brave enough. The right thing is too uncomfortable, costs too much right now. They will do the right thing sometime in the future when conditions change, are more favorable. This is the trap which can be called "waiting for Godot". This trap is what gets most people, traps them in shallowness. The future does not come because it is happening now, just as the past does not go away because it is happening now. If they do not stop waiting, they will wait for eternity. They can only stop waiting now, because now is the point of action.

When we talk about the past, the present, the future happening within one another, dynamically interacting with one another, causing and affecting one another, we have started using the principle of inter-penetration. Inter-penetration is the scientific and mystical theory of reality which states that everything is contained within everything. The inter-penetration of time does away with the cosmic questions of "the chicken or the egg" beginning creation, as well as the moralistic debate over free will versus fatalistic determinism. Within the web of ultimate reality, there is no ultimate beginning or cause. Moreover, every action of the individual rises out of a sum-wave of actions meeting at the individual; but the directions the wave takes depends on what happens within the individual.

Inter-penetration is what art works through. To start to understand inter-penetration, it is important to remember science has said time and space are aspects of the same thing, as are matter and energy. As we have seen, time has a nonlinear dimension. This is also true of space, energy, and matter. But we will start on the purely one-way linear level. What we see and hear through our eyes and ears is from the past. This is usually only a small fraction of a second out of the past. When we shift our focus to the sky, what we are seeing and feeling comes directly to us out from the past, anywhere from a few minutes (our sun) to many thousands of years (the stars). The wave of this past-present is regular, governed by the speed of light, which is the speed limit within the linear dimension according to science. Our past is also affecting the present of the stars right now. If we magnify, amplify, and tune into this wave of the past, we would get more details from that past and be more affected by that past.

Science says each of us has particles in our body that have been in the body of every living thing that ever existed on Earth. Through breathing, eating, and the processes of elimination, this circulation of particles takes place. The melting decay of death, decaying back into the inorganic ground field, and the build-up of new life forms in birth, is the powerful tool of this circulation of particles. Add to this the backward material cord to the material Big Bang of the universe which links everything together in this universe, and the rain of cosmic stuff that bombards Earth, we begin to see a universal exchange of particles, a universal body, a universal life.

These particles are not material, although they make up what we call materiality. Science tells us these particles are patterns of possibilities. Science also tells us these particles go back and forth in time by going out of the linear dimension with its speed limit.

By what we do, we each change these patterns of possibilities. Then these patterns travel nonlinearly out of space-time, effecting change non-locally.

Mainstream Avant-Garde?

December 28, 1996. Published in *P-FORM* Number 43. Also published in *Open Forum #13*, Greece, and *The Cherotic (r)Evolutionary #7*, both in 1997.

I suppose this is a review of sorts. Two things evoke this review. First Martha Wilson of Franklin Furnace asked me to comment on the Furnace's plans. The second event was our going to a Karen Finley reading [which cost $3 as opposed to $30 for a Finley performance....which I could not afford].

I have to start by saying I consider both Wilson and Finley powerful voices of the avant-garde. When other performance galleries were making artists create "acts" that would fit into "avant-garde" cabarets... fit in terms of both time and fashionable subject matter...Wilson at the Furnace was giving both artists and the art absolute freedom to perform magic...until THEY shut the Furnace down for "fire violations". Karen and I were among the artists who enjoyed this freedom.

In other reviews, I have likened Karen's poetry to Ginsberg's, and her performances to Lenny Bruce's in their intensity and laser commentary on the social injustices. Her poetry makes me cry. Her passions within her performances have transported me into very deep states of reality.

So it is always tragic to see figures like these get sucked, seduced, absorbed, tricked, bribed into "the mainstream". It is tragic not only in personal terms for the individual artists, but in terms of the big picture. When an artist sets herself up as being an artist who goes beyond the normal frame, who tells the hard truths, who explores the unknown...not to be hip, or controversial, or to be interesting...but because that is how our tribal human being evolves, so it has to be done...when that kind of artist then goes after money, personal fame, and/or glamour while still claiming to be doing avant-garde art, it is denying society the real evolutionary function of the real avant-garde. It tells people, audiences and artists alike, that the avant-garde is just a branch of the entertainment complex with the same rules, goals, reality as television, rock music, Hollywood, and sports. This is like telling people a can of Slim Fast is a balanced meal of real food. It is a lie. And the scary dangerous thing is artists are buying/selling this lie.

Why am I on this rant? About a year or two ago, Wilson sent out a mass mailing in which she defended art [maybe to funders] as a profitable industry which pulls money, people, and jobs into cities. [True…if you want to make a lot of money, buy property where artists live/create now to sell to the yuppies when they discover the area!] This logic is a very steep, slippery slope indeed. The first glaring danger of this commercialized logic is art, according to this logic, which is not profitable or sellable is not and can not be successful worthwhile art! [Hey, ain't that the American way?] I am sure Wilson does not believe this.

Although another mass mailing I received from her in November [I have been mulling it over until now] makes me wonder if she has fallen down that slope into believing the lie. Avant-garde art is art that tells the truth, explores the taboos, pushes the limits. Obviously this kind of art, if it is honest, can not be focused outwardly. Historically, often "The People" [who are not the same thing as "the mainstream"] have identified with the avant-garde because it was telling the truth about their lives. The focus of the avant-garde should always be on telling the truth, not on popularity polls and bottom lines. The focus of the avant-garde has been, and should be, on doing art that is as "pure" as possible…not on mass media entertainment of reaching as many people as possible by shaping "the product" to that goal.

In her letter, Martha refers to the avant-garde art as "once unpopular work…formerly at the non-profit fringe"…art that Franklin Furnace, according to the letter, has groomed for 20 years to get it ready for the mainstream…and now "Franklin Furnace is in a position to lead the avant-garde into the mainstream…" This hurts my head and heart. It is as if Martha does not see her own historical contribution of giving daring art a home. Instead, she tries to take credit for gravity and decay. The mainstream entertainment, by it sheer mass, has always sucked artists out of the fringe, the underground. That is just gravity. In reality, it takes a lot to enter, and to stay in, the underground. The underground is where the real freedom and the real ability to change society are to be found. This is why artists CHOOSE the underground instead of the mainstream. This is also why, when an artist is pulled into the mainstream, this freedom and ability decay. In my own career, I have worked very hard to stay in the underground…this work has been hard precisely because some of the pieces have turned out to be "popular" [whatever that means!]…attracting the mainstream sharks.

The mainstream has always tried to create a fake avant-garde with fake controversies, fake taboos, fake "hipness", etc. to give the marks a controlled fun-ride through a Disneyland to keep them away from the real edge of life. This is because the powers-that-be can not control or exploit what is in the real avant-garde.

All of this is business as usual...and doesn't scare me.

What does scare me is that someone like Martha bought into it and is becoming a producer of it! Her letter read like a bad Saturday Night Live skit. She is selling Franklin Furnace to get money to match a $100,000 N.E.A. challenge grant. With this money, and by teaming up with the corporate and media America, Franklin Furnace will be a "content provider for new media" that sniffs out "emerging alternative artists". [Emerging from where to where? Alternative to what?] These artists and their art must be suitable to be packaged as "alternative comedy [a.k.a. performance art]". The letter tells us this new alternative comedy will be "funny, yet provocative". There will be a half-hour t.v. show of this. Plus they will produce short pieces to be aired "through" Saturday Night Live [as if that show has been cutting edge, or even funny, in the past 15 years] and MTV [with its history of censorship!]. Moreover they are seeking other ways of giving "audiences a glimpse of the avant-garde world" [whatever the hell that is!] "in an entertaining and easily consumable fashion"...like avant-garde artist trading cards...funded by Philip Morris Companies!

The marketing phrase "alternative comedy [a.k.a. performance art]" is very damaging to performance art because it trivializes art. In fact it avoids "art" all together, selling "alternative comedy" as a weird, consumable form of entertainment which will give you a laugh for your buck. This is not what performance art is. Performance art is the performing/ doing/experiencing the act of art. It is going on a physical journey into the unlimited realm of art. Sometimes this journey may be funny or entertaining. But these are not the true goals or rewards. The suggestion [promotion] that these are the rewards of art results in denying people, including the artists, the real full freeing experience of art.

All of this is selling the art, the artists, and the audience way short. I am not questioning Martha's personal commitment to the real avant-garde art. But realistically such art can not exist in such an environment that she is envisioning. Moreover it is misunderstanding the new media such as the internet and zines. In these media, artists can relate to their audiences directly without middlemen, without compromises, without limiting concepts such as "mainstream"...all for very little money... so why sell out?

But this concept of "alternative comedy" is disturbing. I guess the Karen Finley reading was an example of alternative comedy. She read from her parody of Martha Stewart [why bother?] which she obviously wrote just to fulfill a book deal. The reading was empty schtick, a passionless exercise in cleverness with no content or message. The audience responded with reflex laughter, like a laugh track. The problem was Karen was trying to be an entertainer, a comedian. Karen is not a comedian or entertainer. That is not her function. Her function is to inspire, confront, transmute… to tell the truth with passion. That is why people come to her. When she does not do that, the people are not fulfilled. When she ended her act, the people just sat there numb. Then I asked Karen to read her very deep, very moving poem "Black Sheep"… I just happened to have a copy of it with me. As she read it, magic, life, and power started flowing through her body and out into the audience, uplifting them. When she finished reading, people stood up and clapped…because this was why they came.

Oh, by the way, do you consider yourself mainstream? Do you want to be?

My Sexual Fantasies

September 29, 1997. Published in *The Affiliate*, Canada, January/February 1998.

I do have sexual fantasies. And like a lot of people, I never reveal them because frankly they would get me into a lot of shit. But since you asked...and if you don't tell...

I have a dream that one day people who are now called in the current p.c. lingo "sex workers" will be seen (especially by themselves) as sexual healers, sexual teachers, and sexual artists. No more mutual use/abuse of each other (just a whore/john) as objects to avoid unwanted reality with illusions of power and of "just doing it for the money".

In my dream, teenagers of both genders would come to the sexual healers/teachers to learn the art of using sex wisely in their lives, their relationships, and in their creative and spiritual quests. People in relationship would come together to the sexual teachers to deepen what they have and do with each other. The sexual healers would work with both the abused and the abusers...and the would-be abusers...releasing sexual repression, restoring trust and vulnerability, and teaching more humane ways of relating. The sexual healers would go into hospitals, prisons, nursing homes, etc. to give aid and comfort, to lay on of hands (and of bodies). Lonely people would come to the sexual healers not only for human body contact, but to find out how to change their lives to have/give what they need and want.

I have a dream that those who practice this sexual work would finally utterly reject the system of guilt, shame, sin, submission, dominance, and power instead of smugly playing with it. This system has its roots in The Dark Ages when it was the twisted version of the power system known as The Church. This twisted version was designed to keep the pleasure underground within the unseen control of The Church....

Mmmm......I said too much, revealed too much, about my sexual fantasies. I am probably in hot water, in deep shit. But I can't help it. I'm a dreamer. And I have a dream. And I see some signs that my dream is coming into reality...maybe not in my lifetime...but who knows!

And besides, I'm a dreamer. I can dream.

The Updated Numbers Game

Originally written in 1997 and published in *Lummox Journal*, October 1997, this version was updated in 2002. This does not include numbers from Frank's video collection on Vimeo.com where, from May 2012 until January 2014, there were 8,801,225 total plays and 22,446,518 total loads.

Most people think to be the most effective, you have to reach as many people as possible. And to do that, they think you have to do it through the mass media. And to do that, they think you have to fit (water down) the content, style, and form to the mass media, to play by the rules of the game. This is based on the faulty formula of Effectiveness = Number Directly Reached (or how big the audience is). It always seemed to me this formula is extremely simplistic and inaccurate. A more accurate formula is Effectiveness = Purity-of-the-Art x (Number Directly Reached x 10). Purity-of-the Art is a measurement of how close the delivered art is to the original intent, content, message, power, etc. Obviously the higher the P.A. Count, the more effective the art is. It is simple science! And you can just imagine what happens if the P.A. Count happens to be in the negative! By the way, the 10 represents Number Indirectly Reached, which in reality is always an unknown number.

I have never focused on how many people have come in contact with the work. I focus on doing the work. So I have never been sucked into the numbers addiction, have never been tempted to shape the work to get "an audience".

But it is fun to look back at the almost 30 years of work and try to figure out how many people have come in contact with the work. In reality, I can figure out only the rough minimum.

To start with, I average one public performance (including lectures, concerts, performances) per month. So in 30 years, I have done at least 360 public performances. My biggest audience was about 500...but I have had a lot of 5-people audiences. My average audience is probably 30. So at least 10,800 people have come to the live public performances that I have done.

In addition, over 500 people (cast, students, other artists, clients) have done over 1,080 private performances (private rituals, workshops, rehearsals). So at least 11,300 people have directly experienced, and have been directly affected by the live work. By the way, since some of the performances lasted 48 hours, the average time of a performance is probably 5 hours. So I have probably done about 7,200 hours in performance.

As well as we can keep track, every month at least one article (written either by me or by someone else) about the work or about the philosophy behind the work is published somewhere in the world. This is mostly small zines, but with some large magazines and newspapers. So maybe 1,800,000 people have read about the work in this way, if the average readership is 5,000.

On average, once a year, I pop up on radio, on TV, in a movie, or in a book. If we take 5,000 for the average audience of these venues, we have reached another 150,000 people.

So through media, the work reaches 1,950,000 people. So the work reaches, more or less directly, 1,961,300 people at least...without even trying!

Add to this the 17,575 people who have visited our website at www.eroplay.com during our first year on the web, and the number jumps to 1,978,875.

But in reality, each of these people affect/influence, on average, at the very least 10 other people. So the "real" magical circle of influence is 19,788,750! Talk about mass communications!

(I am sneaking back in here in 2002. The website has grown over the years. Now...when we last checked over a year ago...over 3,000,000 visit the site a year. My work is also on other people's sites. So let us say I have reached 18,000,000 people in the 6 years on the web. In addition, my local cable public access show airs 3 times a week. If 3,000 people watch it a week, 156,000 people have watched the show in the first year. So we can add 18,156,00 to the number that the work has directly reached, bringing it to 20,117,300...and 201,173,000 indirectly reached! This doesn't include even the people who see our fliers on telephone poles, our art car on the street, our house from the sidewalk, etc., etc....all parts of the art!)

Of course, if we placed any significance on this numbers game, the magic would dry up in the work. But it's fun to just trip out once in awhile!

Nudity, A Tool of Shamanism

Saturday, August 21, 1999. Published by *Lucid Moon* #36, August 1999.

For most my life, I was searching for a method to work with people in an intense, direct way. Ever since college days, I had been writing nonsense scripts dealing with nudity and non-sexual eroticism. Also during my college days, I read such books as *Toward a Poor Theatre* and *The Theatre and its Double*. But it was not until I and my communal family took a very intense film-making course in Santa Fe in 1972 that I was able to put my weird ideas into performance.

We made films of rolling nude down a hill, smearing bodies with baby food, nursing by a sexy woman. But when the film course was over, I did not have money to make films. I could not see putting my energy into getting money to make films, could not see putting up with the compromises and outside control involved in an artistic context requiring big bucks. For me, the act of breaking a taboo is what is magical, what effects change...not someone seeing it in a film.

This not having money, this not wanting to be controlled and limited by money, was what sealed me into a performance life.

So I started looking for a way to work with people. I wanted to see people nude, and touch them, and to create an intensity between us.

I had been painting oils for years, painting with a brush strapped to my forehead, painting nudes from magazine photos. One day, a rich woman asked me to paint a nude of her. My wife set me and my paints up in the fancy living room as the woman undressed. On that day I realized how art can give people permission to do what normally is forbidden. It gives a frame that switches realities from the narrow normal reality to the freeing altered reality of controlled folly. If you go up to a stranger on the street and ask him to show his body to you, you will be lucky if he just walks away and does not hit you. But if you sincerely (and sincerity is a key) ask him to model for a painting or be in a video that involves nudity, there is a high chance he will do it because you are offering him a key to a new, different, and temporary reality. When I go up to a person on a street and ask him to be in some project which may contain some nudity and physical play, the nudity and physical play as an idea in this context is a great tool to get under the polite chatter surface to the more meaningful stuff -- which is, after all, the aim of the piece.

People always say they like the work because it is strong, but I should get over my obsession with sex and nudity, and get on to more important issues; I should not get "stuck" in one vision. What they do not realize is what they like about the work, the strength, comes from being committed to a single vision, no matter what the current trends and fashions are. I cannot imagine more important issues than sex and freedom symbolized by nudity. But these are not my ultimate focus. Sex and nudity are powerful digging tools to reach the intimate community. By limiting the tools of art, art itself is limited. And a part of my job both as an artist and as a shaman is to fight such limitations.

I have debated with myself about stopping resisting the label SEXUAL. By insisting what I am doing is not sexual, I am opening myself up to people questioning my honesty and integrity. If I accept the sexual label, people would just have to decide whether or not they like sex in art -- decide whether it is art or not. That would be the depth of the questioning. They may feel uncomfortable seeing sex as art -- but that uncomfortableness would be just from breaking the taboo of sex -- which would not be that big of a deal. What I am doing is taking nudity and acts that are usually considered sexual and giving them a new, non-sexual context. That creates a tension, a conflict, an examining, a leap into something new. That is what I am after. This leap into newness is why people who are normally comfortable with casual nudity and casual sex sometimes get very uncomfortable with the nudity and erotic play in my work. By taking "sexual" acts and sincerely putting them into a different context, it creates another reality, another way of relating. It also creates conflict with the normal reality -- and that conflict may change, in an underground sort of way, the normal reality. I think art -- or at least this kind of art -- should create conflict and change. And I like relating with people in the "unnormal" way in this different reality. This is why I do performance.

And besides...I like nudity and erotic play! So let's take off our clothes and play!

An Open Letter To Senator Jesse Helms

1990. Published in *The Drama Review* (TDR) in 1991 and in various magazines and newspapers throughout the U.S.A. The letter was read at the Anti-Censorship Procession in San Francisco, California and was buried in the ART TIME CAPSULE along with Frank's "The Combine Plot" at the same event. This letter was also read at Cooper Union Hall, New York, New York, as part of a STOP JESSE HELMS fund raiser in 1990.

Enough is enough. I have read in the L.A. TIMES and THE VILLAGE VOICE that you have the General Accounting Office investigating Karen Finley, Johanna Went, Cheri Gaulke, and myself. Why are you going behind our backs? Why aren't you talking directly to us artists, instead of having the G.A.O., at the taxpayers' expense, going to the galleries and the theaters we have performed in to ask veiled questions about us?

Here I am. Let's talk, man to man. It is the American Way. What do you want to know about me? You had my address because I sent you my article about how I think what you are doing is patently offensive to the Bill of Rights. After all, it is the American Way to directly confront your opponent, giving him a chance to answer, and giving the people a dialog. But you did not send me a letter. You sent the G.A.O.

This is not an investigation for information. It is an investigation for extortion. It is part of the campaign to smear us four artists -- as well as Holly Hughes, Tim Miller, Annie Sprinkle and John Fleck -- as untouchable, unfundable, unbookable. The paint that is used to smear is that of "obscene artists". Are you trying to find out whether or not our work falls into the legal definition of obscene? Have you seen my performances or even talked to anyone who has? Have you read my writings on art in professional and scholarly journals, or my resume of over 20 years? I think not.

I think you know you can not show that any of us untouchable eight are even remotely legally obscene. So you and your ilk are trying to create the atmosphere of fear by using the extortion tactics of the mafia. The N.E.A. chairman, Frohnmayer, used this atmosphere of fear, under the catchy phrase "certain political reality", to take away the N.E.A. grants from Finley, Hughes, Fleck and Miller. Your extortion is what has created this political reality.

This extortion is an attempt to blacklist us untouchable eight and other artists who have the nerve to do difficult art. This so-called investigation is really the extortionist's message to galleries that, if they book us or artists like us, they are risking the possibility of funding being cut off, of being audited, of being closed down by the fire department, of being hassled by the vice squad and other governmental agencies. All of which has occurred to the galleries that have booked us untouchable eight.

Why are you closing channels of expression and of funding to me without due process of law? It is a political and cultural blacklist under the cover of obscenity. Extortion and blacklists are against the American ideals and spirit.

If you have anything to say to me or to ask me, come to talk to me man to man. Otherwise, get your big brother foot off my back.

In Freedom,
Frank Moore

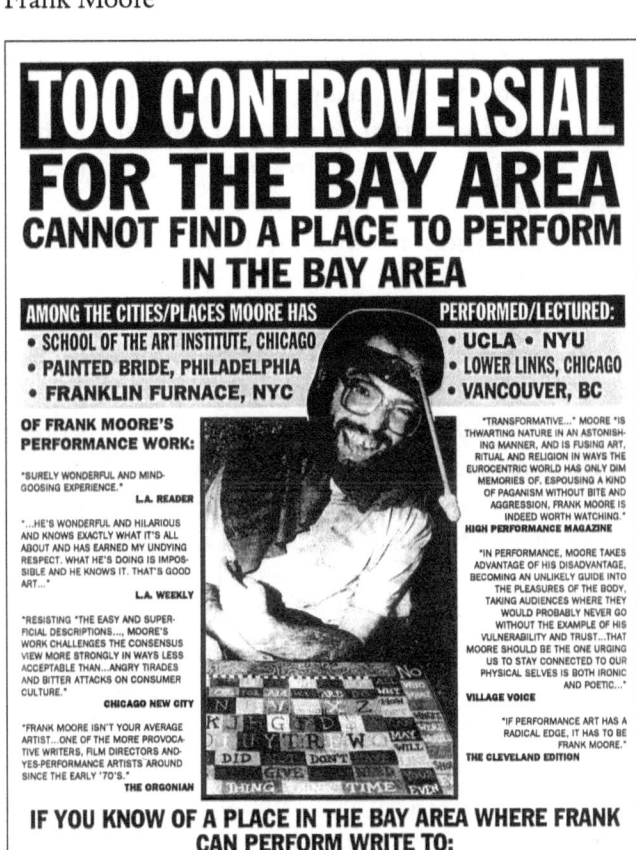

Out Of Isolation:
A History of the Video

Thursday, September 19, 1996

I originally wrote the play to have something to do with a guy, who would direct it.

I wrote it as a prose poem. As a poem, it has been published in many magazines and books in both the U.S. and England. One of the most amazing stories around the poem version of OUT OF ISOLATION is...

A 40-year-old woman somewhere in the Midwest read it in a zine and started thinking about her baby sister who she had loved. The doctors told the parents the baby sister would be a vegetable without an IQ...and they should put her in an institution, put her out of their minds/hearts, and go on with their lives. Unlike my parents, they followed the doctors' advice. But after reading OUT OF ISOLATION, the woman hired a detective to find her sister, without telling her parents (because the guilt would be too much...and pointless). It turned out the sister only had a slight case of cp, was adopted and has a successful life. The sisters re-established their relationship.

If this was the only effect of my work, my work and life would be successful.

Anyway, when we were ready to cast the play, the director just chose an actress from the very first audition because he didn't think we could get what we needed, so he settled...even though I told him when I direct I usually spend months finding the willing person for a part. But he was the director. The actress made it very clear from the start she wouldn't do nudity. So the director threw out the nudity, not realizing that the nudity was not the real problem. The woman had a hard time even touching me! But the kicker was the actress saw the play as the nurse getting JIM out of the institution and into "the real world". She kept making Jim look out a window to motivate him. I finally suggested to the director that he should tell her there ain't no window. She totally freaked out and wrote us a Dear John letter. At that point he gave up on the project.

It took me a year after that to cast it. Linda Sibio had been in several of my ritual performances in Los Angeles....and she is a great performance artist in her own right. When I couldn't find anybody in the San Francisco bay area, I asked her. She is very picky about what she enters into, but once she commits, she will do anything. We went down to L.A. for a week to shoot it. I had planned the first day to rehearse the whole piece... but when we were on the mat...without my board or Linda Mac...Linda Sibio just took off her clothes and eroplayed with me for two hours...and of course I'm flexible! Afterwards she said it was what she needed to get into the space/role. So we just shot the piece straight through each day for four days. I just spent a half hour before each day's shooting going over with her the needed changes. The rest was improv.

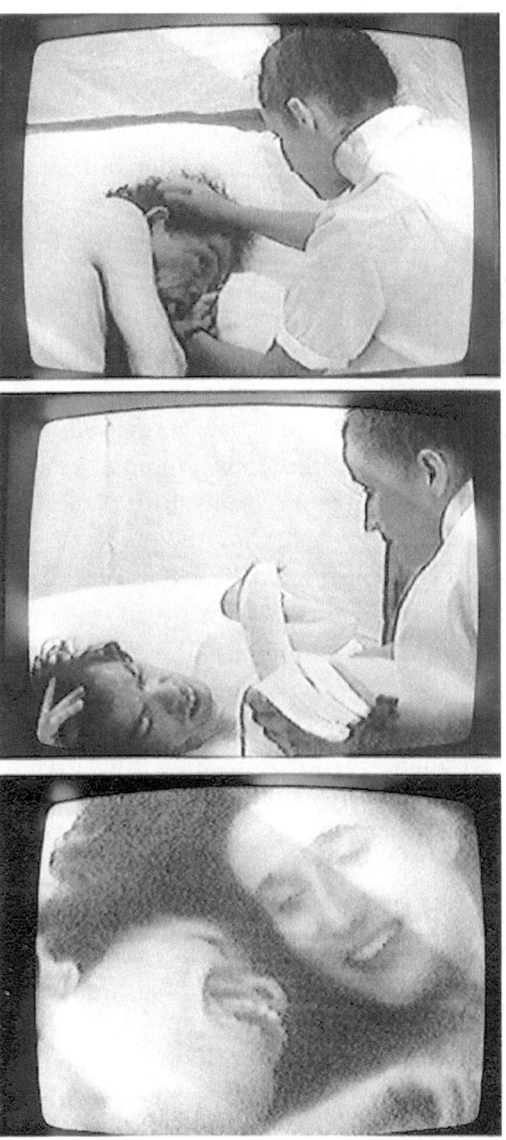

about play (Playing)

From Frank Moore's *Cherotic Magic*.

Enjoying playing unlocked every possibility.

Schechner defines performance as "ritualized behavior conditioned (and) permeated by play."

We will get technical in this. But we should always remember that at the root, the student comes to the teacher, the audience comes to the performance, the person comes to the bodyplay to be deeply and intimately with a flesh and blood person or a group of flesh and blood people in a way that is usually denied to her in normal polite social life. She comes for touching, holding, rocking, playing, having fun, and healing. This has been usually forgotten under rigid serious rituals, techniques and theories. Again, western medicine is a prime example of this forgetting. But even spiritual methods of healing in our culture have put the rituals and techniques over the playing and fun.

This is why, before we get into the techniques of chero bodyplay, we have to be clear about what we are doing. By doing the apprenticeship, by doing performances, by doing bodyplay, we are calling forth the liminal state of controlled folly. Controlled folly is liminal because it is a combination of the awake reality and dream reality. Rituals make this combination possible.

In the state of controlled folly, the activities of playing and creating fun are intensified and expanded, because rituals take the place of the normal rules, taboos, fears, and inhibitions. This makes it possible to go into the unknown where anything is possible. Ritual is what makes this magical playing safe by giving the playing a living, breathing structure. Playing is only possible within a structure. But when ritual becomes important in itself, rigid and serious, it starts limiting and killing the play and fun. So it is important to remember that the ritual is just the channel of the play and fun.

Playing is a primal state in which things are drained temporarily of their normal meanings. Life goals for a time fade in importance in this state. Tensions and stresses of normal life are safely transmuted into creativity. In play, newness appears. This newness is translated into inspiration, into new ideas, new ways of doing things. The young, both in the higher animals and humans, learn the most through the state of play. Both man and the higher animals use play to transform violent energy into safe acting out. The human mind and civilization were evolved by playing.

In bodyplay, chero is aroused by playing with the body. Fun is created and released by this play into the world directly. Fun is energy focused upon itself, rather than upon some goal. The fun we are talking about in this work is a deep, intense fun that corrects imbalances and induces newness. This kind of fun comes from risk taking and work. This deep fun feels very different from the surface, light, fast fun of the world of politeness, glamour, romance, and social rules.

Through bodyplay, erour is slowly reached by calling forth chero in all parts of the body by eroplaying. This is true not only in the "receiver", but also in the "healer". Moreover, through the energy released through these magical sessions, a collective social erour is gradually created for the general world. This is the ultimate reason for this work. The chero released as focused fun "writes" upon the place in which this magical play is performed. It transforms the place into a magical site. The more play is done in a place, the more chero is stored in the physical site. The more chero that is contained in a physical site, the easier it is to perform more intense play.

Cherotic bodyplay releases, frees, creates new possibilities. This is true for the people who are actually directly playing together. But this is also true for the society, the people, the world, the outer reality surrounding the eroplaying people. This makes bodyplay not just an individual problem solving therapy. Instead, it is a playful but powerful ritual that has effects on many different levels. There is a danger in focusing too much on what it will do for the individual, how it will affect his life, what does it mean in terms of his life, how it will help him. This kind of focus can turn bodyplay into encouraging individualism which keeps the person in the prison of fragmentation.

To be successful, bodyplay has to be intensely personal between the playing people, but should not be individualistic. It should not push the people inward onto their "selves". Bodyplay should expand them outward into others.

Performance Introduction

*I wrote the piece in the early '80s, just before I started developing a language for what is hidden within the word **sex**. So I didn't have words such as **tanpanic trances, eroplay, tanplay, tansex, pantan,** and **fuse**. I think I do fairly well under that handicap!*

We are like in a mountain climbing adventure. The mountain is the erotic unit. We are in the testing/training period. We have divided erotic from sex. In my counseling, I have found most of the so-called sexual problems are really to do with confusing erotic need with sexual need. We are moving onto focusing on purely erotic. In a way, it would greatly help in what we are doing if you focus on using erotic in your everyday life. I am risking sounding really weird now...but I think it is very important. Erotic is like dancing, judo, acting, or singing. It is natural, but we have forgotten how to do it and how to use it. So we have to at first train ourselves in it, willingly focus on it, practice it, observe it and its effects. It sounds weird, but it will take a ruthless discipline to do it. Like for me, it is again a split vision. I never think when I go up to a person for the film ...now I am using erotic...but in my other vision, I know I am. If you just practice eroticism as a thing like dance just when we two meet, there is a danger that it will get kinky weird. I want to ask you to start with an aware will to use eroticism in your daily life as a focus...without telling anyone you are doing it. And observe what it does. In general it will make everything easier and more fun. Of course, this is hype, but it is also true.

Also focus on it when you are alone. It will turn you on. Feel your body, feel your humor, feel your giggling. I want to now describe the process. In the beginning, there was politeness...safe but unsatisfying, intellectual...but behind that was attraction, curiosity, wanting to play. Then there was...we want to play. Saying that was a risk. But it opened up pushing back limits...which in itself is an erotic turn-on. But between that time of stating the desire of play and actually physically playing there is usually a tension. And whenever a new limit is being crossed, it seems forced, unnatural...at the same time there is a release which leads to comfortableness. This is what stops most people from getting to the comfort. This is why there needs to be a committed discipline like studying dancing or judo to get beyond the being uncomfortable by freedom. Sexy is something that somebody projects from within. It has almost nothing to do with the body type...what someone looks like. It is rather a nonverbal, nonvisual signal to others that you are ready and willing to get involved on some level with them. It is a nonrational quality that it is advertising. So people who do not have the quality and would not naturally project sexy can learn how to project it. The sexy signal attracts and excites and turns on people...including yourself. But the willingness to get involved with people is what satisfies and maintains. Sexy can be, should be used in all communications.

Just you and I are needed to create the magic that will slow the dragon. But others can add power to this magic. I am the director, I like to direct, I like women, I like to be turned on, I like to scream and be a spoiled bastard...I hope I have not forgotten any bad things...all the rumors about me are true...if all of these things are ok, stay. If not, go. If they become not ok during the piece, leave. But don't interrupt or interfere with the piece. I may be lying. I am saying these things to save time. Time is a vital element of this magic. The longer the time that we are in the piece, the greater the magic. Don't tell anyone about anything that went on in this piece, except if you add that you may be lying.

I will use bits and pieces which I will channel, not knowing why, not knowing how an individual bit fits into the whole. So I can not explain them. In some of these bits I will use some of you, using who you are, sometimes sending you to places outside of the cave of the studio. Some bits only you and I can do alone. Nobody will see all of the parts. But in the end, there will be a whole. I will not use violence to create this magic. You will not be hurt.

We are putting an arrow in the dragon; we are tripping up the plot which has been trapping us for so long. One obvious way is the piece will change us who are involved, changing our lives and relationships... and that change, no matter how small, will cause a chain reaction in the outside world.

But there is another way that what we will do here will effect and affect the outside world. Science has just come up with a theory which explains why one group of a species in another part of the world, with no physical or material contact with the first group, pick up the change. In the past, it would have been called magical. But what some scientists are now saying is that in DNA there is what amounts to a broadcasting unit which both sends out and receives data to and from every member of that certain life form...and perhaps to other life forms and maybe even to unliving material as well. It also has been long known that the observer effects what he observes.

The core of this piece is you and I will set a power erotic wave with each other which will be transmitted on the DNA network. It does not matter if you believe this. But the bits...or rather one of the bits...which I will have people other than you and I do, will create an open channel for our broadcast. So what the other people do in the piece is very important. Now I am talking to everyone else except you. If you feel threatened and want to leave, do so. Don't argue, or judge. Don't try to protect other people in the piece. If you do leave, I am counting on you to honor your commitment to not tell anyone anything about this piece without stating that you may be lying.

Back to the plot which we are fighting against today. If we had freedom to touch each other erotically without limits, without romance, they could not control us, they could not have power over us. They know this. If we know we can do anything we want...that we don't have to wait for enough money before doing what we want...that it ain't true that we have to have talent to do things that we do...then their power over us would vanish. That is why they make commercials promoting ideals and images that you can not fit unless you use their product. "It's so easy to get their attention...it's so easy to lose it...use Head and Shoulders." That is why they keep changing fashions. That is why they say wait for Mr. Right. That is why they say art takes talent and skill...which most people don't have, and say those who are blessed with it must refine it before using it...why they say films must have a certain technical quality before people will see them...why they say don't touch your cock in public, don't stare, don't ask, don't need, don't rub. The people who are on the top and the people who have accepted that they cannot do what they want, have ganged up to preserve this plot of snobs, experts, and morality. It is easy to see why those who are in power want to keep the plot going. But why the schmucks who spend their whole lives not doing what they want, thinking they aren't good enough...why do they want the plot to keep going? Imagine someone like this seeing someone who...like me...is not as smart, skilled, good-looking as they are...so dumb that he don't know that the plot of everything is hard...bumbling through life doing what he wants, making movies and art...playing with sexy girls...all easy. They want to kill him because he, as a symbol, says they could have done what they wanted all along.

The Pipes Of Art

Originally published in 1995 in *The Cherotic (r)Evolutionary* within Frank Moore's column "Frankly Speaking".

Have you noticed there is a plague in all walks of modern life of people forgetting their function as servers? We editors tend to take our position much too seriously (or not seriously enough). One editor of a literary magazine actually charges writers a dollar a poem ($3 a short story) for the "privilege" of having her read their stuff...and they don't get a comp copy if she publishes their work! Then there are editors who come unglued if another zine prints, without giving him "credit", a poem that he had first published...as if he shares ownership rights with the poet...maybe he has forgotten that he had neither hired the poet to write it nor bought it from the poet...he had just published it. Then there are the editors who must think that when a poet sends her work to them, she is asking them for their god-like judgments!

I realize that I and this zine are just middlemen, just a pipe. When the art goes through the pipe, that is when the pipe is important...not before or after. I also realize that, except for when deciding what gets into this zine, my not liking something don't mean shit! (Again, I should say I get way more great art than we can publish.)

I'm honored to be able to be exposed to all of the art!

Point of Responsibility

Excerpted from Frank Moore's *Cherotic Magic*.

Matter is symbol, is metaphor containing possibilities. These packets shape matter. These packets, in turn, are reshaped by each body or object they pass through. This is why we are affected by the stars, for example, (and the stars are affected by us)...and why we affect the Tarot cards or the I-Ching coins we cast...why the physicists affect the subatomic particles they observe. This is the alchemical secret: by reshaping these inner packets, the material reality is reshaped.

These inner rivers of possibilities are two-way on the linear level. This means the magical effects are always two-way. The light of the sun warms us; but we affect the sun through the same channel. Again, we have entered the level of the dynamic web of relationships in which the individual does not exist. In place of the individual, there appear points of personal responsibility in a dance. It is not the sun that warms, nor is it us who are warmed. It is the dance of no dancers, the dance of relationships that warms, and that is warmed. Individualism hides this fundamental truth from most people.

These rivers of inner possibilities do not run only in a two-way linear manner. They also travel nonlinearly. This creates a deep ocean under time-space. In this ocean, there are nonlinear waves of possibility which pass through the points of personal responsibility which most people mistakenly see as individuality. When a wave passes through this, it is possible to personally amplify, mute, or change the wave. This makes the point of personal responsibility the moment of the universal creation. To accept this responsibility of the universal creation, we cannot step back from the ocean to claim the responsibility or judge.

We are then just water drops...individual water drops, not the ocean. To be in the moment of universal creation, in being the point of personal responsibility, we need to melt into being the ocean for all time, letting the dance happen through us, not thinking we are the dancers. In this point of personal responsibility, everything we do, think, and say is universally important, and not in the individually important sense.

Each center of the body is connected to many of the rivers of possibility. The nonlinear flow of the packets of possibilities within these rivers is chero. By transforming, transmuting, the packets of possibilities, it is actually possible to change matter, to change the material world. This alchemical fact is just the opening for the more important fact that reality is created, recreated every second by and within us.

We have said reality creation is a dance and that we are the dancers. But in truth, it is a dance without dancers. If we really take on personal responsibility for the dance, we surrender to the dance, give up individual "control", give up individual linking with the results. By taking on the personal responsibility for the dance, we are the dance. We melt with the dance. We are only the dance. We admit these facts. It is not a question of becoming, but of remembering and admitting. It is a question of being, living, dancing lustfully, without controls or limits in responsibility. In the apprenticeship, this quality is called "extensic". The extensic life dance is beyond morals or limits. It joyfully digs into the dance to the juicy black core.

We have talked about the principle of inter-penetration, the spiritual fact that the universal existence is enclosed in everyone and in everything.

To start to grasp this, we have to remember that the cherotic rivers flowing within matter run in a great many directions, both linearly and nonlinearly, both inward and outward. This is the web dance. The cherotic packets of possibilities, effectively changed within the person, are taken by these rivers throughout the entire web, affecting the entire web.

So you are never hopeless or without effect. You can always shift reality away from doubts, fears, and other mistaken creations. You can always transform, transmute yourself, situations and the universal currents into joyful dancing by extensic melting, which is the heart secret of using erour.

Kinds of transmuting and transforming of situations and of self is the real purpose of alchemical art. You are not the source of effect, the dance of the web is. You melt forever with the dance within personal responsibility. The effect is caused by the everlasting interplay, inner dance, of the whole web of all possibilities with one another, creating seven dimension waves. You must enjoy the dance for its own sake, not some goal as an end. There is no end to the dance. Since the dance is everlasting, the holding-on to any guilt, any doubt, any fear is just creating these things in the whole web, for which you are personally responsible. If you let go of these limited frames, your personal responsibility for them will vanish; moreover, their reality force will fade to a certain degree in the web.

When you admit you are melted into the dance, that you are the dance, and that every act and nonact, no matter how "small", is profound, then reality shifts. The focus shifts from what you do, what you appear to be like, what effect you are having...shifts to enjoying extensically life, claiming any and all responsible act or thought as your own no matter who does it.

Matter is a symbol containing within it packets of possibilities. Chero is the possibilities. The human body-personality is a symbolic system containing possibilities. It is a symbol containing chero flowing nonlinearly through it, breathing through it. The human body-personality is a point of creative multi-universal responsibility because it contains self-awareness. The "self" in this self-awareness is not the individual ego, but the self of the web of ultimate reality of all possibilities. This self-awareness is only beginning to evolve out from the web. This means the on-going act of multi-universal creation has just started. This creation depends on the self-awareness which is flowing through each one of us.

Modern physics tells us that our universe is sitting on the razor's edge between existence and non-existence, leaning slightly on the side of existence. The self-awareness is the slight edge of existence. It is creating existence. This creating is radiating both linearly and nonlinearly from the point of responsibility which is contained within each of us.

Our point of entry into this on-going dance of magical creation is our body-personality in everyday living, everyday relating.

We think our body is contained, enclosed, limited within our skin. In reality, the skin is not the borderline marking the difference between inside and outside, marking off what the individual (or any other object) is. As we have seen, there is an energy field of thoughts, emotions, and other psychic material. This field usually comes out a quarter of an inch from the skin. This field is as much a part of the body as anything within the skin. The skin is the eighth center of the body, the center of relating, of touch, of melting. It is the center which connects the first and the seventh centers together, creating a circle out of the horizontal linear order.

The skin is not a fence of individualistic ego. Instead, it is the connecting organ of the body, our body. This body does not end at the skin. This body, our body, extends both outward and inward throughout the multi-dimensional, multi-universal existence which is being created by self-awareness. What we normally think of as our body is in reality only a small part of our body. It is only a symbol of personal responsibility which lives within us creating. We are now entering the secret of inter-penetration.

When we look at our body within the physical world, we can easily become aware of physical trails. At least they at first appear to be trails we leave just as the snail leaves a shining trail as it travels along the sidewalk. After we begin to recognize the existence of such trails, we begin to quickly see more and more of these trails. Body smells, dead skin falling or rubbing off the body, fingerprints, sweat, shit and piss are just some of the most obvious of these trails. There are many hundreds of these trails, mostly unknown to modern man. Each of these trails has volumes of information and possibilities about us and about our connection to the web of existence. In fact, each of our trails contains us. The scientist can clone a body copy from a single cell. A cat can read the emotional state of another animal by the smell of the piss left hours before. Everything leaves these traces of its existence in the reality. Our homes are filled with these traces of ours, which is why our homes have feelings of us, smells of us.

These trails are really meltings between our body and rest of the web of ultimate reality. These meltings are the breathing of chero, the blood veins of chero running both linearly and nonlinearly throughout the entire reality web. This implies that the whole web of ultimate reality is one living organism which extends beyond time and space. What is usually thought of as the individual's ego/personality/being is a connection in relationships of responsibility, of creation, and of change.

When reality is seen in this way, what looked like trails of individuals left behind within space and time become channels of cherotic breath and cherotic blood of possibilities. These channels are physical, although not necessarily material. We have just listed some of the more obvious material trails. But thoughts are physical trails too. These thought trails, these melting webbings, are made of many, many different kinds of conducting materials, such as chemical, electrical, vibrational, and many materials that we have not yet either discovered or connected to thought. Thought is focused in the sixth body center, that of wisdom.

Post Porn, Post Sex, A New Art Movement

The Harmony Theater on a side street in the village is usually the venue for strippers. But for four nights in June it was the site of an expression of a new art movement, an art movement that is being born and will probably take several years (if not a decade or two) to break through the gloomy pessimistic view of the performance world of the last fifteen years. This talk about a new art movement would seem dangerous and pretentious in a review about a "sexually" explicit show. But it is not this reviewer who puts the show into this lofty context. It is the artist and her peers. As we leafed through the program before the show, we came across a manifesto. Manifestos are often signs of artists who are taking themselves too seriously, who are choking on their own self-importance (imagined). So it is a bad sign, a sign of a boring evening ahead if the artist hands you a manifesto before you see the work.

But this manifesto is different. It talks about an art movement which "celebrates sex as the nourishing, life-giving force" which these artists use, in the self-empowering "attitude of sex-positivism" to "communicate our ideas and emotions...to have fun, heal the world and endure." This is a declaration of war on the censoring forces of anti-art, anti-human, anti-sex, anti-fun, anti-love, and truly anti-life forces of darkness in power in the world today. This document was signed by some of the leading artists who use sex in their work. But this movement needs a better name. These artists call themselves Post Porn Modernists. This is very limiting because it links them not only to dying deadening porn, but to the glum post modern art movement, setting themselves up to be just a reaction, just the limb of a dead tree. They need a name like Living Pleasure Artists.

This is also my main criticism of the show itself. It was called Annie Sprinkle--Post Porn Modernist. The work was more than that because Annie is more than that. The stage set was Annie's bedroom, Annie's world. But Annie's bedroom world is not limited to the stage, not to a private bedroom, not to a private booth with a one way window in a XXX theatre. This is because Annie has been expanding out of the massage parlor strip joint, porn screen into the worlds of art and spirit. So the bedroom we see on stage keeps changing, pulling us in, including us.

We never are sure what we are experiencing--a play, a one-woman sex show, a performance with audience-participation, a monologue, a magic tantric ritual. This not being sure created an electric reality which wrapped us into Annie...deep inside Annie Sprinkle.

When we first see Annie, she is like a corporate yuppie explaining to us with the help of charts, graphs, and slides why the sex business was a great career move for our young Annie. This seemed very similar to the whitewash rationale of the porn business.

But just as we were about to dismiss Annie, it became clear that this was not just a self-justifying monologue about the inner world of a sex star written by some male ghost-writer. It was much more than this. It was billed as a one-woman show. For anyone who has followed Annie's career (and for those who have not, the biographic thread in this piece provided the needed background), the show was the logical next step. She is someone whose spirit has reached out of sleazy hard-core flicks to inspire by humor and human warmth. She is someone who has teamed up with Veronica Vera, sister sexual evolutionary and author of the manifesto, to claim control over their sex art by publishing their explicit magazines, and selling bottles of their own piss by mail. Annie's "innocence" has a wide streak of clever business sense. She went on to become a writer and a photographer, as well as directing an erotic video. Over the last six years, she segued herself into the performance art world to the point that she is the subject of much serious critical discussion. This piece encapsulates this. Many sections have been performed before as individual pieces. Done separately, they have been cute, daring, but lack a certain depth of magical insight. But in this production, Annie weaves these pieces with new creations into a nonlinear magic carpet that breaks through the merely shocking, merely vulgar, merely taboo-breaking, into the cosmic realm of personal touch where by laughing, crying, being turned on, we become channels for new alternatives.

So we are sitting in this strip joint, watching this explicit show. But it will not stay on stage. Annie will not stay just a sex object. She is a sex object. Everyone is...at least everyone who is healthy and happy. But Annie is not just a sex object. She uses her sex, her porn/hooker/sex background to make the people in the audience see they are sex objects, but not just sex objects. Annie can do this because she does not deny, hide or underestimate the sex/porn/tacky/child aspect of her soul as so many do. She may, in the future, be seduced away from this, her power. But in this performance, she exploited this erotic power.

It was billed as a one-woman show. This was not true. The audience was her leading man/woman. She talked to us, involved us, enveloped us. The play vanished, and an experience took over. She had us doing tantric breathing and exercising our inner genital muscles. It felt silly and tacky and dumb, as Annie appeared to be. Dumbly innocent and pure. But as shamans will tell you, magic is dumb, tacky, silly, innocent and pure. Annie, at different points, invited the audience onto the stage to play with her universal tits, peer into her deeply to glimpse her pink clam cervix. She was always talking to us, responding to us, making love to us, pulling us into an enveloping reality that kept getting deeper and wider...first the porn reality, expanding into Annie's reality, and finally into the liquid world of melting forms of tantric magic.

The play melted away. Annie became more than herself, more than her Sprinkle identity. She was talking about her reality, about herself, but not just talking about herself. By transforming herself into a symbol of what we all could be, she was offering a working alternative to the workings of the normal world. This melting away of the play expanded the performance into an all-enveloping environmental experience, a magical ritual. I do not think Sprinkle is aware of the full range of her work. She is guided by feelings, by spirits and the muses. She may be tempted to polish up her act, to package it, to stick to the rehearsed script. If she falls into this temptation, she will lose the power of the soft magic that comes through her body and personality. Then she would be just another clever woman performer. What made the piece and Annie special were in the little things...the way she stayed in full view talking to us as she changed clothes...her giggling because the douche water kept leaking out of her long after that scene had ended...the love of people that bubbled out of her very being.

Photos flashed on the screen, before and after photos, first of Annie. This slide show revealed that Annie Sprinkle is a self-creation of a shy, awkward, fat, Jewish girl named Ellen from nowhere, U.S.A. Annie has and is everything that Ellen dreamed of. But Sprinkle never stops at biographic monologues, which are self-indulgent. Her slideshow quickly included before and after pictures of very average women who transformed right before our eyes into different people, into sex goddesses. Some were professional strippers and sex queens. But a lot of them were housewives, nurses, artists whom Annie and Vera transformed into their secret, hidden selves. The clear message is that this self-creation, self-transformation, is possible for anyone...and not just for sex goddesses.

Still a nagging feeling remained. All of this was too neat, too nice, just so many rationalizations of a porno victim who denies all the pain and hurt. This feeling floated around through her cute bosom ballet...and through the outrageous, taboo-breaking, jack-off scene reading the bible. The floating, nagging feeling was the lack of deep human emotion, the lack shared by porn, new age spiritualists, and hard-core feminists. But Annie took aim on this feeling. She said most of her experiences in the sex business have been good...but...then she took us on a nightmarish journey through all the sweaty spermy dirty hurt, sucking rubber cocks faster faster deeper deeper in factories with bodiless angry male voices screaming at her about pain, about cunts and bitches, making her into an object, not a sex object, no sex in this nightmare, just sucking until gagging, puking, screaming, body shaking. We then knew Annie Sprinkle is a great actor, both physically and emotionally, to channel this vision.

Then we watched Annie quietly transmute all of this negativity into personal strength, into a human wisdom, all within her body. She grows, expands, becoming a shaman. She is now ready to perform the final ritual. Her body has become the temple, the universe. By turning her body on into a holy orgasm, Annie by means of pleasure, pushed the world a little back on the track. Suddenly, we were in the primal cave, the sex temple, with our dead friends, many dead of AIDS, watching something sacred. As her orgasm rose, her magical presence expanded to embrace everyone in the theatre. I then knew I was experiencing one of the best performances. Annie believes that sex heals cosmically and personally, physically and emotionally. I left the Harmony warm and satisfied and happy.

What does Annie do for an encore? She invited members of the audience to pose for a Polaroid with Annie's tits on their head...at five bucks a shot. Every shaman knows that you should not leave people out in the ozone.

I end this with a word about language. I have said I do not think Annie has a full understanding of what she is working with. The problem is language. We say Annie works with sex and has an orgasm. But the orgasm we are talking about could have been centered in the liver rather than the genitals, could have lasted for over an hour. It was for healing, or magic, or even other reasons. All of which is not what the normal person means when she says sex and orgasm. It confuses and limits using those terms. There may be many different states, many different forms of physical energies, waiting to be discovered, but which are being masked under mislabels of "sex" and "orgasms".

Platform For Frank Moore's Presidency 2008 *I GET RESULTS!*

I'll do away with welfare and social security. Instead, every American will receive a minimum income of $1,000 a month. This amount will be tied to the cost of living and will not be taxable.

We will have universal prenatal-to-the-grave health care and universal free education with equal access.

I'll do away with all tax deductions for over $12,000 income. Instead, there will be a flat tax of 10% on annual income of less than one million dollars for an individual and less than five million dollars for a corporation. But the flat tax will jump to 75% on annual income exceeding these limits.

I'll cut the military budget by at least half.

Public mass transit will be free, 24/7, and reliable.

All patents and copyrights will expire in 20 years. Inventions, products, etc. which are developed with governmental money and/or public institutions can not be patented.

All businesses selling their products in the U.S. will have to certify that their products were manufactured in accordance with this country's labor, wage, environmental, and safety laws...that they meet or exceed these...no matter where they were produced.

Each city and each "media market" will have at least two public access channels on radio, broadcast television, cable, AND satellite!

Election day will be a paid holiday.

I will push for complete public funding for all political campaigns and the banning of political contributions and the use of personal wealth in political campaigns.

The President should have a line veto. But the Congress can overturn this line veto by a simple majority. Also, bills should be limited to 5 pages in length and/or limited to one subject.

An individual taxpayer will be able to direct her taxes to what functions she wants to support. But corporate taxpayers should not have this option.

Every corporation should come up for a renewal every 25 years, at which time it must prove that it has been operating in the public interest. If it fails to do this, it loses its right to exist. Corporations that have existed before this policy will have 10 years before they will have to prove they are worthy.

Government should leave marriage to churches. Instead, any two or more adults who have been living together for at least 2 years should be able to register as a "family".

* * *

The end of hunger, poverty, and discrimination in this nation will be my main focus domestically. This will also shape my foreign policy.

The minimum income and the minimum/livable wage, linked to the cost of living, will rise every time the congress members vote themselves a pay raise…will rise by the same percentage of their raise.

Education should be federally funded, based on the number of students, adjusted to special needs of each student, in each school district. But schools should be locally controlled. The equal access of education for every student will be insured by the federal government.

I will call for a major rebuilding of America. We will repair our school buildings and will build needed new schools. I will encourage a society of small villages connected by mass transit. Within these small villages, people could walk or bike to work, to school, to shopping, to entertainment, etc. Mass transit will combine these small villages within 15 miles radius into dynamic communities. Living in these villages will end gridlock traffic, will cut greenhouse gasses, will cut stress and isolation. Housing for all incomes will be included equally in each village.

We will encourage electric cars, fast trains, clean sustainable decentralized energy generators. I would shut down all nuclear generators.

I will destroy 10 percent of our nuclear weapons each year to reverse the nuclear arms race.

We will stop giving/selling arms to other countries. All private arms sales should be illegal.

Now my policies are pro-business. The universal education system will provide business with a superior, flexible work force. The minimum income and the universal health care will remove the business's burden of providing health insurance and pensions to workers. In reality, this relief will be much more than any tax cut could give. Moreover, the minimum income will make the starting and maintaining a small business much easier. This is also true for small family farms. The minimum income will encourage independent invention and artistic pursuit, on which true progress depends.

* * *

The primary function of the government should be the protection of the health, the civil and human rights, the freedoms, and the general welfare of the people...instead of the protection and the promotion of corporate profits and interests. The government should exist to serve the people, and not to make a profit on the services to the people. My administration will be governed by these basic principles.

I will bring the troops home from Iraq immediately. Moreover, I will change this country's self-image from that of THE SUPER POWER/ WORLD LEADER to that of a member of the global community.

Prisons should be only for violent or otherwise dangerous criminals. Prisons should be a part of the health and educational system and should include drug rehab programs. This should also be true for the new creative in-community programs for non-violent criminals for paying-back, rehab, and education sentencing. These programs will be more effective and much less expensive and harmful to the community on every level than the current human warehouse system. Flexibility of sentencing should be returned to judges. I will ban the death penalty.

The use of drugs should be legalized and taxed. Pot and spirits should be sold over the counter to adults only. Tobacco and other addictive drugs should be sold by prescription only. Free drug rehab programs should be readily available.

All of the opt-out schemes should be illegal. If a corporation wants to sell your information, it first should directly and clearly get your permission. Before this happens, all such information is a part of your privacy, not the property of a corporation.

The selling/buying of debt should be illegal. Moreover, there should be a maximum interest rate of 10 percent on the original principle over the lifetime of a loan.

I will forgive the loans to the so-called third-world countries over the original principle.

We will use half of the money we will save by cutting the military budget to pay down the national debt. I will reduce the pollution caused by obscene corporate profits.

I will also reduce the federal government while raising services to the people by getting rid of welfare, social security, the so-called war on drugs, etc., and by the cuts in the military, the I.R.S., prisons, etc.

THIS PLATFORM OF MINE GIVES YOU AN OUTLINE OF WHAT WE WILL DO TOGETHER, OF WHAT I SEE THIS COUNTRY AND THE WORLD BECOMING...IT IS DEFINITELY POSSIBLE, IF WE ARE WILLING. YEP, IT IS RADICAL. BUT IT JUST MAKES SENSE! DOESN'T IT?

-- Frank Moore

Reclaiming Public Reality

1997 version. Originally published in *The Cherotic (r)Evolutionary* issue # 1 as "Nonlinear Bits" in 1996.

We went to the movies...Pasolini's Arabian Nights at Berkeley's alternative theatre. Eating candy, drinking Coke, rubbing each other, pleasure maintained almost until the end of the movie, then quiet coming, thrilling gentle pleasure explosions. Just an ordinary night at the movies. Rubbing for enjoyment, just like eating popcorn. Taking public reality back into personal reality is the magical effect of such public acts, which are made invisible to the surrounding reality by the personal everyday nature of such acts, instead of being reactive confrontations. The reason closest to the surface for such acts in public places is the physical expression of enjoying of friends and lovers and humans just being together. But these invisible private/public acts of pleasure become a powerful force for effective political/social/cultural change when they collide on their own with life-denials. The effectiveness of such personal pleasure acts, which are in reality sexual or cherotic magic, is in the fact that they are not reactive, confrontational, or an exhibition of specialness or difference. Not wrapping ourselves in the glamour of being kinky, perverted, or evil and thereby falsely creating ourselves into an elite above the common human. Being reactionary always chains you to the old reality to which you are reacting.

Instead, these acts of personal magic are creating the alternative reality which we want, reclaiming freedom by acting free, calling forth yin energy by using yin energy. The fact that the feminist movement in the '70s and '80s on the whole didn't use this channel of change created limits to the transformation of gender.

This is reclaiming public reality, returning it to personal freedom. We have done these rubbing good feeling acts of humanness and subversion at baseball games, in the middle of the sidewalk in the afternoon, on trains and planes. For months, five of us sat in the middle of a coffeehouse, playing cards, drinking coffee, kissing, rubbing one another into a pleasure trance. Just everyday human living.

Because our attitude to our playing is that it is just everyday human living, we were invisible. No one saw, noticed, or complained. Because the art of invisibility is tricky, I am stopping short of advocating such radical acts unless you are prepared for any outcome. Such invisible action does not have to be at this degree of revolutionary intensity to be effective. Every time you kiss or hug or laugh or smile out in the "public" world, every time you wear colorful sexy revealing clothes, or do not wear a bra (or just wearing one), or any lusty joyful act, you are performing a very powerful magical/political action the effects of which can not be deleted by any linear means.

The Rehearsal

The idea I have could be called **the rehearsal**. You would play an uptight actress who for some reason agreed to be in a piece that is over her head, beyond her limits. This is the first rehearsal. The piece starts with her doing the piece with my character...so the audience thinks we are just doing a piece. But then she pulls out of her character, hitting a block. She starts questioning my motives as the director [revealing I'm the director]..."Oh, this is just a trick for you to get fucked!"..."I can portray INTIMACY without taking my clothes off!" But she psychically knows what I'm saying. So you will do both of our parts of our dialog. At some point she goes back into the ritual...until she reaches another block, then the dialog continues... But it gets deeper, more expansive, more personal each time.

That is the structure of the piece. And below is the physical backbone ritual.

A DANCE RITUAL

1/26/03

Lower the lights.

Squat in the center of the room, holding yourself very tightly, rocking, fully dressed, maintaining boundaries, making whatever sounds, all tight, all "self-contained".

When you are ready...it doesn't matter how long this takes...let yourself expand into the room, while still squatting and rocking. Relax.

Let yourself expand into me when you are ready...it doesn't matter how long this takes...and take me into you when you are ready...it doesn't matter how long this takes...all the while squatting and rocking.

When you are ready, move around the room, making deep sounds within a relaxed freedom. Slowly remove your clothes... when you are ready...it doesn't matter how long this takes. Let yourself expand outside of the studio, taking everything into you.

When you are ready...it doesn't matter how long this takes...dance with me, drawing everything in the room into the rapture state of our combined being, making deep sounds within a relaxed freedom.

When you are ready...it doesn't matter how long this takes...sit on me and rock/rub our combined being into a rapture state, making deep sounds within a relaxed freedom. Remain in this state.

Audrey Rubinstein Interview

A very short version of this interview titled, "We Misfits Are Still Needed": A Performance Conversation with Frank Moore, was published in *Adobe Airstream Magazine* in October 2013.

Audrey: Dear Frank, I wanted to speak to you in person, but that will have to wait until I am in Berkeley or you are in Santa Fe. Thank you for agreeing to be interviewed. I admire you and would like the opportunity to understand your performance work in greater depth.

Can you describe the type of performances you are creating now? Has your performance changed/evolved over the years?

Are there any projects that you've not yet realized that you are burning to create?

Frank: Ah, "Where is your work heading? What do you want to do next?" It is not my work. It is not my choice. For me, it is not a question of a next thing. It is a growing, evolving vision. I am carried along in this vision. A performance does not have a beginning or an end. It is just a tiny bit of the vision. The vision braids around itself, flowing on. I do not know where the vision is taking me. I have not been down this vision before. I just follow wherever the art and the magic lead. I could not have planned anywhere near as rich a life that following has opened up. I never know what will trigger what, what will bloom into years long projects, etc. I just jam, play, and enjoy!

In a way what I do in my monthly performance series today is close to what I did in my first performance workshop in Santa Fe in the early seventies.

I used my communal family of four as a core to start a weekly drop-in workshop held in my friend's Santa Fe pre-school. I never knew who would show up each week. People from my street performances, free-spirits who heard rumors about this naked happening, a Wait Until Dark cast of straight actors whose director required them to come, all were thrown into this crazy experiment. I never knew what I was going to do because I never knew who I would have to work with, or what I would have to deal with. This madhouse gave me a flexibility and a trust that the vision would guide me to create a temporary communal reality from those who were there. But the casual drop-in format placed a limit on how deep the intimacy could get. In my communal family, we were creating a way of being which was an underground base for the art. This base was a powerful influence. But it wasn't yet the clear focus of the work.

In May 1973, the end of this stage was a twenty-four hour performance. I became aware of the magical quality of extended time lengths when I attended an all-night peyote ceremony of the Native American church in Taos. [They dug a hole in the ground in the teepee for me to sit in.] Time was as powerful as the magic medicine in creating a group reality trance. To try this time factor, I took my cast to Albuquerque to do what amounted to a 24-hour performance. For the first six hours, we approached people on the campus of the University of New Mexico, people with whom we would like to play, inviting them to an audition that night in the College Art Department for a happening. Then, after dinner, we did the workshop exercises with the 12 people who showed up. Slowly taboos were broken, a community of performance magically appeared... which was lucky because I could only book the room until midnight. Then I had to truck the performance across the city to the University of Albuquerque. The sense of community was strong enough that everyone came along. At dawn, as we stepped out of the studio, there was the crisp feeling of being born into a new world. In the late seventies I was doing forty-eight hour performances!

But more about Santa Fe later. What I do in today's series and what I did in that first workshop look very similar because they are! But the performance is always changing. Sometimes the change is when I see that something has stopped working. Like by the nineties I had developed a loosely scripted ritual. But the audience started to know what will happen, started coming for a social [pickup] shallow scene. There was no magic, risk, push!! So I had to stop using any script and do a totally improv ritual!

I became sucked into performance not to tell stories, not to paint pictures for others to look at, not even to reveal something about myself or about the state of things, and certainly not for fame or fortune. It was simply the best way that I saw to create the intimate community which I as a person needed and that I thought society needed as an alternative to the personal isolation....

I have always wanted to bring dreams into reality.

I was lucky. I was never under pressure to be good at anything, to make money, to make it in "the real world", to be polished – and the other distractions that other modern artists have to, or think they have to, deal with. So I could focus on having fun, on going into taboo areas where magical change can be evoked. I couldn't do anything THE RIGHT ["NORMAL"] WAY. But I always have been so dumb that I didn't realize I couldn't do whatever I was pulled to do. So I just figured out how I could do things MY WAY! So I have done pretty much every kind of art in every kind of role in almost every kind of venue. And I took it for granted because I thought it was easy and I always had fun! So it's hard to say what my art is!

There are all kinds of art. There is art that calms, art that pacifies, art that sells, art that decorates, art that entertains. But what I am committed to is art as a battle, an underground war against fragmentation. The battle is on all realities. The controllers have always tried to fragment us. Fragment us from each other. Imprison us in islands of sex, color, religion, politics, classes, labels, etc., etc., etc., etc., etc. -- they fragment our inner worlds, they blow our individual realities apart, and play the pieces against one another. They are us, or a part of us. They are the controllers, the politicians, the sexists, the women's libbers, the pornographers, the censors, the moralists, the church, the media, the businessmen, educators, the victims and the powerful.

They are us. They have divided us from our power, from our beauty, from our lust for life and pleasure. They have divided us from most of reality -- divided dying from living -- sex from living, sex from pleasure. We are kept in boxes of fear, of mistrust. We are kept waiting -- kept waiting to do what we want -- waiting for enough money, enough schooling, for everything to be right. We are kept waiting and protecting and hiding and suffering.

This is the time to do battle with the boxes.

As artists, our tools are magic, our bodies, taboos, and dreams.

This kind of art can be bubbles of childhood -- hidden places where you can play and explore -- it is the kids' under-the-covers world, the playhouse, the treehouse, the cave, behind the barn, playing doctor, cars at drive-ins before going all the way, Huck Finn's raft, tepees. People are afraid of this area of lusty exploring that they think they have out-grown -- but they are sucked into it.

But this kind of art can have a more heavy-duty magical side to it that shocks, offends, and breaks new ground. This side is what is locked in, the subconscious, the womb, the underground, hell/heaven, pleasure/torture, the coffin, the grave, birth/death/rebirth, dream/nightmare, the hidden world of taboos.

249

Artists of this breed need to be warriors who are willing to go into the areas of taboo, willing to push beyond where it is comfortable and safe to explore and build a larger zone of safeness. They need to be idealists, willing to live ideals.

Truth is we here always have several projects going at one time and more are popping up all the time. A lot of them turn out to be multi-year projects requiring major work which radically change our life. For example, in the nineties I was publishing an underground zine THE CHEROTIC [r]EVOLUTIONARY, which had become a well respected venue for all kinds of artists over three years. Then I [who can't talk] got a regular radio talk show on one of the first internet stations. Well, we quickly started our own online radio station for various reasons [I exposed things about the other station]. LOVE UNDERGROUND VISIONARY REVOLUTION [LUVeR] quickly bloomed into a 24/7 community with shows from people around the world. So I had to stop the zine so I could do LUVeR! I did not plan to do a radio station just like I had not planned to do a zine! I just follow! LUVeR lasted for almost fifteen years until the record industry forced me to shut down LUVeR last year! I still do my SHAMAN'S DEN show [which started streaming as live video very early on].

Audrey: I am curious about your childhood, where you grew up? What you dreamt about....

Frank: My first stroke of good luck was I was born spastic with cerebral palsy, unable to feed myself, walk or talk. Add to this good fortune the fact that my formative years were in the sixties -- my fate was assured!

During the first year, it became more and more obvious that things weren't "normal". The doctors told my parents that I had no intelligence, that I had no future, that I would be best put into an institution and be forgotten. This was a powerful expectation with all the force of western science and medicine as well as social influences, behind it. It would have been easy for my parents to be swept up into this expectation. Then that expectation would have created my reality. I would have long ago died without any other possibilities.

Instead, my parents rejected this expectation for the possibility they saw in my eyes, for what for them should have been true. This rejection of the cultural expectation of reality could not be a one-time choice. They had to passionately live their choice every day, every minute, or the cultural expectation would have sucked them and me into it. It fought them at every new possibility they opened to me. Their passionate commitment to how they thought things should be attracted people to me who kept opening new possibilities for me.

So I came out wanting to communicate with people any way I could… With my eyes at first! But soon with my noises, physical movements, laughing, etc. I just let people know I wanted to be with them, wanted to play with them, etc. This was a great training to be an actor! This was how I communicated until I learned to spell [I don't know when that was!].

Actually it was my mom, Connie, who insisted to ignore the doctors. Connie was the black sheep of a Mormon family in Utah who had married a non-Mormon guy who was in the air force. Grace, Dad's step mother…my grandma…supported my mother in keeping me, in treating me as a normal kid. I think they out-voted Dad! We lived in Dayton until I was 8 on the Air Force base. Granddad Frank and Grace lived in Mansfield…over 2 hours away. To give Mom breaks, they took me to their house for a week at a time.

I named my left hand "Mike" and my right hand "Ike". They have different personalities from each other, move differently, etc. Mike is a smooth dude, somewhat sneaky, but in control if non-linear. Ike is very emotional, prone to outbursts, jerky…and shy. They have always had issues with each other…always the soap operas. Kids live in realities like this. I thought people who talked/thought in terms of "handicap" just didn't see Mike and Ike…and the other body characters…didn't understand their inner/inter logics!

Because Dad was in the Air Force, we moved a lot, both around the country and to Morocco and Germany. Each time we moved, Mom had to battle to get me into school [either regular school or special schools which often said I was too severely handicapped for them to take]. So I grew up knowing doing battle/struggling was how to open new possibilities up! Sometimes the school took me, at least with Mom doing something like coming to feed me or taking me home in the afternoons to continue the lessons. Other times, the school refused to take me at all. So Mom had to teach me at home! All of this taught me that struggling with flexibility is a great life style. True, when I was home taught I felt isolated. But even in those times, I made friends and was in the Scouts and went to church and to the teen club just to be with kids!

We moved to Redlands outside of San Bernardino and I got into a special education program. It was in a wing of a grade school campus. There were two classes, one for grade school kids and one for junior high and high school kids like me. There I had a board with the alphabet divided into four lines. The other person would point to each line and I would nod when he got to the right line, etc., a slow process! [My family just said the alphabet.] The doctors dictated I should learn to type with my hand... The normal way to type! I, my teacher, and my therapists all thought it was the wrong direction. But back then doctors were gods. So three times a week they taped a peg in my hand, put me into a standing box [I am not sure how that's normal!], and for an hour I tried to get the peg through holes on a thick plastic key guard to an electric typewriter... Me sweaty, rubbing my wrist raw. In the year, I may have typed a few words! But I quickly had a practical idea. Put a pointer on a headband... My therapists and my teacher [women] wanted to try my idea. But the doctors [men] vetoed the idea. So for a year I was losing ground on my school work. They were getting ready to drop me from the school because I couldn't keep up. Meanwhile the news that next year the class would be moving onto the regular high school campus! Then we had a substitute teacher who tried my idea in art class, putting a brush on a headband. It worked! So my regular teacher ignored the doctors and rigged a pointer from tinker toys and an elastic band. It kept flipping down, hitting my nose. But within five minutes I was typing on an electric typewriter, without any key guard or any other special equipment. Everything then changed! So I started to paint and write at the same time! Btw, the first thing I wrote was a paper on a one world democratic socialist government! And the rest is history!

Talking to people through my board has intimate qualities. It slows people down, bringing them into a softer, smaller, more focused reality. It also reveals things about them through Freudian slips, etc. Through the years I have designed the board around the other person who is reading the board, rather than around me.

In high school, I started hanging out with the few leftist students on the campus. And I started writing a political column in the school paper for my journalism class. This started me on commenting on everything. Most people who read my column didn't know I was disabled, just a radical before being a radical was in fashion. I got shit for debating a G. I. who was in Vietnam. He responded to a column I wrote in the school paper. We went back and forth in the paper... People accused me of undermining his morale. I was sat down and told I was ruining the opportunity of the crips [my word for the disabled] who would come after me [it was the first mainstream special education class on a regular high school campus] by being a radical. They wanted to use me as their poster crip because of my high grades. I didn't buy it! I said I thought the goal was to procure the right to be fully human for crips [and for everybody else]... Including being political! So I continued doing what I was doing! I was interested in the big deep picture, not in being a disabled artist.

Funny, that was only a couple of years after I got them to try my idea for my head pointer for typing and talking. Now I was causing trouble with my writings! And writing for underground papers opened a lot up for me for years. After high school, during the summer before I went to junior college [which almost didn't take me because I drooled!], I had my brother drop me off at the head shop THE MIND VENDOR every Saturday. A lesbian couple ran the shop. They also put out an underground paper THE MIDDLE EYE which I quickly started writing for! When the cops shut down their shop, I started hanging out at their house. This included me in the small underground community in San Bernardino! This opened everything up for me! This community was made up of artists, musicians, poets and radicals of STUDENTS FOR A DEMOCRATIC SOCIETY, THE BLACK PANTHERS, and THE PEACE AND FREEDOM PARTY.

My personal roots are in the idealism of the '60s. That was when I broke out of personal physical isolation. I looked for a way to bring about the ideals for me and for society as a whole. The normal channels obviously would not work for me.

So all I had were my fantasies. I read novels like The Magus and Steppenwolf. I started wanting to create other alternative/altered realities just like the magicians in those novels. I read the Beat writers and the French Surrealists, Lenny Bruce and Mort Sahl and Abbie Hoffman, listened to Dylan, watched the hippie movement grow. I wished I could be a hip artist living in San Francisco instead of being stuck outside San Bernardino reading, listening, watching, waiting. All of this brewed inside of me. From my high school year days, I had been writing nonsense scripts dealing with nudity and nonsexual eroticism, always with roles for me to play! I read how-to books about directing, acting, film making, etc. I read such books as Toward a Poor Theatre and The Theatre and its Double. I read THE REALIST, published by the Yippie satirist Paul Krassner, who now is my good friend! I read about THE LIVING THEATER, Allan Kaprow, Anna Halprin, etc. Little did I know that I would in a few years meet in intimate ways most of my heroes, and that they would feel that what I was doing was the continuing of their work! When I was doing my OUTRAGEOUS BEAUTY REVUE in the late seventies, it turned out that a writer who was interviewing me was the writer who did the piece in PLAYBOY about THE LIVING THEATER which I read in the late sixties! I took this as a sign I was doing something right! I also read STRANGER IN A STRANGE LAND and wondered about the possibilities of group relationships.

[I do believe I just answered your question about who are my heroes!]

But I didn't think I could get people to let me direct them in the rituals in my head. It was not until 1970 that I started trying to live out my inner visions. I tried to get the ok at Cal State, San Bernardino, to produce my all-nude play on campus. To my surprise, the college said yes. But I couldn't get actors. [In the early eighties they had me do a performance there!]

I was offended by such things as body doubles for nude scenes in movies and actors in live plays wearing flesh-colored tights in lusty scenes. My play was a statement against this perverse attitude. I wasn't really into sex itself in my art. I just wanted to see nude bodies on stage -- not sneak them in to a love scene -- and see them do things like paint their bodies with baby food. I learned it can be hard to get people for weird things.

Also in college, I started doing political pranks. For an example, I had my friend Steve Emanuel [who I still do things with] push me into the Marines recruiting office on campus. I spelled out to the confused recruiter that I wanted to join [I was extremely serious!]. Finally the poor guy said I could not do what the Marines do. I replied I could push "the Button"!

Audrey: Tell me a little about your connection to Santa Fe.

Frank: During the time of the Kent State killings, I saw my life was heading back into isolation if I did not make some radical changes. I was about to get my degree. I knew that once that happened, I would be stuck at home without much contact with people. I had tried to move out several times before. But gravity pulled me back home every time! At the time several of my friends were living at what they thought was a hippie commune. So I was hanging out there on Saturdays. But then the actual owner returned to sell the property. So my friends had to move. But the owner saw things in me and I continued to visit her, showing her my poetry and oil paintings [I painted one for her called VANITY]. Louise Scott had been a Beat in the fifties and transitioned to hippie. I told her my tale of woe. And she said I could live with her and her two kids and move to Santa Fe with them after she sold her San Bernardino property. But I had tried to move out before. I figured I needed a lot of miles between me and home when I moved out again. So I dropped out of college and hitched to hippieland in Santa Fe to wait for Louise to come, which we thought would be in a week or two. It was two months! I stayed in a DIGGER style commune crash-pad THE CENTER which was in an abandoned shopping mall in town. At first I just crashed there, eating the two free meals served every day, getting a different person each day to help me [feed me, take me to the bathroom, push me to THE PLAZA, get me down to the floor mat to sleep, etc]. There were always people glad to do whatever I needed! So I found out I could live in raw life without any money, etc! I even visited quite a few of the communes in northern New Mexico, including THE HOG FARM, MORNING STAR and THE THEATER OF ALL POSSIBILITIES. When Louise and her kids finally arrived, we lived together communally with a few others. We never had much money... But what a fun life!

I was known as UNICORN then because of my head pointer. I wrote a column, UNICORN SPEAKS, in the underground paper. Basically I was hanging out with the artists, musicians, poets, hippies and political revolutionaries in cafes, bars, coffeehouses, etc., helping to plan both political and art events.

But in a year, I found this life too comfortable! So I hitchhiked to northern Massachusetts to a commune, the Brotherhood of the Spirit. There I danced with the communal rock band, Spirit in Flesh, having fun, hitching/touring the East Coast. I even danced on stage at Carnegie Hall and got written up [with a photo] in CREEM MAGAZINE! After that start, it was all downhill from there [just kidding]!

My first major performance began in that spiritual commune in which I lived. This commune was itself a liminal altered state in which 350 people went around doing their everyday duties, but talking about who they were in past lives, going into trances, channeling spirits and other things that I, skeptic, thought were weirdnesses better suited to cheap horror movies than to real life. But the people would not listen to me when I tried to tell them this spiritual business was spacing them out of this human life. But then one day, when I was typing, a spirit who later introduced himself as Reed, came through me, typing, "You are not typing this, Frank." At the beginning, I thought I made Reed up to get the people to listen, and to start creating my ideals in the world. But I may have been taking more credit than I deserved because Reed and two other spirits/characters/persons took on reality for themselves. People waited for the next "lecture" to come through. The spirits talked to people, guiding them (and me) to create a new personal community. Even when I left the spiritual commune, reading the new lectures for the people around me became performances aimed at them. People started seeing Reed and the others in their dreams. The question of whether Reed is "real" is not a useful question in shamanistic performance -- that is, performance for change. Reed is real whether he is a spirit floating around somewhere, or my alter-ego, or a conning fiction which I used as an invisible puppet. His reality is the change he created in the outer world.

Reed lasted for three years as an active performance. He as a performance contained the qualities which shape all my work. It was aimed at building a personal community which by its very existence threatens the established order of isolation and fragmentation. Its parts, the lectures, used the people around me to get to universal concerns. Reed was a framed process running parallel to, but braided with, my normal life.

So after a year at the BROTHERHOOD [during which I had gotten married], I moved back to New Mexico with Debbie my wife to build a personal community. In Albuquerque, because of my REED writings, SILVA MIND CONTROL [a new age outfit] wanted to back me to open a commune. So I, without any money, was driven around in a big RV by a couple of real estate agents showing me huge hotels, etc. for sale for a week! Talk about a surreal performance piece! But the deal exploded when I exposed shady practices of SILVA!

So I went back to college at New Mexico University. Debbie and I developed a relationship first with JoAnne and later with Ray. We four eventually moved in together as a tribal relationship and moved to Santa Fe again!

I was still looking for a way to work with people. I got into the Moving Image Lab at Anthropology Film Center on Upper Canyon road. It was a very intensive in-depth film making course which was nine to five every day for four months. I made films of rolling nude down a hill, smearing bodies with baby food, nursing by a sexy woman. But when the film course was over, I did not have money to make films. I could not see putting my energy into getting money to make films, could not see putting up with the compromises and outside control involved in an artistic context requiring big bucks. For me, the act of breaking a taboo is what is magical, what effects change...not someone seeing it in a film.

This not having money, this not wanting to be controlled and limited by money, was what sealed me into a performance life.

So I again started looking for a way to work with people. I wanted to see people nude, and touch them, and to create an intensity between us.

I had been painting oils for years, painting with a brush strapped to my forehead, painting nudes from magazine photos. One day, when I was selling newspapers in The Plaza as an excuse to talk to people, I told what turned out to be a rich woman I painted oils. She asked me to paint a nude of her. So Debbie set me and my paints up in the fancy living room as the woman undressed. On that day I realized how art can give people permission to do what normally is forbidden. It gives a frame that switches realities from the narrow normal reality to the freeing altered reality of controlled folly. If you go up to a stranger on the street and ask him to show his body to you, you will be lucky if he just walks away and does not hit you. But if you sincerely (and sincerity is a key) ask him to model for a painting or be in a video that involves nudity, there is a high chance he will do it because you are offering him a key to a new, different, and temporary reality.

So I sat on the center plaza, "selling newspapers". But selling papers was only a context. The context for me was an excuse for watching people, talking to people who had the slowness and the insightful curiosity to stop and talk...a way for me to ask them to model for me. These special people were my real targets for my street pieces. They saw past the mask of the cripple. The masses used the mask of the cripple to relieve their guilt, to reinforce their fragile superiority of being "normal", to make themselves feel better by throwing money (up to $20 a throw) at the less fortunate at whom they would not even look. The third type of person was made up of the poor and the kids who gave money as a pure spiritual act. When the special person stopped to talk, a crowd gathered around to listen. Money fell on my board while I was asking the special person to model.

The newspaper selling quickly fell away. All I had to do was sit there on the sidewalk, being available to talk. It did not matter that I dressed fancy, or had a sign saying, "I don't want money; I want you." The money kept falling. But I did discover that there are special spots and special ways of sitting which attract people. Sit at a slightly different angle, or on a spot a few feet away from the special spot and you become invisible.

I have done these street performances across the country. I have gotten tickets to the Joffrey, filled a couple of workshops, got my cameraman for one of my films, all from the street pieces. I almost caused a riot in front of Caesar's Palace in Atlantic City, N.J. The crowd did not take kindly to the casino guards trying to push me away because I was taking Caesar's money.

I painted a lot of the special people from the street performances. I noticed the changes in the people when they took off their clothes; how they relaxed, how they started talking on a deeper level about important personal things. After I got a taste of direct interpersonal acting out of erotic dreams, painting became too static. I began a series of private performances called Nonfilms. I asked the special people from the street performances to come to my home, into my study which was my first cave. Within this cave, cut off from the normal reality, we created scenes which no camera would shoot, nobody would see. Although I had played with my friends before in nonsexual eroticism, this was the first time I tried to use "sexual" acts in a nonsexual art form. I was surprised with the power that this released. Because of these scenes, the people started talking about their lives during these sessions and said it helped their other relationships. Not one person minded that there was no film. These nonfilms were the base for my career in relationship counseling.

I first noticed the nonlinear effects of private performance in these secret rituals. People whom I approached on the street came to me weeks after the nonfilm, the person usually reported changes in his life, in his relationships, in how people were towards him...all of which amazed him (and me too) because he hadn't told anyone that he had done the ritual. Part of the change in how people related to him can be explained linearly by the change in the person emotionally and even physically caused by the performance. But this does not explain how things "just happened" to him, things that were improbable, things that we both linked to the ritual.

In the eighties I started videoing these nonfilms when the VHS home equipment first came out. I didn't care that there was no place to show these videos. I got shit for using the VHS [among many other things]! I didn't care! The important thing for me is always the doing the art with people, not who will see it! So we just put all of my videos in the closet. When the internet finally arrived, I was ready! I was one of the first artists who used the internet to show my videos! Those nonfilms in the closet now get watched by thousands a day!

I don't have a choice about what the art is like, can't change it to suit the art fashion to keep up with the times. It is a living monster pulling me along in its zigzag evolution. Real art is like that. Art is a calling, not a career.

The nonfilm pieces were active physical mutations of the psychic, literary lectures of Reed. Both the Reed lectures and the nonfilms were created around the particular people in my life to call forth an alternative reality to the normal one. I do not function all that well in the social, political, casual, sexual, economical, competitive world. So I look to performance to create a world of community, intimacy, and human intense interaction. For me, art is a matter of survival.

But I began to see the nonfilms were magical intense nonsexual one night stands which were not building a sense of expanding community, the heart of the vision that controls my art.

I was not satisfied with these nonfilms because they were brief relationships that did not go anywhere. What I wanted to do was create intimacy -- that is, a situation in which anything is permissible, where people feel that secure. I didn't want to connect this intimacy with romance or sex because that would set limits. But that "anything is permissible" did mean a wide open erotic freedom.

I somehow stumbled upon a book, Environmental Theater by Richard Schechner, a book about a theater of active involvement and participation, of nudity and intimate physicality, of risk-taking and change. It was right up my alley. Richard's insights and experiments were inspiring to me.

But it seemed to me the Performance Group of Richard's was not well-versed in, or committed to, a living communal intimacy, so they retreated from the edge when they were expected to live the personal intimacy they were acting out. My years of communal living and spiritual study gave me needed keys to take what Richard had done forward. The book fit so well with my own experiments, philosophy and vision, it became a base of the next stage of the work.

And I have already talked about the workshop and the twenty four hour performance which came out of all of this. After that performance, my tribal body of four plus around five people from the workshop moved to N.Y.C. to continue the work.

Audrey: You are well known as one of the NEA funded artists that was targeted by Jesse Helms in the 1990s, which resulted in the NEA no longer funding performance art. What do you think about the growing embrace of performance art by large museums, collectors, and the public?

Frank: I have written a lot about what I call THE COMBINE PLOT which leads artists on a chase of college degrees, of skills to operate high-tech art-making machines, of money or positions that will give them the opportunity to do art, even when the style, the subject matter, and maybe the content of the art is dictated by this chase, by the combine plot. When the news came out that I was on the hit list I wrote this:

> "I see in the press that Sen. Jesse Helms and Rep. Dana Rohrabacher have nominated me, along with Annie Sprinkle, Karen Finley, Johanna Went, Cheri Gaulke, as well as other unnamed artists, to be the next target in their war on art. By doing so, Dana and Jesse have given us artists a platform from which to fight the plot. Because doing battle with the combine plot is one of the main functions of an artist, I am flattered to be nominated as one of the top ten on the new McCarthy hit list. I was feeling left out. All my heroes in the past were banned, jailed, harassed for their work. Artists such as Finley who I respect have been fighting the censors for years. My ego was crushed when I saw Rohrabacher on CNN label Annie Sprinkle a threat to the established moral order. After all, my work is as threatening as hers. But days later, someone sent me the NEW YORK CITY TRIBUNE (Feb. 5) special report that named names, and my name was there. What a relief! I only wish Dana and Jesse had invited me to testify. Jesse, I am available."

It was not about stopping funding artists. Annie Sprinkle had not even tried to get NEA funding when we were targeted. And I just had gotten an NEA fellowship of five thousand dollars years ago! It was my first and last spin in the Grant Game. I felt fine about applying because back then they based it on your past work, not for some future project. There were no strings on how I used the money. I always had the iron clad policy of not giving the control of the art away to the government, corporations, audiences, cast members, venues, etc. So I only do art that we here can afford to pay for ourselves. But in the end of the year of that fellowship, I began to have an addicted feeling, thinking about applying for more grants, etc. rather than just doing art. So I said FUCK THIS SHIT and went cold turkey! That addiction to getting outside money really shut off a lot of possibilities!

About five years before this targeting, I was pissing other artists off by warning them they were opening gates for such an attack by giving other artists shit for not doing politically correct enough work. So I was expecting such an attack. But I didn't think I was a big enough fish to be one of the targeted! But I was ready, ready to ride the bull for years, ready to use the platform and power that being targeted gave me to battle with censorship, repression and suppression, and to have fun doing it! Being targeted is just a part of the job of doing the kind of art I do!

The core goal of this attack was to politically deball all art. All of us targeted artists [gays, women and me] were using nudity and eroticism for radical political social change.

When an artist sets herself up as being an artist who goes beyond the normal frame, who tells the hard truths, who explores the unknown… not to be hip, or controversial, or to be interesting…but because that is how our tribal human being evolves, so it has to be done…when that kind of artist then goes after money, personal fame, and/or glamour while still claiming to be doing avant-garde art, it is denying society the real evolutionary function of the real avant-garde. It tells people, audiences and artists alike, that the avant-garde is just a branch of the entertainment complex with the same rules, goals, reality as television, rock music, Hollywood, and sports. This is like telling people a can of Slim Fast is a balanced meal of real food. It is a lie. And the scary dangerous thing is artists are buying/selling this lie. Avant-garde art is art that tells the truth, explores the taboos, pushes the limits. Obviously this kind of art, if it is honest, cannot be focused outwardly. Historically, often "The People" [who are not the same thing as "the mainstream"] have identified with the avant-garde because it was telling the truth about their lives. The focus of the avant-garde should always be on telling the truth, not on popularity polls and bottom lines. The focus of the avant-garde has been, and should be, on doing art that is as "pure" as possible...not on mass media entertainment of reaching as many people as possible by shaping "the product" to that goal.

The mainstream entertainment, by it sheer mass, has always sucked artists out of the fringe, the underground. That is just gravity. In reality, it takes a lot to enter, and to stay in, the underground. The underground is where the real freedom and the real ability to change society are to be found. This is why artists CHOOSE the underground instead of the mainstream. This is also why, when an artist is pulled into the mainstream, this freedom and ability decay. In my own career, I have worked very hard to stay in the underground...this work has been hard precisely because some of the pieces have turned out to be "popular" [whatever that means!]...attracting the mainstream sharks.

The mainstream has always tried to create a fake avant-garde with fake controversies, fake taboos, fake "hipness", etc. to give the marks a controlled fun-ride through a Disneyland to keep them away from the real edge of life. This is because the powers-that-be cannot control or exploit what is in the real avant-garde. To pull this off, the government, corporations, whatever need us artists. WE ARTISTS DON'T NEED THEM!

Seeing art as THE PRODUCT, with marketing phrases such as "alternative comedy [a.k.a. performance art]", is very damaging to performance art because it trivializes art. In fact it avoids "art" all together, selling "alternative comedy" as a weird, consumable form of entertainment which will give you a laugh for your buck. This is not what performance art is. Performance art is the performing/doing/experiencing the act of art. It is going on a physical journey into the unlimited realm of art. Sometimes this journey may be funny or entertaining. But these are not the true goals or rewards. The suggestion [promotion] that these are the rewards of art results in denying people, including the artists, the real full freeing experience of art.

All of this is selling the art, the artists, and the audience way short. Moreover it was misunderstanding the new media such as the internet and zines. In these media, artists can relate to their audiences directly without middlemen, without compromises, without limiting concepts such as "mainstream"...all for very little money...so why sell out?

Btw, I am always willing to sell out for fifty grand a week!

So the NEA became a part of this long before Helms targeted us. But when he forced the NEA to add a clause to its artist contract, the NEA became useless to artists like us. The clause was basically a loyalty oath to the established order, promising to do no art that could offend anybody! Some artists like Rachel Rosenthal sent their NEA money back, refusing to sign! But most artists signed, not embarrassed to admit that they did that weak of art! And that was the death nail of the NEA to individual artists.

Audrey: Your work deals with the body, erotic play and sexuality—themes that a person with cerebral palsy is not usually identified with. Are you able to get away with things that more traditionally able-bodied artists are not?

Frank: Mmmmmm... Who is doing the identifying? Who are the artists with cerebral palsy who don't deal with the body and sex? And why don't they? Don't they deal with life in all of its dimensions?

I have always claimed whole LIFE with all of its issues, etc. as my canvas and subject matter. I have claimed all kinds of art and all channels of communication as my tools! Having cerebral palsy is one of my tools. It is a great shortcut and adds additional dimensions to what I do. For an example, when I get on a stage at a punk club to sing, everything is blown open, the old reality with all the limits have been shown up as lies because a dude like me shouldn't be a rock star! So my body is like a booster rocket even before I open my mouth! But then I need to deliver, get results! I always do!

There are always all kinds of pressures to change the content, the tools, and the focus of the work. People always say they like the work because it is strong, but I should get over my obsession with sex and nudity, and get on to more important issues; I should not get "stuck" in one vision. I can never figure out why they LIKE the art if they think that!

What they do not realize is what they like about the work, the strength, comes from being committed to a single vision, no matter what the current trends and fashions are. I cannot imagine more important issues than sex and freedom symbolized by nudity. But these are not my ultimate focus. Sex and nudity are powerful digging tools to reach the intimate community. By limiting the tools of art, art itself is limited.

When the artist is rooted in private rituals, it becomes clear that she is not an agent for society, or some political movement, or the art galleries and art "experts", or even for her own individualistic imagination. Instead, she is an agent of gods, of dreams, of visions and myths. This causes reactions in society, especially when the piece is public. Karen Finley in the eighties was criticized for limiting her audience because she offended them by her words, anger, nudity. An artist who is rooted in the private channels is not affected by this attempt to curb the power of the art by strapping it to audience acceptance and agreement. The power of a Karen Finley is the taboo-breaking energy she releases into society. This societal pressure to tame art down, which usually sounds very reasonable and comes even from liberal sources, is very hard for the artist to resist who is not familiar with the hidden channels of change.

Audrey: Is nudity and eroplay always a part of your performance?

Frank: Well, in my performances, like in my life, the possibility of nudity, sex, and everything else is always there on the table to appear at any time. This turns up the importance of everything that does actually occur into an intensive altered state. I never know what will happen!

And in reality all my life is my performance, using all kinds of channels of communication [both linear and non-linear]. Funny! I probably have reached a lot more people than any other performance artist. And me, not caring how many people the art reaches!

Audrey: Is the glass half full or half empty?

Frank: My cup runneth over! It always has!

Audrey: As a younger performance artist, I am interested in a dialogue between our generations. What are your impressions of the '80s and '90s generation of artists as opposed to your own. This, of course, is a very broad topic, but perhaps you can rap on the subject a little.

Frank: In the seventies and the early eighties, the calling of art became the career of art. The passion and idealism became the studying of the trends of what will be "in" next. The passionate vulnerability that creates magic was replaced by a cool and clever intellectualism. We artists got seduced by high tech. We got seduced by the modern media, by the quest for large audiences.

I think performance was being ruined by trying to package it as entertainment, as off-beat cabaret. Some performance is entertaining. Some performance is cabaret. That is great. But when you try to package performance into a neat cabaret format, as I think is the trend, to make performance acceptable and profitable, it becomes a hip form of nightclub watching or groovy T.V. watching. If you limit performance in time and space for acceptability, it stops being performance.

I like doing cabaret and video. They are great mediums in themselves. Of course, video, cabaret, computers, etc. have always been a big part of what I do.

But when I am doing cabaret or video, I am always aware of the limitations built into their formats. When someone watches a video, he knows that he will remain passively watching from the outside; the video will not literally pop out into his reality, or physically drag him into the T.V.

When someone goes to a cabaret, he knows there are certain limits involved such as that each act must end before another begins; but in performance, anything is possible. A performance can last for a minute or it can last for days. Performance can start in one space but then move to another. Performance can be storytelling, it can be a guy threatening you with a baseball bat, it can be a guy hanging by his skin, or throwing food, or anything. In performance all things are possible. And that is what gives you an extra edge to create dreams.

Performance, like any avant-garde art, is the way society dreams; it is the way society expands its freedom, explores the forbidden in safety, loosens up. Society needs its dream art, just as an individual needs to dream or will go insane. Our moral majority society, bent on going backwards into the violent blank rigidity of a censored mind, needs taboo-breaking dreams to get back to freedom. Performance is perfectly suited for this dream role. At the present time, our society is at a fork in its growth. It can go deeper into high tech impersonal isolation, or it can rediscover the magic that happens when physical and emotional humans actively and directly link up with one another. Art can either just follow society, just recording the trends, or it can take a pathbreaker role. I am talking to you artists who are not as lucky as I am to have a physical reminder that they are misfits of society whose job it is to push back the limits of society. This is a reminder that we misfits are still needed.

Performance art, the art of performance, is rooted in the private games of babies where every move and gesture has its own meaning to the baby -- it is rooted in the creative and the destructive games that a little kid does when he is all alone -- games that adults still do, but will not admit to doing, even to themselves.

One of the main criticisms I get is that my art is old fashioned, a throwback to the '60s. I find this funny because the roots of the art are much more old fashioned than that, going back to the cave.

Performance obviously goes much farther back than 1909 when it became a formal art form. The Futurists were reacting to the bankruptcy of formal art, with its gallery power scene, the elitism of art, the money, the politics, and the social scene of art. This is a true but a one-sided view of why performance appeared at that time.

I think performance came into existence to fill a void in western life. The void was the lack of magic and inspiration. The two areas of creativity, theatre and religion, that traditionally were the source of this magical inspiration had long ago moved from magic to entertainment and politics. This void also gave birth to psychology during that same time period. I often get the criticism that my work is really psychology and therapy, and not art. When it is realized that psychology as a formal science and performance as a formal art were born at the same time, this criticism can be answered. Performance and psychology are both involved in spiritual healing by digging into the hidden mysteries of life.

The dynamic of seeing art is not the fundamental dynamic of art. The doing of art is art's basic dynamic. The doing of art and having other people see the art work are two separate dynamics, events, rituals. The seeing of art is what the viewer or listener does in her head. The doing of art is the ritual of creation, is what the artist does. In reality, this ritual has more to do with the act of doing than the act of creating. When a child first draws crazy lines on the wall, he is not trying to create something... but to do something for some effective purpose that our linear logic cannot grasp. The crazy person does his insane rituals, not to express himself but to keep the sky from falling or to make pain go away. And it works. The sky does not fall down. Maybe it is because of the rituals of the insane.

The very act of doing changes the whole universe. This is a key principle of magic. By doing a ritual or by speaking a spell, you can effect change. Painting a picture, doing a dance, writing a poem, any act of art can be a magical ritual, the doing of which has nonlinear effects. Seen in this way, most acts of creation are private rituals done in personal caves.

What we usually think of as works of art are aftermaths of art.

The problem with our modern frame of art reality is not that we make art to be seen, but that we have forgotten (or have been made to forget by those who control what is to be seen and what is not) that the power of doing art is the main power of art. The private performance is a way to regain the magical power of the doing of art. Defining what a private performance is is an interesting way to enter the magic. I define it as a ritual that is not for an audience. It is something that has to be done, something you may not even want to do. One of the easiest to frame as a private performance is a shaman going to his secret spot to do rites nobody will see to open himself up for channeling visions that he cannot personally use or tell anyone about. We have seen other obvious private performances -- the child, the madman, the artist alone doing art. We can add things like doodling, singing in the shower, playing invisible drums to the radio when you are safe alone in your room. It is something that has to come out. It is something too silly, too taboo, too sacred, too intense, too raw, too vulnerable to be done in public, to be expressed. This may be where real art begins. This kind of doing by one person is clearly private performance. It has an element of secrecy and undercover. I can remember singing on my bed along with the radio, quickly stopping when anyone opened the door, not wanting to be exposed, not wanting to lessen the magic. And now I sing in rock clubs.

The hidden ritual not only kept me from insanity (some people will say that makes it therapy, not art), but opened nonlinear routes of possibilities not only for me, but for everybody. The private performance gives the artist freedom from limits and shoulds and morals, so that she can go beyond where the society or culture or the consciousness has reached, to connect to the universal power. By doing this she brings a new universal area into this reality.

Audrey: I think you are terrific Frank. I see that you ran for President?

Frank: Well, are not all political campaigns performances? That doesn't mean they are not serious. My performances often start with something seemingly trivial then grow by themselves very quickly into forces unto themselves. The campaign started with a t-shirt of The Three Stooges. Michael ["Mikee"] LaBash, who is one of six people I live with within a tribal relationship and who is our graphic/web designer, had a

CURLY FOR PRESIDENT t-shirt. For Christmas 2006 Mikee made me a FRANK MOORE FOR PRESIDENT shirt. When I wore it, people started asking me what my platform was. So I wrote a platform up. Everybody who read it got excited, overflowed with hope, saying it expressed what they felt and wanted. They didn't see a performance artist in a wheelchair. They didn't check the odds of my winning. Instead they saw someone who they could excitedly vote for… somebody who shared their dreams, who talked deeply about what really affects their lives. Their reactions placed on me a responsibility to mount a serious campaign, to commit and surrender to it…and to hang on no matter where this ride would go. I never know where a performance or a project will evolve to.

In one of my speeches from the campaign I said that I started running basically because none of the prominent candidates were talking honestly and directly about the state of things, were committed to fundamental change, and had a clear plan to create a humane, sustainable, and just plain enjoyable society. So I took on that role. My running for President created an excitement for how possible it is to bring our dreams for our society into reality… to remove fear and isolation; to get the boot of big corporations off our neck; to provide everyone health care, life-long education, a minimum income, and a livable wage; to restore our rights and freedoms; and to bring our troops home! We everyday people know the real state of the union! But more importantly, we have the sense of what is possible! We need leaders who share our dreams and who do not sell us short. Or sell us out!

This excitement extended overseas, and we received much more coverage of the campaign in Europe than we did locally, although there were a handful of great interviews and articles about the campaign here in the U.S.. In Europe, there were great articles written about the campaign in France, Germany, Poland and the UK, and an appearance on Swedish TV!

We did many local events and attended many different local festivals during the over two years that I ran for President, and they were some of the most effective pieces I have ever done … Here is what I wrote about the campaign coming to the "How Berkeley Can You Be" Parade in September of 2007:

"The whole day blew me out. Linda and Mikee took turns pushing my chair close to the lines of people along the parade route so I could shake hands, look into people's eyes, hear their responses, interact one on one…all of which would have been impossible if I sat on a truck. I was moved when people thanked me for running, when whole sections started clapping and chanting, "GO, FRANK, GO!" Erika, Corey, Alexi, and sometimes Linda or Mikee gave out over 1,200 copies of the platform. And people didn't throw it away as is common, but started reading it, shouting out planks they were moved by. I can see that "pressing the flesh" can be addicting! And a lot of people are devoted viewers of the public access shows of Suzy and mine. "I WATCH YOU EVERY NIGHT!", "WE TIVO YOU!", "I LEARN FROM WATCHING YOUR SHOWS!"

Camping out in our beautiful booth, which we put up for most of these events and festivals, was only slightly less intense. We were a visual magnet, decked out with banners, t-shirts, buttons, bumper stickers, peace flags and platforms. And people got the tribal body that the 6 of us are together!

By the "official" count, I received a handful of votes, spread across a number of states, Maryland, Illinois, Kansas, Georgia, Utah, West Virginia, and of course California. But the "official" count for write-in candidates is always just a small part of the picture, because so many of the states that actually accept write-in candidates for President will never actually count or record the votes unless the number of votes becomes large enough to contend with the "major" candidates. For instance, we know directly that I received votes in New York, but there were 0 votes counted for me in NY.

The campaign also had a direct effect on the electoral process for write-in Presidential candidates in a number of states. We not only forced several states' elections divisions to learn their own system, we also challenged and/or changed procedures and requirements in other states both before and after the election.

For much much more information about the campaign, with great photos and video from the various events, visit: http://www.frankmoore-forpresident08.com/index.html.

Audrey: Thanks for sharing your being/art/love with the world~

Shamanistic Art

Text for the *Shamanistic Art* brochure in 1988.

Shamanistic Art is a focused use of rituals to call forth dream trance in which reality can be reshaped in nonlinear ways.

I became sucked into performance not to tell stories, not to paint pictures for others to look at, not even to reveal something about myself or about the state of things, and certainly not for fame or fortune. It was simply the best way that I saw to create the intimate community which I as a person needed and that I thought society needed as an alternative to the personal isolation....

Art can give people permission to do what normally is forbidden. It gives a frame that switches realities from the narrow normal reality to the freeing altered reality of controlled folly. My live ritual art offers people a key to a new, different, and temporary reality. Within my performances, this kind of awake dream is created. Cut off from the normal reality, we create magical rituals...magical rituals are called forth from the people. Within these rituals, we explore a nonsexual physicality, EROPLAY. By using eroplay, the innocent child within the body is released in a playful energy. Within this altered reality, intense emotions can be released, intense acts can be performed, outside the normal slots. The people often start crying, or laughing, or telling deep personal secrets, or start intimate sensual acts, safely beyond sex. I never know what will happen when I enter this altered reality of performance. This not knowing keeps what I do exciting and new for me, keeps me flexible and vulnerable. Within the magic state, dramatic changes take place within the bodies and emotions of the people. Moreover, most people come back to say that somehow the trance reality powerfully affected their normal reality and relationships in nonlinear ways which we do not understand.

In performance I allow myself the freedom as a channel of inner forces, to say and do whatever comes to me, no matter how off-the-wall and outrageous it seems. I use nonsense, blatant insults, humor, and the holy obvious, lusty playing and breaking of taboos to break into the altered reality of controlled folly. I use the bigger-than-life mask-character of the trickster shaman to reach this end.

In the performance there is no actual sex nor harming violence. This creates a safe environment in which people can allow one another to trust, to be demanded of.

Providing adult playgrounds is one of the basic goals of my work. I think playing is a safe, mind-altering drug. I use child-like playing to get people out of their old personalities, old mind-sets and old worlds. By playing, we die and are reborn.

The ritual performances are battling the social fragmentation and isolation through underground channels, avoiding standard rules and criticisms and values. What appears to be happening...or in some cases, what appears not to be happening...in the ritual is really a cover, a distraction of people's attention, so that the hidden magical trance can take them over. A trance can be cast by showing them something outside of their reality. I have cerebral palsy, so I have a body that stands out from the normal reality. Little kids often become frozen on the spot when they see me, my special body, in a cafe. I just greatly magnify this trance process in the performances by introducing many of these trance inducing images, weaving them into a subtle spell. Within this inner trance, the real magic happens.

The performance is a dream which guides me as the shaman artist. I have to be open enough to use everything and anything that the dream gives me.

As playing is a safe, mind-altering drug, so is extended time. The usual length of these ritual performances is from 5 to 24 hours, but the longest has been 48 hours. This magical time spell melts the people who come to the performance as strangers into an intimate tribal community, and transports us into the dream world where all things are possible, where nothing behaves normally, not even time.

This long, complex dream performance melts the normal reality with dream reality to form a liminal state. In this liminal state anything is possible and anyone can be a conspirator in this dream production. This is not only true for the people being led through the ritual, but for everyone, including me. This dream force can begin even days before the actual ritual.

Within the liminal state, what usually is unbelievable, corny, tacky, suddenly becomes extremely powerful. Things like water become potent magical drugs just through words. Within these temporary living myths, time becomes very plastic, as do other forms of reality. Time within the dream reality has the nasty habit of shrinking.

Another tool I've discovered in these prolonged spells is to hide the most intense rituals by performing them inside a locked box, hidden cave, or secret tent. In this way, the unseen ritual affects the people on the feeling level directly, without being filtered by the mind.

Goals brought into the dream state from the everyday world become limitations because the dream's vision will lead us into a much deeper, richer soil of realities than goals would allow. So we enter the dream to experience the dream, to receive what the vision has to give us. This frees us from our linear prison.

These dream performances have magical effects on every level. This is the ultimate function of the shamanistic art. To deepen this magical effect on the world and to develop a shamanistic community based within the modern western world, I have set up a shamanistic performance school, THE UNIVERSITY OF POSSIBILITIES. This school presently contains ten apprentices who have signed up to train for a certain amount of time. The focus of this school is to create a mythic life as an alternative to the world we see around us. The mere existence of this mythic life and these shamanistic dream performances will subvert, change, the normal world. Creating this mythic life is done through performing privately. This school has already deepened my public pieces.

Frank Moore has been performing, directing, writing and teaching Shamanistic Art since 1973. He has Master's degrees in Psychology & Performance/Video. He now resides in Berkeley, California. He conducts shamanistic performance rituals throughout the year.

Annie Sprinkle's
Post Post Porn Modernist

A review by Frank Moore, April 1994. Published in *The Cherotic (r)Evolutionary* #5, 1995.

Annie Sprinkle invited us to her POST POST PORN MODERN-IST one-person show last Saturday. I saw it years ago when she did it at an N.Y.C. strip theatre...and I wrote a review of it which was published in ART PAPERS. In the review, I pretended I was just someone who had come to the show (in reality we were staying at her place, watched her rehearse the last ritual, and Michael [LaBash] painted her vibrator). I could not do that now because she has put me into the show for my "famous tongue"...and listed me in the program credit as one of her performance teachers...which is very flattering because she is the best performance artist I have seen and her show is the best I have been to. I said this in the old review. But the ritual that is this show has become much deeper, much more human. Annie very quickly shattered the limitations of a stage show, very quickly created an intimate community from all the people in the space. It is the community that really does the ritual, using Annie's life as the pathway. The ritual never stops, not even during the "intermission" (Annie stays on stage for people to have their picture taken with her bare breasts on their heads...at $10 a pop). The show's last section, a very magically powerful ritual, did not end, Annie did not leave the stage, until way after the last audience member had left (I, as a performer, watched each person somehow decide it was time to go).

Annie's messages are clear in the show...sex and the body are good... people do not have to be victims...and the more happiness and pleasure you have, the more happiness and pleasure you are creating in/for the world.

Unfortunately the new age goddess haunts the show just below the surface, producing a sublayer or a hidden message of separation and isolation which really runs in conflict with both Annie's basic nature and the community that her show calls forth. The new age goddess is basically a corruption of the original goddess which is the yin principle which is within all of us no matter what our gender. The original ritual journey or task was to reunite the yin and yang principles into the original creative life force, and to apply, along this major journey, the yin principle for the tribal welfare. One of the powerful characteristics of the original goddess has always been an unlimited inclusiveness. This is also true of Annie personally, and it radiates from her show. But both the original goddess and Annie are being misused, distorted, by the forces of exclusion as an excuse and a justification of elitism, separatism, discrimination, fear, and isolation. These forces of exclusion are the main cause of today's world conflict.

One of the problems is "goddess" is being personalized, then given a gender. It is common today to hear women saying, "I am a/the goddess." It has the protection of being politically correct. But if we change the words to "I am a/the male god", or "I am a/the white god", or "I am an/the american god", the fascistic dangers of this kind of logic become more obvious. Moreover, the new age goddess has more to do with Mother Mary than the original goddess. It isolates women once again high upon the pedestal.

Annie's story is one of self-discovery...both her personal self and our collective self. Her method is to isolate and define aspects of herself, give each a name and a personality, and then live each to the hilt. So far, she has discovered Ellen, Annie, and Anya. In the past, Annie has described Anya as the goddess, which attracted the confusion. Recently she has started describing Anya as a sacred prostitute. Although this term is also misleading...created by one culture projecting its morality into the past onto another culture...it is not gender-driven...after all, Annie introduced me to the audience as a sacred prostitute. What is really meant by the term is a cultural role of a magical channel between this and other realities by means of, among other techniques, expanded sex.

Annie is only in the middle of her story. Before it is all over, I think she will discover many more aspects within herself...and will then combine all of the aspects together. I'm looking forward to that climax!

States Of Tanpan

October 1, 1997. Published in *The Symposium* issue #1, Greece, July 1998.

In the late '70s I started to realize that one of the things that was undermining my work was the English language. There was no word, no name, for the force I was dealing with. This fits the designs of the established powers that are out to isolate and censor us. So my first task was to create a new word. It was EROPLAY.

Our mind needs labels, words for something to be able to think about the thing clearly. There is such intense physical play, and such a force or energy, and I have labeled it EROPLAY. But before this, there has not been a word for it. Usually the word SEX has been the catch word for people to dump almost everything sensual, romantic, physical, or for showing more skin than usual. Cars are called sexy. Poses that do not show the sex act are called sexual. Wearing certain things, moving certain ways are all called sexual, even when it is not leading to the sexual act -- even when there is no intent to have sex.

In magic, words have power. To create a word for something is to create the possibility for it to exist in our reality -- for it to happen. Even for us who intellectually knew eroplay existed as a separate thing from sex, it was hard before the word EROPLAY to talk about it clearly, to think about it clearly, and to experiment and play with it without sexual undercurrents and fears creeping in. This was because we had to use words like LUSTY, SEXY, and EROTIC to attempt to talk about it. In our language, all of these words have sexual connotations. In magic, words create. So if you use sexual words for nonsexual playing, the sexual words will set a false sexual confusion. This is why the word EROPLAY itself is important.

Eroplay is intense physical playing and touching of oneself and others. Eroplay is also the force or energy which is released as the result of such play. It is also the happy, playful attitude towards life that comes from such play. Eroplay is not foreplay, even though foreplay is eroplay.

Kids play very physically both with their own bodies and others' bodies. They get turned-on by this play, turned-on both physically and mentally. This turn-on is not sexual in kids. Studies have shown that babies who are held, touched, and played with are more healthy and alert, weigh more, and have a lower rate of death than babies who are denied this eroplay. Studies also show that old people who live alone, who don't get physical and emotional contact, are less healthy and die sooner than people of the same age who live with others and get that physical contact.

When we grow into adulthood, eroplay is linked to sex, maybe to assure procreation. But there may be different results when eroplay is connected to the sexual orgasm. This difference may be caused by the mixture of chemicals released in the body during eroplay with other chemicals released in the body during orgasm. Foreplay is eroplay, but eroplay is not foreplay. We may need a certain amount of straight eroplay (not connected to or leading to sex) to be as healthy as possible.

Orgasm may start a patterning process in our brain, which is an intense bonding between people. Free love did not take into account this psycho/physical process.

Foreplay leads to orgasm -- eroplay leads to being turned-on in many different ways and in all parts of the body -- including, but not limited to, physical arousal. It can be different every time. Skin touching skin seems to be what releases the full impact of eroplay.

Eroplay can be intense. It is like when you rub a puppy on its belly and the puppy goes into a state of rapture, both totally turned-on and relaxed. To use something that is not normally confused with sex, eroplay is the blissed-out, warm, relaxed, turned-on, totally satisfying feeling of a good head rub. The same feeling comes from playing with ears. Eroplay is that intense feeling throughout the entire body.

Sex seems to be connected to mating; whereas the combination of both physical and psychic forces released during and after eroplay seems to be connected more to communication and attracting people to you.

What stops most people from physically eroplaying without connecting it to sex, without sexual undercurrents or expectations, is the inability to see where eroplay ends and sex begins. Foreplay is eroplay, but eroplay is not foreplay. The difference between foreplay and eroplay is one of intent -- physically there is no difference. It is the same pleasurable, physical, turned-on feeling.

But there is a difference physically between eroplay and sex. Eroplay is satisfying in itself, in relaxing intensity. There is no build up of pent-up energy in one climactic act. In sex, however, there is a point where foreplay (eroplay) ceases to satisfy and energy gets pent-up and built-up to be released in the sex act. This build up is a clear and broad dividing line between the turn on of eroplay and sex.

Eroplay starts when the possibility of physical eroplay arises -- the possibility of the breaking of the normal rules, social conventions, and morality.

Eroplay is not just physical activity. The possibility of physical eroplay is enough to start releasing whatever chemicals and other forces that physical eroplay will continue to release. Talking and thinking about eroplay will excite, will turn you on, even physically. This seems to be a natural part of eroplay, an innate part.

Eroplay is fun!

Eroplay is innocent and childlike.

Eroplay's focus is on physical enjoyment and pleasure for its own sake. This is one reason why eroplay is taboo in our society where religion teaches physical pleasure for self is bad.

Eroplay connects you more with your own body and with other people. It decreases isolation and alienation. It increases self-trust and trusting of others. It makes you harder to be controlled. This is another reason why eroplay is taboo.

Because the after-glow of eroplay attracts people to you, you get more opportunities in all aspects of your life. And because eroplay relaxes you and gives you more energy, you are in a better position to use opportunities.

Because eroplay is not focused on goals other than physical enjoyment in many ways, and because it does not lead to a mating life, eroplay would be much harder to use to sell products than sex. This is another reason why eroplay is taboo.

Because of all of this, eroplay leads to a definite life-style with all these characteristics. The life-style looks strangely like the love generation, but without drugs or free sex.

Eroplay is intense nonlinear physical touching, rubbing, licking, exploring for physical pleasure for its own sake. Eroplay is foreplay which is released from the linear goals of reaching genital orgasm.

When I first wrote about eroplay, I lumped both the physical and psychic play and the energy released by that play as eroplay. But that has made it hard to talk about both the energy and the play as clearly as I have wanted to. I have since started calling this attracting, pleasurable, healing energy of excited calmness "chero".

In the western culture, chero is known as "sexual energy" or as the "sexual urge". This is because in this culture, adults usually call chero forth by means of sex and use chero mainly for sex. However, sex is just one way to use chero. Moreover, sex is just one of the ways to call forth chero.

Chero is the life force. It is what attracts. Chero is what attracts other people to you. It is what the shamans used to heal and melt other realities into the normal reality. It is what Tantric Buddhists used to reach the higher spiritual spheres. They used the sex act to arouse chero, which they then used in their spiritual quest. Sex is a cherotic act. But Chero is by no means simply a/the sexual energy. There are many ways of calling forth chero, and many ways of letting chero direct or guide you.

One of the oldest ways of calling chero up is what I call "vere". Vere is what most writers would call the use of pain to attain spiritual ends. But vere is no more pain than eroplay is sex. Vere is physically different than the normal pain, releasing different chemical and psychic reactions in the body. Vere and eroplay are related. Because of the crudeness of the language, it is very difficult to explore these realms.

In magic, masks are important. These masks could be created out of material, or paint, or tattoos, or facial expressions. Magical masks are not meant to be a hiding, a covering up, or a protection. Rather, they are meant to reveal, to liberate, to call forth the deep personality which is usually hidden in normal society. They are vulnerable masks.

In my work, nudity is such a vulnerable mask. In itself, physical nudity does not always mean you are vulnerable. But in the context of this work, it takes you out of the social, polite world. It physically changes you slightly (I will get into these changes later). It signifies the willingness to use every part of yourself in the work...holding nothing back or in reserve, holding no part too private or sacred not to be used in the work. This is on all levels of your being, from your body to your psyche. Most of my students are now into healing and/or performing. But the work is bigger than these channeling contexts.

Nudity also gives us direct access to the energy channels of the body. In time we will have the access of nudity even with our clothes on. But it will always be easier to arouse chero through eroplay with physical nudity.

The physical health and lifestyle advantages of using eroplay to arouse chero in your body are caused by the physical and psychic changes in the body started by aroused chero. Over the years of experimenting, we have often noticed that people's physical appearance changes, sometimes radically, after they eroplay. Their physical features soften, the way they hold their bodies relaxes, their bodies have a glow very similar to the glow that many pregnant women have. All of these signs are visual, physical signals which attract open people to the chero-enriched person...and thus attract more opportunities to him. It is also important to point out that these changes are temporary, lasting from a few hours to a few weeks depending on the physical and emotional environment. Continued release of chero is needed to have these changes be longer and longer lasting.

There are other changes that occur during eroplay. By touching, rubbing, rocking, moving, the energy centers of the body are randomly activated, releasing a flood of blood with chemicals that produce the sense of well-being in all parts of the body. This is a warming well-being. This is deepened by the special breathing that is gentle laughing. This is why eroplay is playful and fun at its most healing level. Laughter has its own special healing quality.

Sometimes the release of chero is blocked by confusion and guilt when the person feels the pleasurable, turned-on feeling which he in the past associated with sex. But now he feels it in a nonsexual, nonromantic situation. If he can just let the pleasurable turn-on wash over him without thoughts, it carries him to a new realm of relaxed enjoyment.

Eroplay as a spiritual, healing technique balances chero through all the energy centers throughout the body. This is different than other techniques such as Kundalini Yoga in which the energy which I am calling chero is raised through a very dangerous process from the base of the spine to out the top of the skull. In eroplay, chero is called forth in all parts of the body, creating an energy center out of the whole body.

There is a widely held misconception that the physical and the spiritual planes are in opposition to each other, that to reach the spiritual, you have to avoid the physical. This is overlooking a great number of disciplines that use the physical in various aspects to reach spiritual treasures. The physical is one aspect of the spiritual, the aspect most accessible to us.

As we eroplay, many changes take place. The changes are both physical and psychic. We have already talked about some of the physical changes. One of the physical signs that can occur is the male erection when certain energy centers (and not necessarily the cock) are aroused in certain ways. This male erection has become the most sexual symbol in our culture and perhaps the most taboo. The female erection is not outwardly visible, and hence is usually ignored. But in reality, the "sexual" organs are no more or no less sexual than any of the other energy centers in the body. In eroplay, erection should not be thought of as sexual or a turn toward sex. This region of the body is just one of the main centers of energy.

The other physical changes caused by the arousal of chero through eroplay are a slight enlarging of the pupils, a slight change in scent from the sweat glands and nipples, the chero blush, and a difference in body tone. All of these are so slight that they usually are only picked up on the subliminal level. The changes in one body can be transferred to the bodies of others through these subliminal sensory signals. This is one reason why physical nudity is important in this work. It gives these signals a more direct channel to affect others.

But to understand better what is happening when chero is aroused by eroplay, it should be remembered that the physical is only one aspect of what we are. Around our physical body there is a force field made up of thoughts, emotions, and other psychic material. This field is usually a fraction of an inch out from the body, but we have the ability to broadcast this psychic force outward.

When we release chero through eroplay, we focus this force, and with the willingness to be unlimited, we radiate this force outward, creating a rapport into which others can be drawn. This rapport has physical, mental, and psychic qualities.

In my performances, this rapport, in the form of an altered reality or a spell, is created by arousing chero between two people by rubbing bodies, by rocking together, moving together, making noises. These two generating people are sometimes isolated in a tent or a box. But the rapport generated physically and psychically by these two leaks out of the enclosed space, putting those on the outside into an altered state. The deeper the chero rapport is between the two, the more complete the outer reality will be.

At first, the generating chero rapport may feel uncomfortable, forced, and/or strange to the apprentice. This is because we are using things that in the western culture are usually contained only in sexual and/or romantic contexts. The apprentice should not be thrown by this forced, uncomfortable feeling. It is the breaking of old patterns. It is one of the first stages of this work.

Each energy center "breathes" several kinds of energies in and out, very much like the lungs-nose breathe air in and out. Each center both takes energy in and projects energy out. Some energy centers are commonly thought of as one-way channels. The eyes obviously let in visually the outer world to our brain, our mind, our inner reality. But the eyes also visually let out what is happening inside us, who we are, and our personal power into the world. All of the centers work on this breathing principle.

In eroplay, the centers are randomly opened up so that this chero breath can be free and deep. Eroplay creates a complete cycle of chero. This cycle is created when you touch your own body. But it becomes more dynamic when this chero cycle is between two people. This interplay opens and relaxes the centers of both people, letting them both cherotically breathe deeper and easier. This deep, easy breathing is what is healing. (We will get into the difference between healing and curing later.) Both people get healed in this interplay and the energy released through the interplay helps to heal the outer world. This is important to understand because many people think healing is a one-way helping/giving channel. Because of this, they are careful "not to give too much". "I must protect myself and my personal power; maintain my own space, my control over the situation." This attitude is thought to be individualism.

But in reality, it robs the individual of her power. It isolates her, fragments her. It makes her think she has something to protect, to hide, to defend. It makes her think that she is some limited, weak, fragile being that has to be guarded. All of this is wrapped up in the glitter packaging of individualism and specialness. This attitude makes the chero breath shallow and one-way. It makes the person fragile. Vulnerability is not fragile. Vulnerability is a rubber ball. It gives very easily, but it bounces back to its original shape after it undergoes pressures of hard knocks, and it keeps rolling on the path.

Chero healing as eroplay is a two-way channel whether in play, art, magic, or everyday living. It must be this way to be effective. To create this deep two-way chero breathing you must be willing to both deeply project and deeply take in chero with anyone who is willing to do the same. This willingness will be a demanding screen which will protect you far more than any defensive wall built by fear and doubt.

To understand what eroplay, chero, and bodyplay both are and do, it is necessary to have some idea what sex is and does. The sexual urge is the urge to merge with, to combine with, to become one with another. Sex is a physical symbol of this becoming one. This being one is a long-term process of bonding. Sex is a combination of eroplay as foreplay, sexual intercourse, orgasm, ejaculation, and erection. Each one of these may release different chemicals into the body with different results. Sex is the sum of these parts.

We have mentioned how sexual intercourse within the normal social context of the modern western context starts and promotes the bonding patterning in the brain which creates the merging oneness with one of its functions being child-rearing. If the reality of the relationship does not match this being a living unit, then it will, sooner or later, cause very painful confusion which usually translates into jealousy and rejection. In this materialistic culture, the being one with another turns into owning one another. "I am you" becomes "you are mine".

Because eroplay does not have any kind of physical intercourse, it is not about becoming one with another. It is to communicate, to share, to exchange on all levels by connecting the centers through physical contact. Because eroplay is not connected with producing children, there is not ejaculation or sexual orgasm. In sex, orgasm combined with intercourse and ejaculation, shoots energy as well as the sexual material outward into another's body. To ensure sexual mating, the sexual orgasm is felt in the "sexual" organs as violent peaks of intense releasing pleasure in the middle of the well-being of eroplay pleasure. These two kinds of pleasures create a physical trance. Although orgasm is felt in the "sexual" organs, the actual orgasm happens in the brain.

In eroplay, there is no peak of released chero outward. Instead, the level of chero is raised within the body, creating a physical trance which I call "ontonse". Ontonse can be as intense as an orgasm, but ontonse is not a peak of chero; instead, it is a high plateau. When ontonse fades, the extra chero produced stays within the body, healing and calming. This extra chero slowly radiates out later as an attracting force. We call this force "erour". Erour usually is called sexual power.

Within ontonse, creativity and magic can be done. Ontonse can be felt in different parts of the body or in the entire body. Since ontonse is not a peak of chero, it can be maintained and turned into a doorway to deeper dimensions. Since chero has been hidden within sex, it has been difficult, because of social-moral taboos, to use ontonse directly as a healing magic. This is what the student will learn to use.

The hands are transmitters of chero. This is because your hands are the only parts of your body that can touch almost all of your body. They are healing wands of chero. Laying on of hands is powerful magic. But rubbing body centers together is much more powerful, therefore more taboo. This magic requires two or more people being physically intimate together.

Having an orgasm in each center of the body has a different effect, each opens a different door than having an orgasm in another part of the body. For example, it is fairly common for nursing mothers to have orgasms while they nurse. In this context, the orgasm should not be seen as sexual, but as an aspect of human nourishing love. By just revealing this hidden fact of the capability of moving the site of orgasm around the body, of using the different aspects of the orgasm other than the usual sexual, it opens up a richer, more complex, more empowering life. But this is only the beginning. This is true of all of the functions that are traditionally limited to one part of the body. You see with your heart, belly, mind, cock/pussy, etc. You do not see just with your eyes. This is another way of saying that light, as an example of all sensual forces, has many more aspects than the ones we have been told about. Light, and every other sensual force, interacts with all of our body centers, exchanging cherotic packets of possibilities, creating a total interactive experience.

In body play within cherotic magic, we used what is normally called sex as our access point into the deeper magical dimensions. We stated that the orgasmic intercourse act is confusing within all relationships except in a relationship of creating a committed life together.

This confusion is caused by the biological patterns set off in the mind by the act of orgasmic intercourse. But most of the confusion, the jealousy, the possessiveness, and the other manifestations are caused by the casual use of sex.

This casualness has been caused by the artificial funneling of this aspect of the cherotic energy exchange into the genitals, into intercourse. This funneling has been a major aspect of the life-denials. What we were left with was an artificial choice between having sex, that vague concept, or being celibate. In reality, both of these "choices" focused the chero only through the genitals, only through the medium of intercourse, or the refraining from orgasm and intercourse, on the "sexual" level. What this does is forces people to use only one channel, called "sex", to fulfill all of their needs, to express and exchange/express all of their physical chero. Moreover, this one channel is tightly controlled by life-denying morals, glamour, and romantic expectations, creating an extremely complex game maze of illusion. This is like taping up all of the keys except one on a piano, like denying a painter all colors except yellow. What can be created, can be expressed, is extremely and artificially limited. This limiting is the root of casualness.

Within the magical experimentation in which I have been involved for over 25 years, it became clear that each component of physical play had its own alchemical, biochemical, physical and psychic effects and properties. The orgasm that is felt in the genitals within intercourse begins a long-term bonding pattern within the brains of the playing lovers. When this is realized, it becomes obvious that using this type of orgasmic sex in any other relationships than in the context of a long-term relationship would be counterproductive. It would be like removing a screw with a hammer. This removes the distorting morality that has hidden most aspects of experience from us.

In my magical experimentation, the first "new" form of play to be drawn from the veil of sex was "eroplay". Eroplay extends well into the everyday communication exchange between you and the rest of the world. This is the real meaning when somebody says everything you do, every communication, is sexual. But this real meaning is hidden the second it is revealed, by using the word "sexual", herding us back into the accepted, life-denying, controlled channels of relating. Instead, we should say everything you do is cherotic. Eroplay is for communicating, for getting to know, to reveal, to exchange, to be vulnerable, to play, to enjoy, to explore. For this reason, eroplay, even at its most intense naked physical play can be done with anybody you like and enjoy...can be done in clarity in even social situations once it has been clearly and purposefully taken out of the usual sexual context. Romantic monogamy, celibacy, and sexual sex all hide this primal channel of satisfying successfully these needs of play, exploring, and communicating...hide by misdirecting these needs into channels which are not capable of satisfying, or even holding, these types of living needs. The result of this is frustration, isolation, and draining the energy of creation away from the personal level along with personal responsibility. In short, the result is life-denial being created by the dimension of power.

But eroplay is only one of the states of physical trance long hidden within sex by the life-denial of power. Each state has its own aspects, nature and effects. Each state is complete within itself, although one state may contain the other states within its special context. For example, sex contains eroplay as foreplay within it. But there is not a linear ladder. That is, eroplay should not be seen as a step towards sex, something less than sex. If you look at eroplay and sex in this way, the true qualities of both will be hidden from you.

We have said orgasm as the physical sensation can be located in each of the body centers, including the skin. Each center has its own special effect. So where an orgasm occurs has its own magical effect and context. Moreover, when we realize it is possible to feel an orgasm in different centers, or even in all of the centers at the same time, we begin to see that even orgasmic sex is a much more rich and complex experience. This is not the place to go into these orgasmic sexual states in detail. But it should be again pointed out that genital orgasmic sex, especially when it includes intercourse, is suited only for long-term living relationships when done within the normal social and cultural frame. This is because of the bonding pattern this sets off in the brain.

Ontonse is the fairly regular level of implosion of cherotic energy into the body during physical trances such as eroplay. Cherotic energy is the nonlinear stream of the subatomic packets which our body breathes in and out through every center of the body. Ontonse can be physically as intense as an orgasm. But because it is a level implosion of chero, rather than a peak explosion as the orgasm is, it can last much longer than the orgasm. Its effects are different than orgasm. Ontonse can arc between two eroplaying bodies, creating a united body during the trance time without genital intercourse. When ontonse occurs on a regular basis, eroplay has been transformed into "tanplay". Since you can not work linearly toward having an ontonse as you can to some degree work toward having an orgasm in sex, you can only enter the tanplay state by enjoying play for itself, enjoying being with the other person just for being with that person. Then the state of tanplay will settle in. Tanplay is a state of close friends... warm, slow and gentle...willing to go anywhere the tanplay takes you. Because the ontonse arcs into the body, it can effect people not physically within the tanplay. A lot of the formal cherotic magic takes place within this tanplay trance. Tanplay is serious folly.

The student should enter the following two physical trances only at the direct bidding and direction of the shaman, the teacher. The shaman within these two trances may use the student's body as his own to accomplish things he can't in his own body. The student might be playing both for/as herself and for/as the shaman.

In one of these states, "tansex", orgasm has not the linear goal peak quality it has in sex. In tansex, both orgasm and ontonse are just two of the many possible ports that the play may carry the ritual into. Tansex, although it can be intense, has a magical evenness to it. Everything has an equal value. If there appears a linear goal such as to have an orgasm, this transforms tansex into some other trance state with different effects. Tansex has a nonlinear relaxed floating quality of things just happening following the playing without forcing or trying. As in the other physical trance play forms (other than sex) that we have been talking about, there is no genital intercourse within tansex. The effect of tansex in the normal reality is to express and to explore the depth of a long existing friendship. Because of this, it only makes sense to be in tansex only within a friendship which has lasted for two years. This is within the normal western cultural reality. During the apprenticeship, however, the student should regard tansex as a ritual to be performed only upon the direct instruction of the shaman. In this magical ritual, the student is acting both as herself and as the shaman.

But within the magical work of apprenticeship, as in all magical work, another reality is working under the surface. Within this Cave of Lila, the shaman works with these altered states of physical trance, without the limits of morals, for different magical nonlinear change, in a totally different non-individualistic context than the normal cultural context. We will call this context "tanpan". Within tanpan, all of the aspects of this physical play/trance, including that of intercourse, are drained of both their normal and hidden meanings and qualities, so that they can be used by the magic through the shaman to effect both local and non-local changes. During the apprenticeship, both tansex and tanpan must be kept within the disciplined ritualistic context of controlled folly within the Cave of Lila. By doing this, the tanpanic relationship between the student and the shaman will not conflict with, threaten or weaken the student's relationships in the normal cultural frame. This is because this tanpanic relationship exists and is contained within the different, special, magical reality. However, this does not deny the fact that entering any magical experience often will shake to and beyond the breaking point any relationship that is not solidly based. But magical work can only strengthen a relationship that is solid.

Tanpan Defined

SOMEONE ASKED ME WHAT IS TANPAN. TO ANSWER, I HAD TO FIRST DESCRIBE SOME OF THE OTHER PHYSICAL TRANCES OF PLAY.

Eroplay is intense nonlinear physical touching, rubbing, licking, exploring for physical pleasure for its own sake. Eroplay is foreplay that is released from the linear goals of reaching genital orgasm.

Tansex is another state of physical trance play. As in eroplay, there is no genital intercourse. However there may be orgasms in tansex. But the orgasm in tansex has not the linear goal peak quality it has in sex.

Pantan combines various kinds of orgasm [explosions of energy] with ontonse [a regular implosion of energy] within an intensely small/intimate nonlinear play. These explosions and implosions feed off one other, creating a sustainable state of enjoyable pleasure. The sustainable state of pantan can become the context of your whole life. Pantan is the state of turn-on, aroused enjoyment of life and of being together. Within pantan, creativity, inspiration, a sense of awe and newness, etc. always are at work.

The shaman works with these altered states of physical trance, without the limits of morals, for different magical nonlinear change, in a totally different non-individualistic context than the normal cultural context. We will call this context **"tanpan"**. Within tanpan, all of the aspects of this physical play/trance, including that of intercourse, are drained of both their normal and hidden meanings and qualities, so that they can be used by the magic through the shaman to effect both local and non-local changes. These physical trance rituals of tanpan are magical rather than personal [even though they have a personal root within them and will powerfully affect personal relationships]. As such, tanpan is dangerous and should be done within respect, outside of romance, social, and glamor. Tanpanic trances arouse the state of pantan to the surface of being.

THEN SHE ASKED IF NUDITY WAS TANPANIC.

In itself, nudity is not tanpanic. When the social charge of distortion is removed from nudity, nudity by itself isn't even particularly "erotic". It is enjoyable. It is easier to call forth the tanpanic trances when nude. But nudity is, or should be, just a part of everyday life.

Two Parties

1995. Published in *The Affiliate*, Canada, in January 1996.

Annie Sprinkle has come out with an over-sized deck of playing cards with Annie's erotic photos of women famous in the sex subculture [she says she'll do a deck of men which I'll be in].

To promote the deck, HBO threw a private party which they filmed for their show REAL SEX. 100 people famous in the sex world were invited. Big bucks! A lot of food, booze, even blackjack tables [which were the most fun thing of the party].

BORING!!!

Everybody spent the night running up to one another to say a big HI!....then running away. There was a phony strip poker game with famous strippers sitting around a table bored. Every 20 minutes there was a fanfare, bright spot went on, HBO camera went on, a woman got up on the stripping block, and squirmed out of an item of clothes, then sat back down. Very unsexy! And they had so many clothes on, by the time they were approaching nude, nobody cared, nobody was watching...except the HBO camera.

The high point was when Annie did a great Charlie Chaplin-style strip. But it was too much for the other artists who were billed to perform to follow. They bowed out after her act.

The whole party showed how in-grown at least this level of the sex world has become. There is even a level of not liking/enjoying sex in this circle. Sex has become again the means to power, fame, money...and the means to avoid relationships, intimacy, needing other people. One woman actually said, "I don't like sex, I like faking it!" Most of the people just nodded their agreement.

Annie is beginning to feel this shallowness. The day after the party she called us and said her new focus is to get a relationship like Linda, Michael, and I have.

Now for the party of real slut artists who have fun with sex in both their lives and art. The next weekend, our friend, Barbara Golden had a party to celebrate her new cd/book package at the HOTEL UTAH in San Francisco.

She invited her musician friends to play covers of her songs. Barbara had us go on first [even before my guitarist had arrived] so that we would set the level of outrageous freedom for the other acts.

I had Bonnie on trumpet, Corey on piano [they are my ISOLA-TION cast], and Toyoji Tomita on slide trombone [he has played with John Cage].

I sang CLIT ENVY straight....Bonnie sitting on my chair. As I sang BONER BOY, I played with Michael's appropriate parts...if you get my drift. Then for TRASHY GIRLS, my voice became a horn. Linda did a going all the way strip to it which brought the house down.

The other acts were great musicians of very different styles, getting down funky...everybody getting inspired by the others...everybody eating Barb's food.

For the finale, Barb had us do an encore of our TRASHY GIRLS strip act.

It turned out the sound guy was the HOTEL UTAH's booking guy who has refused to book me, calling my demo video tape the most disturbing thing he has ever seen [I'm flattered!]...and why don't those [disabled] people stay in their place?! He sat through my set mouth open and hands over ears. After my set, he told the bartender, "After that, I need a drink!" I'm flattered!

What Price Fame

Written on October 18, 1997. As published in *Movement Research Performance Journal #16*, Spring 1998. Also published in *The Cherotic (r)Evolutionary #8* in 1999.

I don't know why artists think fame is all that hard to get, or something worthy of seeking. Why, it's as easy as falling off a log, as easy as dying. You just have to surrender to the forces of gravity and decay. The mainstream entertainment, by its sheer mass, has always sucked artists out of the fringe, the underground. That is just gravity. In reality, it takes a lot to enter, and to stay in, the underground. The underground is where the real freedom and the real ability to change society are to be found. This is why artists CHOOSE the underground instead of the mainstream. This is also why, when an artist is pulled into the mainstream, this freedom and ability decay. In my own career, I have worked very hard to stay in the underground…this work has been hard precisely because some of the pieces have turned out to be "popular" (whatever that means!)…attracting the mainstream sharks.

The mainstream has always tried to create a fake avant-garde with fake controversies, fake taboos, fake "hipness", etc. to give the marks a controlled fun-ride through a Disneyland to keep them away from the real edge of life. This is because the powers-that-be can not control or exploit what is in the real avant-garde.

About every five years, the fame makers "discover" me, want to make me famous. I always play along. But I also always do "the wrong thing" to keep my work surfing just below the "fame wave". Fame cripples art. But the sub-fame level is where the hidden channels of effecting, healing, changing, dreaming, myth-giving powers lie.

It is easier to stay in this sub-fame level when you do private performances than when you do public performances…because in public performances layers of seductions, limitation, consideration, taboos, morals, ways of being politically correct are laid on the art and the artist by either the powers of the establishment or the "alternative" power systems of the present society or both. But I like the challenge of doing very public work without surrendering to the fame manufacturers.

When I do a public piece, I am not swayed by how many people come or by how many walk out, because I am still functioning, and rooted, in the channels of magical change that I became aware of by doing private performances. This rooting in private rituals gives the artist freedom from, and weapons against, the corrupting concerns of money, fame, competition, good taste, acceptance, and the search for an audience. This freedom is important in shamanistic art, which is art that acts for non-linear change, because, by bringing new dreams, new myths, new visions into society from the universal underworld, it radically changes society. By being linked to a power system, be it establishment or alternative, the artist is trapped in a basic conflict of interest, because she has aligned herself either with protecting the social system or with a certain manner of change, when her true job is to carry the new visionary myths from the gods into this world through her body.

When the artist is rooted in private rituals, it becomes clear that she is not an agent for society, or some political movement, or the art galleries and art "experts", or even for her own individualistic imagination. Instead, she is an agent of the gods, of dreams, of visions and myths. This causes reactions in society, especially when the piece is public.

Karen Finley is criticized for limiting her audience because she offends them by her words, anger, nudity. An artist who is rooted in the private channels is not affected by this attempt to curb the power of the art by strapping it to audience acceptance and agreement. The power of a Karen Finley is the taboo-breaking energy she releases into society. This societal pressure to tame art down, which usually sounds very reasonable and comes even from liberal sources, is very hard for the artist to resist who is not familiar with the hidden channels of change.

So it is always tragic to see artists who are known for doing underground, shamanistic, and/or risky art get sucked, seduced, absorbed, tricked, bribed into "the mainstream". It is tragic not only in personal terms for the individual artists, but in terms of the big picture. When an artist sets herself up as being an artist who goes beyond the normal frame, who tells the hard truths, who explores the unknown…not to be hip, or controversial, or to be interesting…but because that is how our tribal human being evolves, so it has to be done…when that kind of artist then goes after money, personal fame, and/or glamour while still claiming to be doing avant-garde art, it is denying society the real evolutionary function of the real avant-garde. It tells people, audiences and artists alike, that the avant-garde is just a branch of the entertainment complex with the same rules, goals, reality as television, rock music, Hollywood, and sports. This is like telling people a can of Slim Fast is a balanced meal of real food.

It is a lie. And the scary dangerous thing is artists are buying/selling this lie.

Another example of society's attempt to rechannel the change coming from shamanistic art is what an "art expert" told me: "Your work is… not art…(because) it doesn't address the concerns…(which are a) part of the current art dialogue, whether it be mainstream or 'alternative'…curators and presenters are (not) obliged to show it." She went on to say that I should stay "in (my) own sphere", and that I don't need the public channels that galleries represent. Which is true. But galleries and the people who think what is in galleries is the full range of art need the artists, not the reverse. The magic of private performance is needed to expand the narrow, shallow river of "the current art dialogue", controlled both in content and depth by the art experts. Fortunately, there are galleries which are willing to go into the magical unknown represented by private performances.

Another way society tries to deball the magical power or private performance is to co-opt it by absorbing it back into the normal reality. What happened to Paul McCarthy is a classic example. Paul is, or was, the best of the modern shamanistic performers. In the '70s, he did performances in run-down motels. He transformed into a rubber-masked trickster who called forth realities of vomit, of messy meals of dog food, mayo and catsup…of wearing women's clothes…of hard-ons dangling out of girls' underwear fucking dolls, tubes up asshole and down throat and up the nose…, of fucking alone in a motel bed in mayo…, of walking bloodied barefoot on glass. Friends watched via video in another motel room. But most ran out in shock. This shock is a special kind of shock. It is not the shock of when a youngster uses obscenity or when a guy exposes himself. It is not a reaction or an aggressive act. It is more like culture shock. It is a reality shock. It is when two different realities come together, collide, and combine. This happened around Paul's pieces. Most people could not handle it. But the shock released incredible amounts of uplifting energy.

By the early '80s, Paul had been discovered by the art scene. He was invited to the San Francisco Art Institute to do a performance. The big hall was packed with students. Paul did his rituals, which in the past would have cleared the room, shocked and physically disturbed most people. But this time, the audience laughed and clapped at everything this clown did. They even drank catsup with him to show how hip they were. There was no shock, no magic, no colliding of realities. Paul stopped, defeated. He was cut off from his private, magical roots by being transformed from an outlaw magician into a hot artist.

He told me the day after, he felt the loss of the magic but did not know how to get it back. After a few more performances, he stopped performing...which is a great loss to us all. He was defeated because he underrated not only the importance of his private magic, but how much it threatened normal reality.

About Frank Moore

Frank Moore was an American performance artist, shaman, teacher, poet, essayist, painter, musician, and internet/television personality who experimented in art, performance, ritual, and shamanistic teaching from the late 1960s until his death in 2013 in Berkeley, California.

Moore is perhaps most well known as one of the NEA-funded artists targeted by Jesse Helms and the GAO (General Accounting Office) in the early '90s for doing art that was labeled "obscene". Frank Moore was featured in the 1988 cult film Mondo New York, which chronicled the leading performance artists of that period. He is well known for long (5–48 hours) ritualistic performances with audience participation, nudity, and eroticism. But he has also become well known for his influential writings on performance, art, life, and cultural subversion, for his historic influence on the San Francisco Bay Area music and performance scene, and more recently for his performance/video archive on Vimeo.com that has been viewed by over 8 million people worldwide.

Moore coined the word, "eroplay" to describe physical play between adults released from the linear goals of sex and orgasm. He explored this, and similar concepts in performance and ritual as a way for people to connect on a deep human level with each other beyond the social and cultural expectations and limitations, and as a way to melt isolation between people.

Moore has been an underground counter-culture hero and artistic inspiration for decades. He was born with cerebral palsy, could not walk or talk, and wrote books, directed plays, directed, acted in and edited films, regularly gave poetry readings, played piano, sang in ensemble music jams, and continued to lead bands in hard core punk clubs up and down the west coast until his death. He also produced a large collection of original oil and digital paintings that have been shown across the United States and in Canada. Moore communicated using a laser-pointer and a board of letters, numbers, and commonly used words.

Performance artist Annie Sprinkle considers Moore one of her teachers, and Moore performed with a host of performance and punk figures of the underground since the 1970s like Barbara Smith, Linda Sibio, The Feederz, and Dirk Dirksen - The Pope of Punk.

Frank Moore first came to be known in the 1970s as the creator of the popular cabaret show, the Outrageous Beauty Revue. In the 1980s he became one of the United States' foremost performance artists. In 1992 he was voted Best Performance Artist by the San Francisco Bay Guardian. In the early 1990s he was targeted by Senator Jesse Helms. From 1991 to 1999 Frank Moore published and edited the acclaimed underground zine, The Cherotic (r)Evolutionary.

In addition to his books, *Cherotic Magic, Art of a Shaman, Chapped Lap, Skin Passion* and numerous other self-published pieces, Frank Moore was widely published in various art and other periodicals. In artist Pamela Kay Walker's book, *Moving Over the Edge*, Moore is one of the artists featured as having "greatly impacted me and many people through their artistic expression and their lives."

Frank Moore's award-winning video works have shown throughout the U.S. and Canada, and in 2001 Moore began producing shows for Berkeley's public access channel, Berkeley Community Media, Channel 28. His shows continue to play weekly, throughout the week.

In 2011, Frank launched his online performance and video retrospective on Vimeo. At the same time, he created the EROART group featuring videos by eroart artists from all over the world.

Frank Moore's Web of All Possibilities, www.eroplay.com, features a growing archive of his audio, video, visual and written work, as well as the work of other artists. He founded Love Underground Visionary Revolution (LUVeR) in 1999, a webstation combining live streaming and on-demand libraries of audio and video programming, described by Moore as a "non-corporate, d.i.y., totally uncensored, noncommercial, nonprofit internet-only communal collective with 24-hour 'live' programming (by amazing people) with 'no-limits' content." LUVeR ran until 2012.

In 2006, Moore announced his candidacy for the 2008 election for President of the United States. He became a qualified write-in candidate in 25 states. His campaign was responsible for reforming the write-in candidate qualifications and procedures in many states. His platform videos are available on YouTube.

Moore also hosted his regular internet show, "Frank Moore's Shaman's Den". Moore described it as a show that "will arouse, inspire, move, threaten you, not with sound bites, but with a two-hour (usually longer) feast of live streaming video. You might get an in-studio concert of bands from around the world...or poetry reading...or an in-depth conversation about politics, art, music, and LIFE with extremely dangerous people! But then you may see beautiful women naked dancing erotically. You never know, because you are in The Shaman's Den with Frank Moore." Video and audio archives of all of these Shaman's Den shows are available online.

Frank Moore performed regularly in the San Francisco Bay Area up until his death.

His students and the people influenced by his life/work continue his vision.

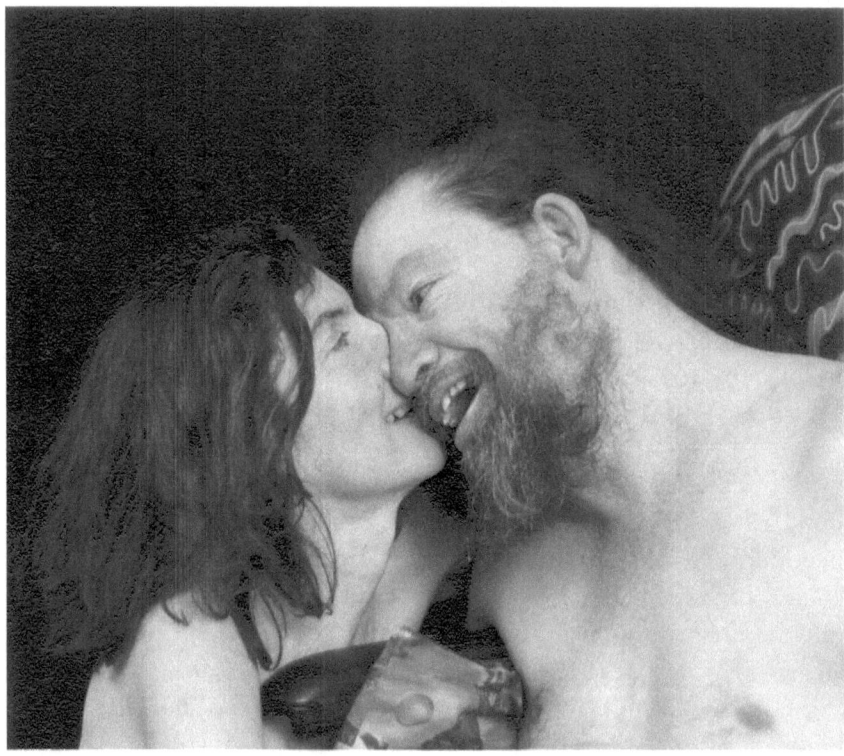

Linda Mac and Frank Moore. Photo by David Steinberg.

Frank Moore online

Frank Moore's Web Of All Possibilities
http://www.eroplay.com

The Shaman's Cave
Performance archives, writings, articles and more
http://www.eroplay.com/Cave/shaman.html

Vimeo.com
Online video and performance retrospective
http://www.vimeo.com/frankmoore

Vimeo.com - EROART
A group created by Frank on Vimeo.com for EROART
http://www.vimeo.com/groups/eroart

Frank Moore's Painting Gallery
http://www.eroplay.com/Cave/painting-slideshow/paintings.html

Frank Moore's Shaman's Den
Includes an archive of his online show
http://www.eroplay.com/underground/shamansden.html

The Cherotic r(E)volutionary
http://www.eroplay.com/contents.html

2008 Presidential campaign platform videos
http://www.youtube.com/user/frankmooreforprez08/videos

Frank Moore on Wikipedia
http://en.wikipedia.org/wiki/Frank_Moore_(performance_artist)

Credits

Book design & layout
Michael LaBash Graphic Design
http://www.designbymikee.com
http://www.lavapen.com

Editorial assistance and organizational maestro
Linda Mac

Proofreading
Corey Nicholl

Cooking our amazing meals
Alexi Malenky

For always loving us
Erika Shaver-Nelson

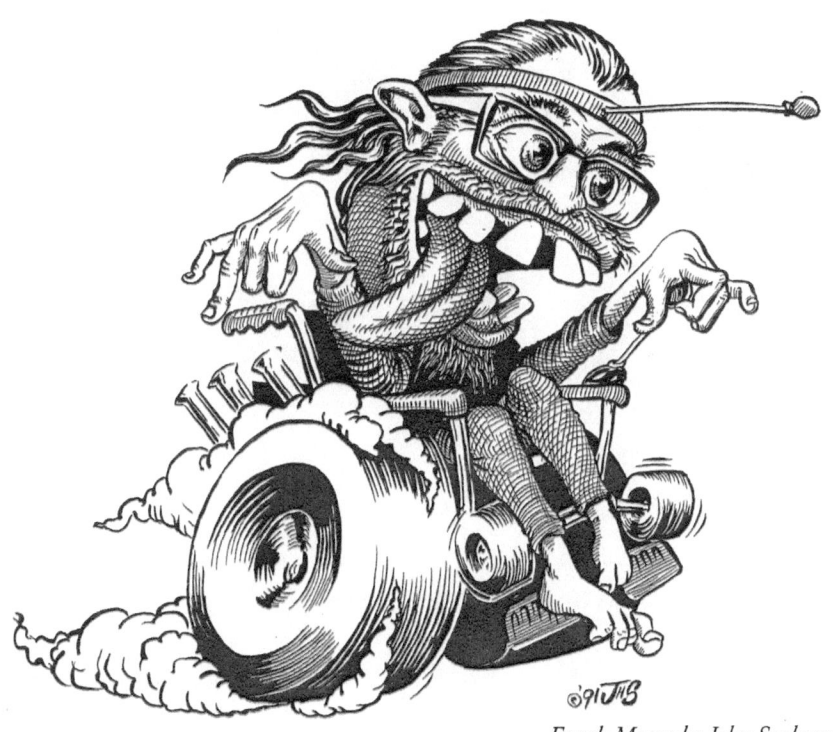

Frank Moore by John Seabury

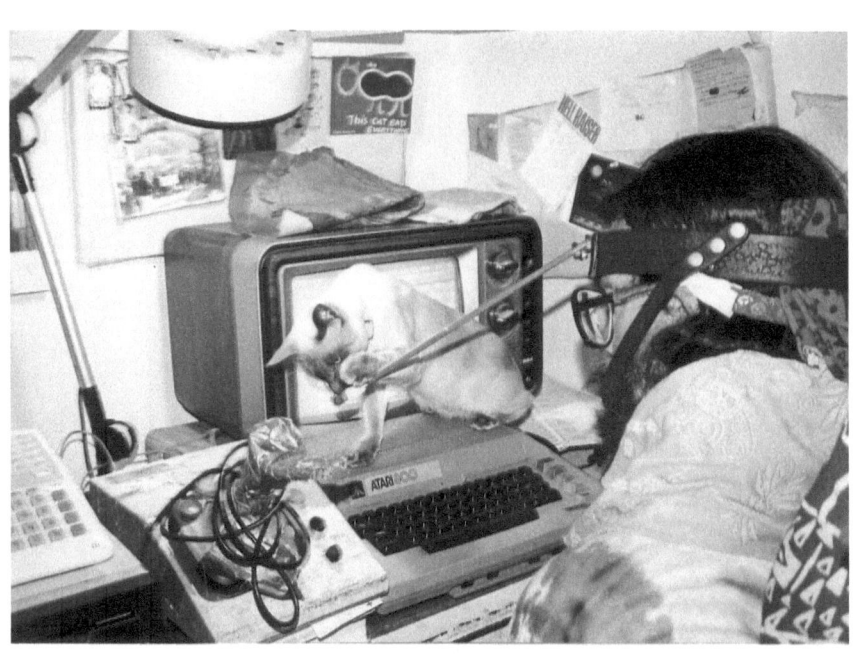